IMAGE COMICS, INC.
Robert Kirkman—Chief Operating Officer
Erik Larsen—Chief Financial Officer
Todd McFarlane—President
Marc Silvestri—Chief Executive Officer
Jim Valentino—Vice-President

Eric Stephenson—Publisher
Corey Murphy—Director of Sales
Jeff Boison—Director of Publishing Planning & Book Trade Sales
Chris Ross—Director of Digital Sales
Jeff Stang—Director of Specialty Sales
Kat Salazar—Director of PR & Marketing
Branwyn Bigglestone—Controller
Sue Korpela—Accounts Manager
Drew Gill—Art Director
Brett Warnock—Production Manager
Leigh Thomas—Print Manager
Tricia Ramos—Traffic Manager
Briah Skelly—Publicist
Aly Hoffman—Events & Conventions Coordinator
Sasha Head—Sales & Marketing Production Designer
David Brothers—Branding Manager
Melissa Gifford—Content Manager
Drew Fitzgerald—Publicity Assistant
Vincent Kukua—Production Artist
Erika Schnatz—Production Artist
Ryan Brewer—Production Artist
Shanna Matuszak—Production Artist
Carey Hall—Production Artist
Esther Kim—Direct Market Sales Representative
Emilio Bautista—Digital Sales Representative
Leanna Caunter—Accounting Assistant
Chloe Ramos-Peterson—Library Market Sales Representative
Maria Eizik—Administrative Assistant
IMAGECOMICS.COM

EAST OF WEST

JONATHAN HICKMAN
WRITER

NICK DRAGOTTA
ARTIST

FRANK MARTIN
COLORS

RUS WOOTON
LETTERS

EAS

W

ST OF

EST

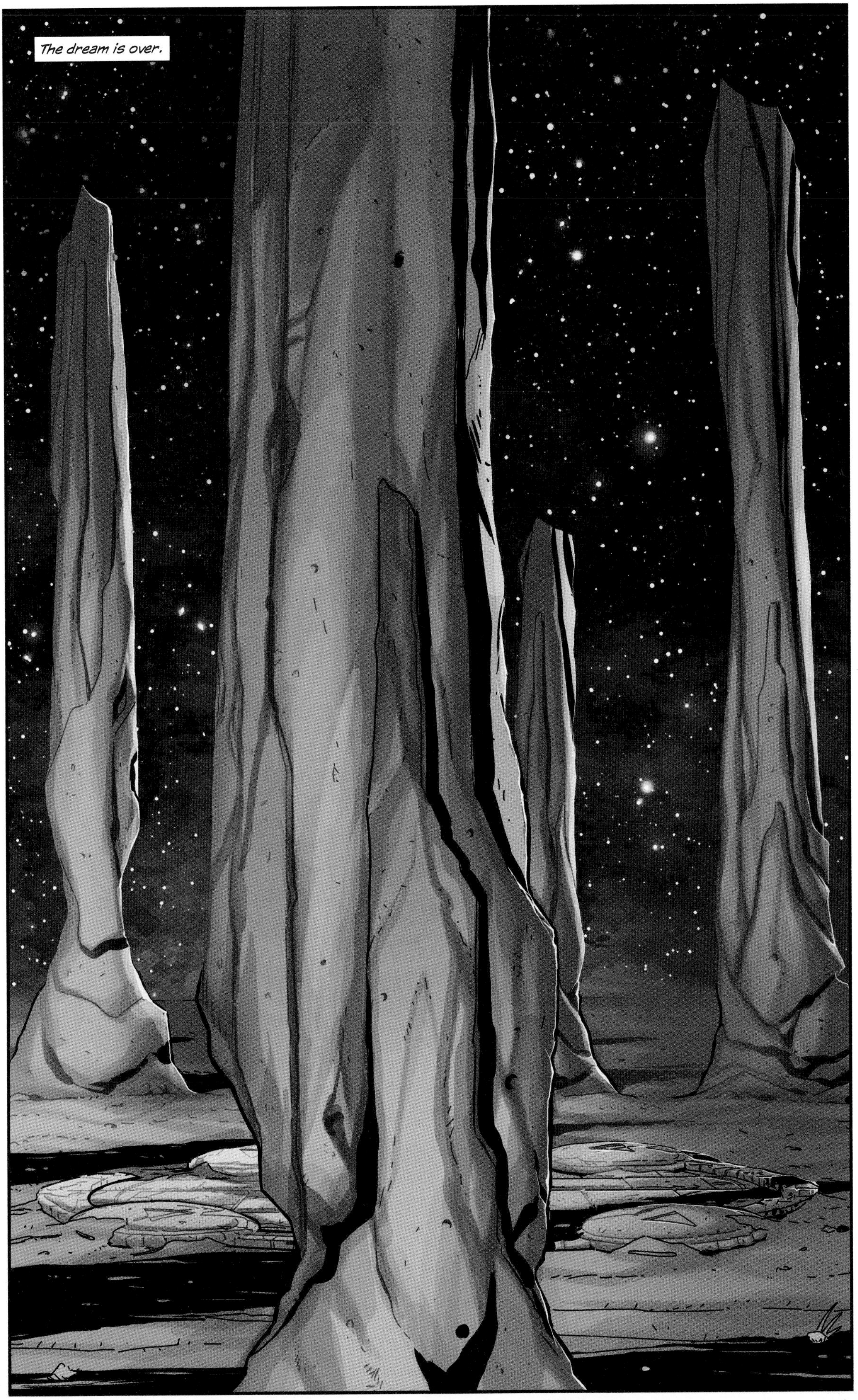
The dream is over.

KRAKA
BOOM

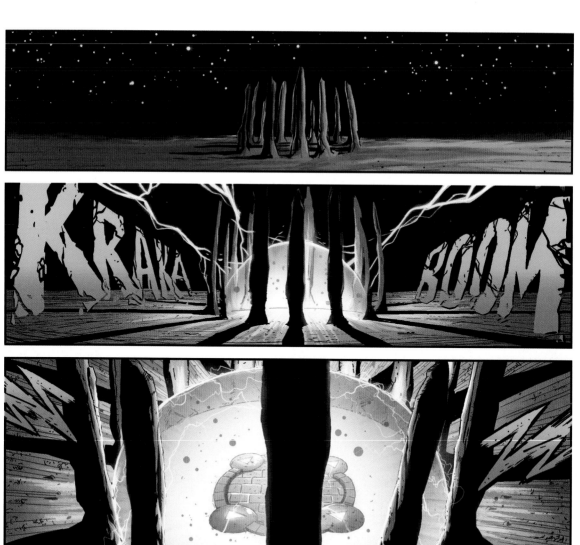

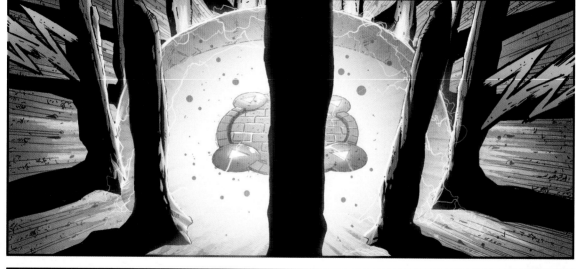

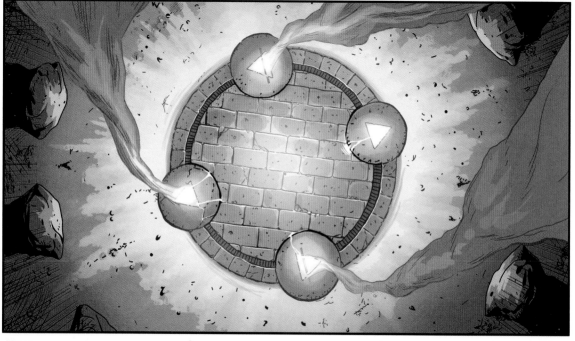

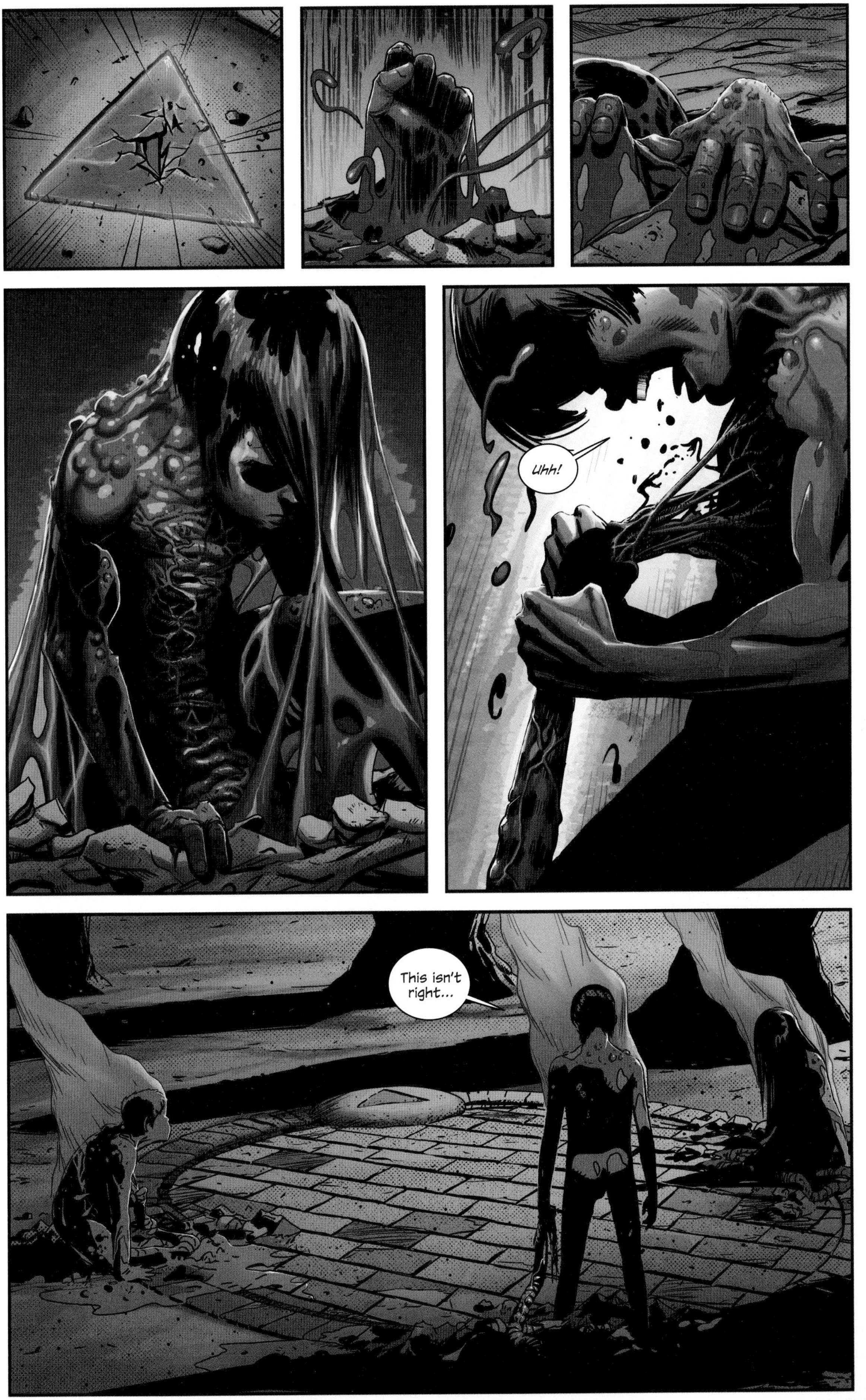
Uhh!
This isn't right...

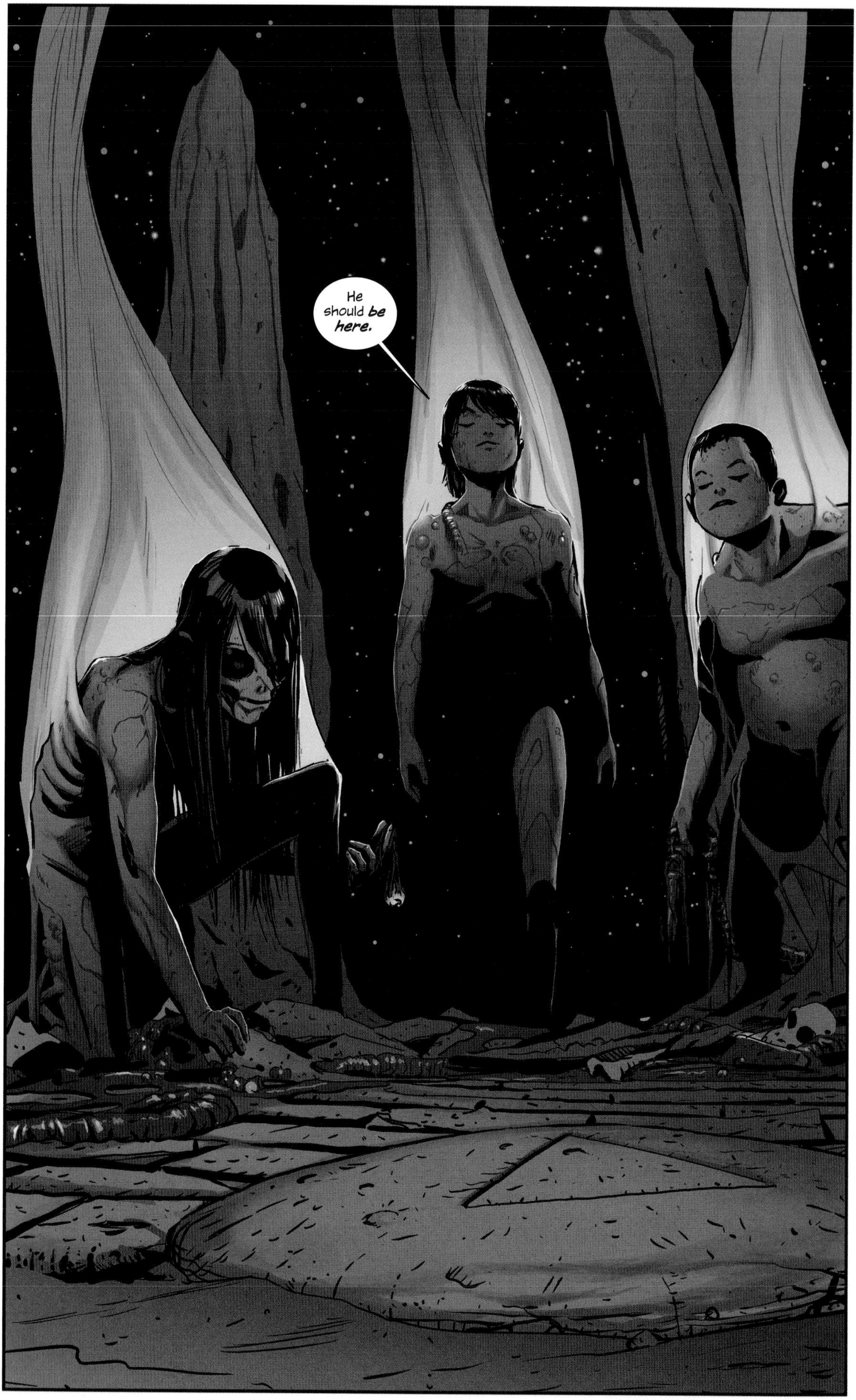
He should be here.

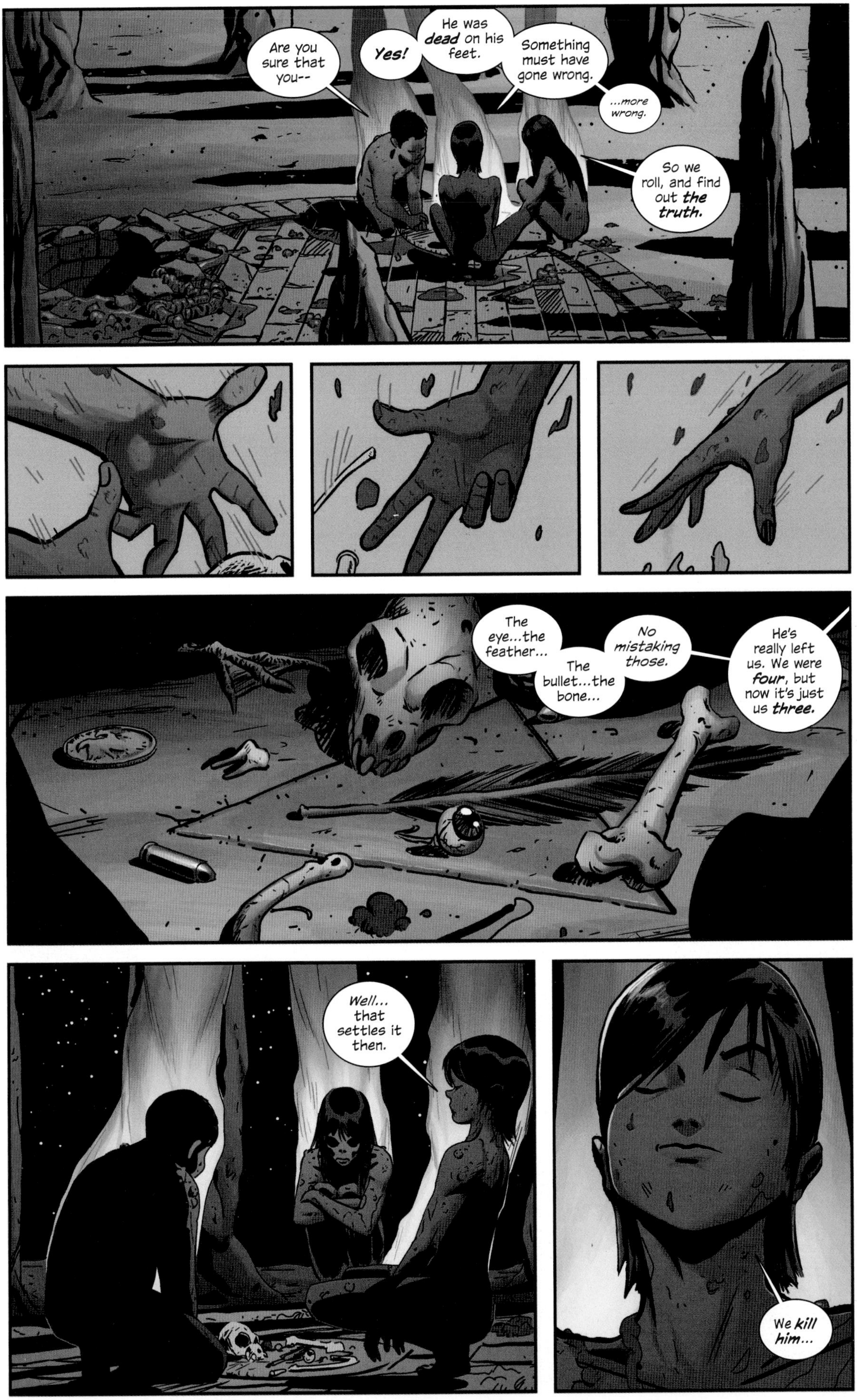
Are you sure that you--
Yes!
He was dead on his feet.
Something must have gone wrong.
...more wrong.
So we roll, and find out the truth.
The eye...the feather...
The bullet...the bone...
No mistaking those.
He's really left us. We were four, but now it's just us three.
Well... that settles it then.
We kill him...

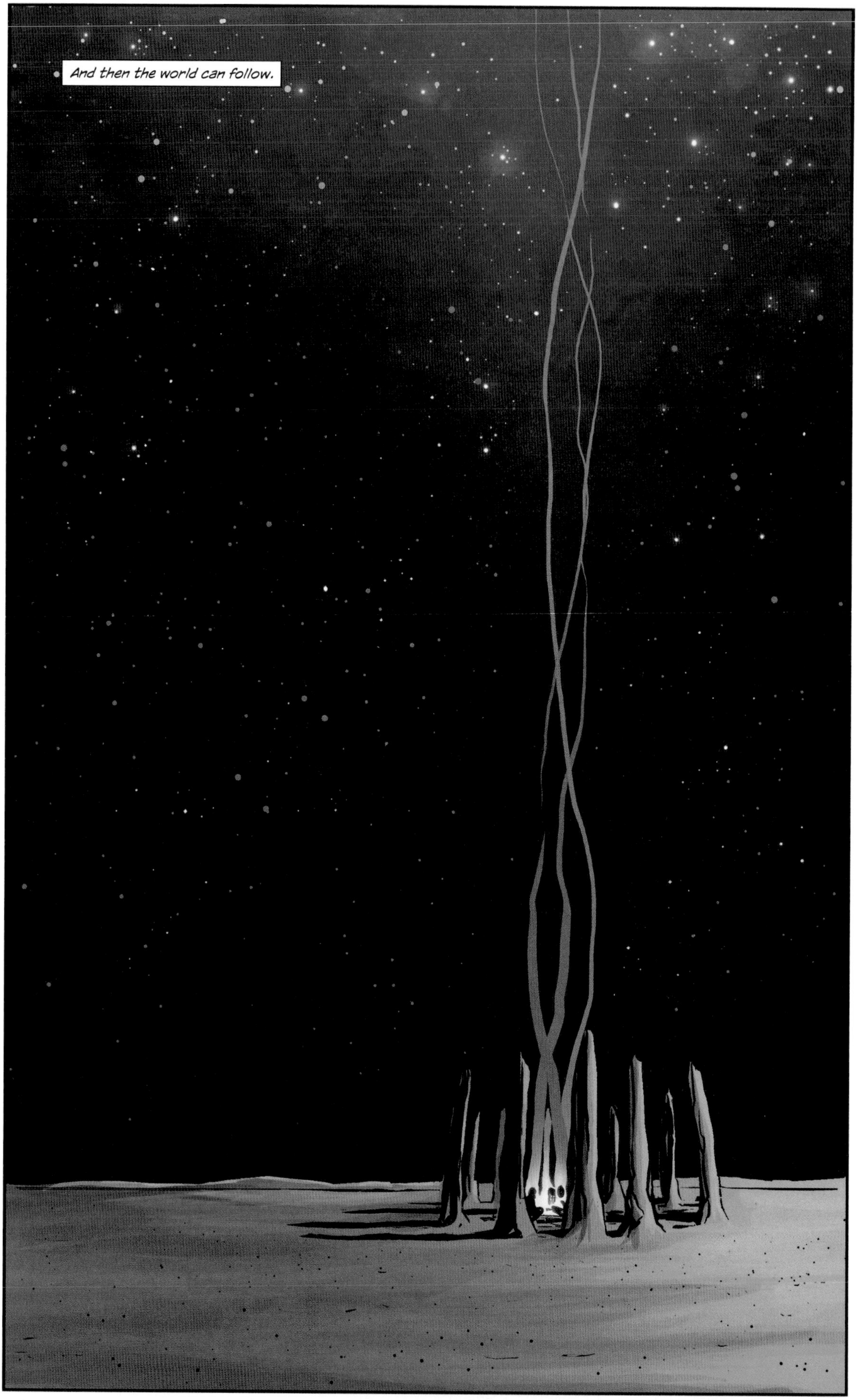
And then the world can follow.

THE THINGS THAT **DIVIDE US** ARE
STRONGER THAN THE THINGS THAT
UNITE US.

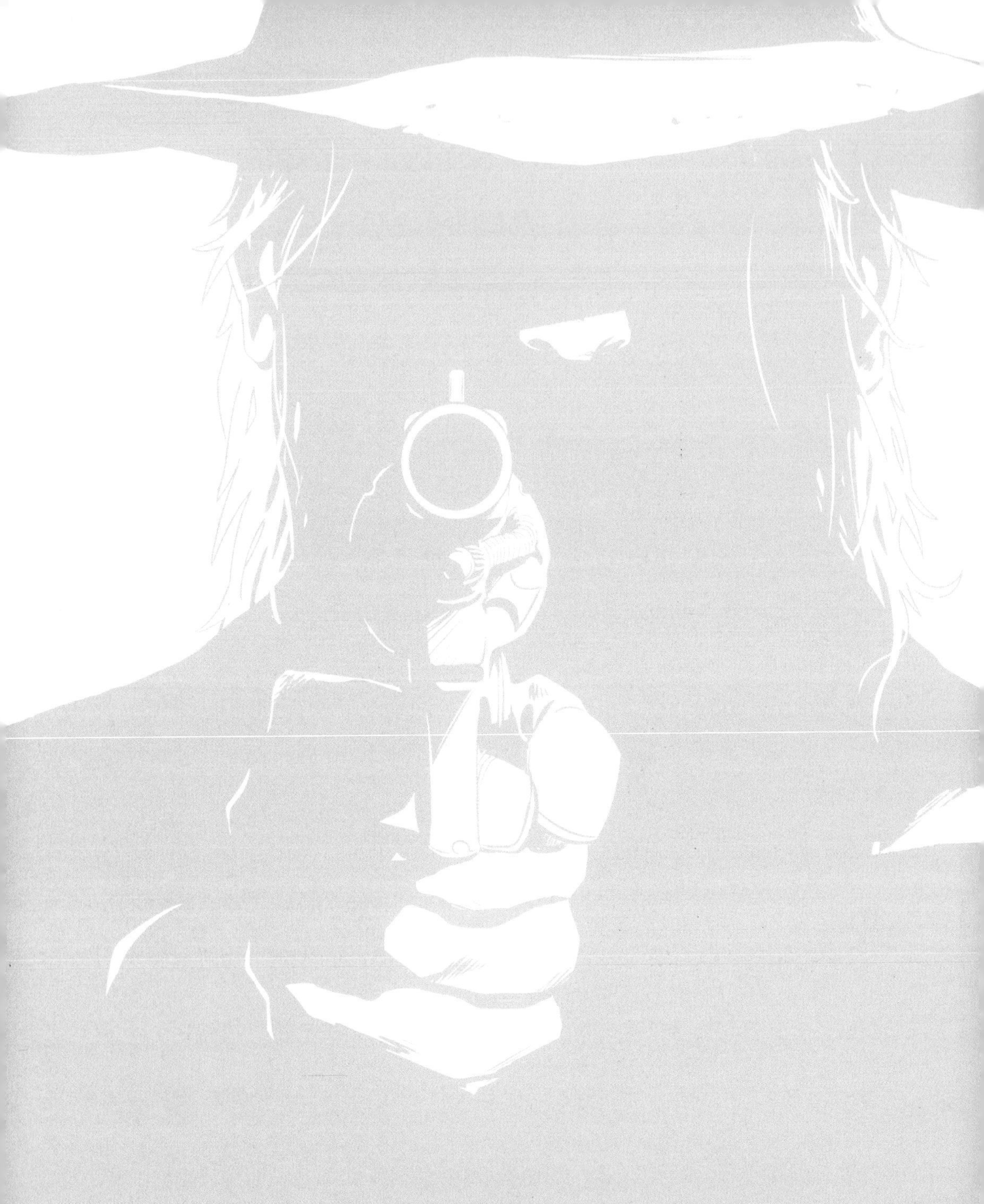

01

ONE: OUT OF THE WASTELAND

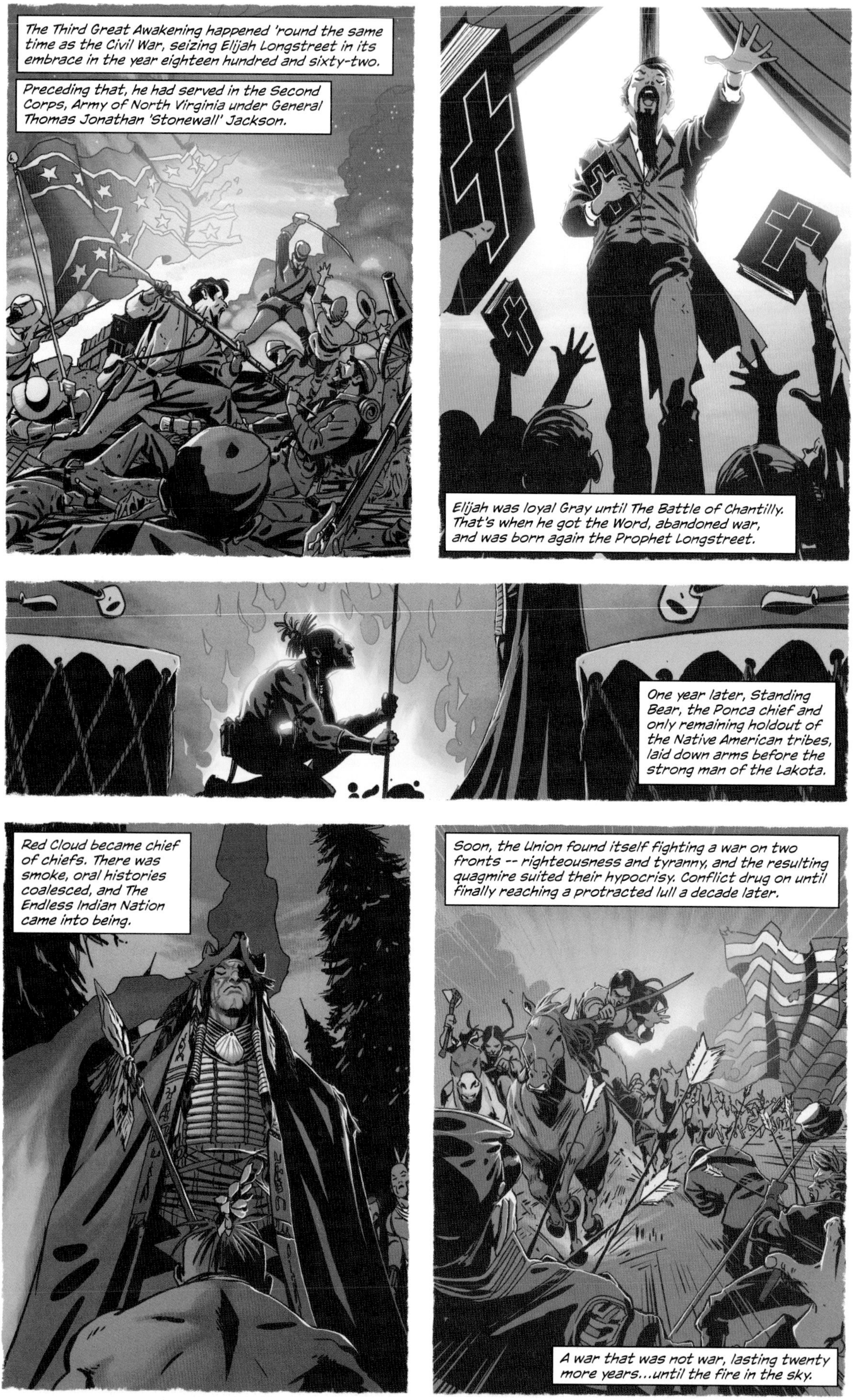
The Third Great Awakening happened 'round the same time as the Civil War, seizing Elijah Longstreet in its embrace in the year eighteen hundred and sixty-two.
Preceding that, he had served in the Second Corps, Army of North Virginia under General Thomas Jonathan 'Stonewall' Jackson.
Elijah was loyal Gray until The Battle of Chantilly. That's when he got the Word, abandoned war, and was born again the Prophet Longstreet.
One year later, Standing Bear, the Ponca chief and only remaining holdout of the Native American tribes, laid down arms before the strong man of the Lakota.
Red Cloud became chief of chiefs. There was smoke, oral histories coalesced, and The Endless Indian Nation came into being.
Soon, the Union found itself fighting a war on two fronts -- righteousness and tyranny, and the resulting quagmire suited their hypocrisy. Conflict drug on until finally reaching a protracted lull a decade later.
A war that was not war, lasting twenty more years...until the fire in the sky.

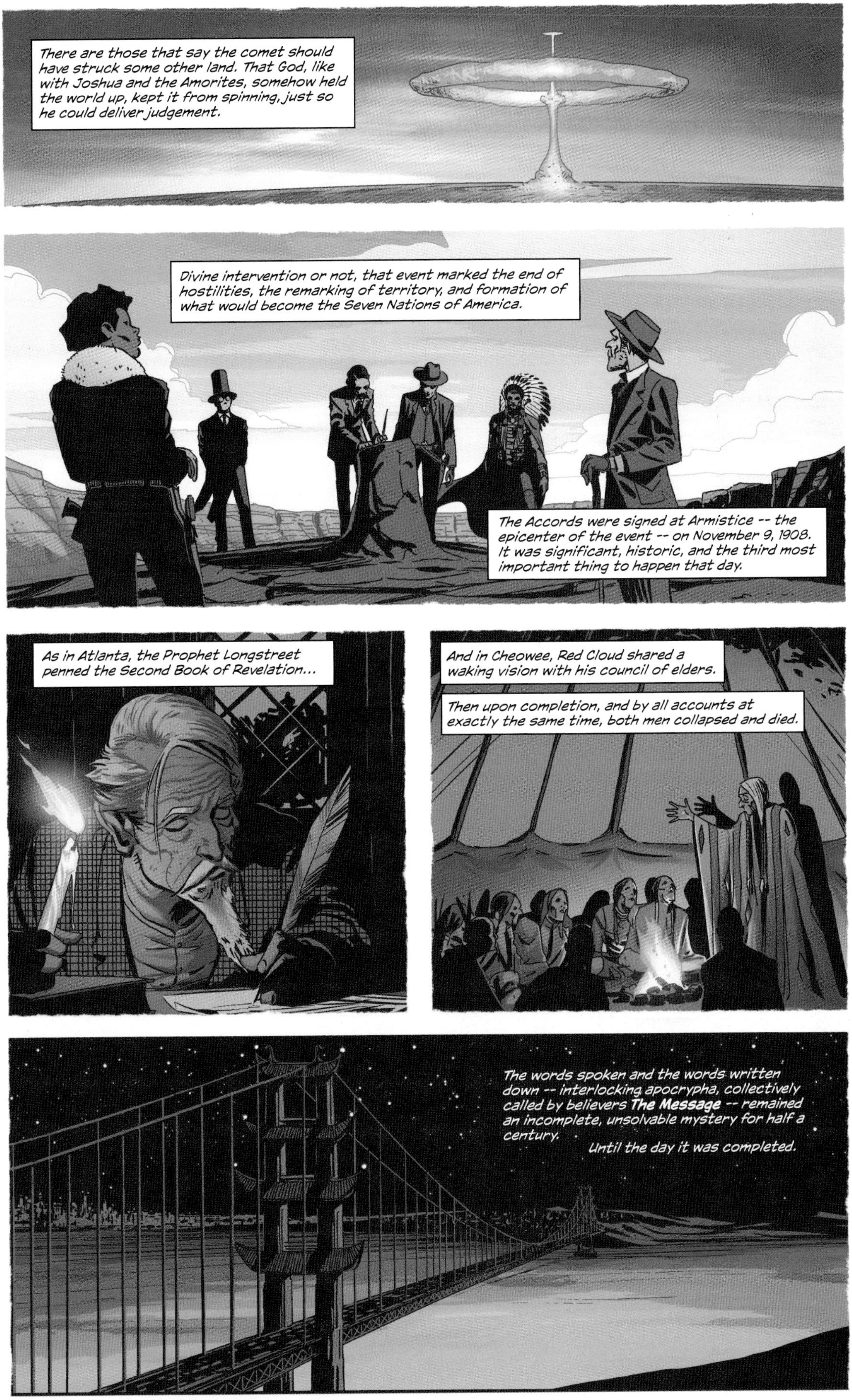
There are those that say the comet should have struck some other land. That God, like with Joshua and the Amorites, somehow held the world up, kept it from spinning, just so he could deliver judgement.
Divine intervention or not, that event marked the end of hostilities, the remarking of territory, and formation of what would become the Seven Nations of America.
The Accords were signed at Armistice -- the epicenter of the event -- on November 9, 1908. It was significant, historic, and the third most important thing to happen that day.
As in Atlanta, the Prophet Longstreet penned the Second Book of Revelation...
And in Cheowee, Red Cloud shared a waking vision with his council of elders.
Then upon completion, and by all accounts at exactly the same time, both men collapsed and died.
The words spoken and the words written down -- interlocking apocrypha, collectively called by believers **The Message** -- remained an incomplete, unsolvable mystery for half a century.
Until the day it was completed.

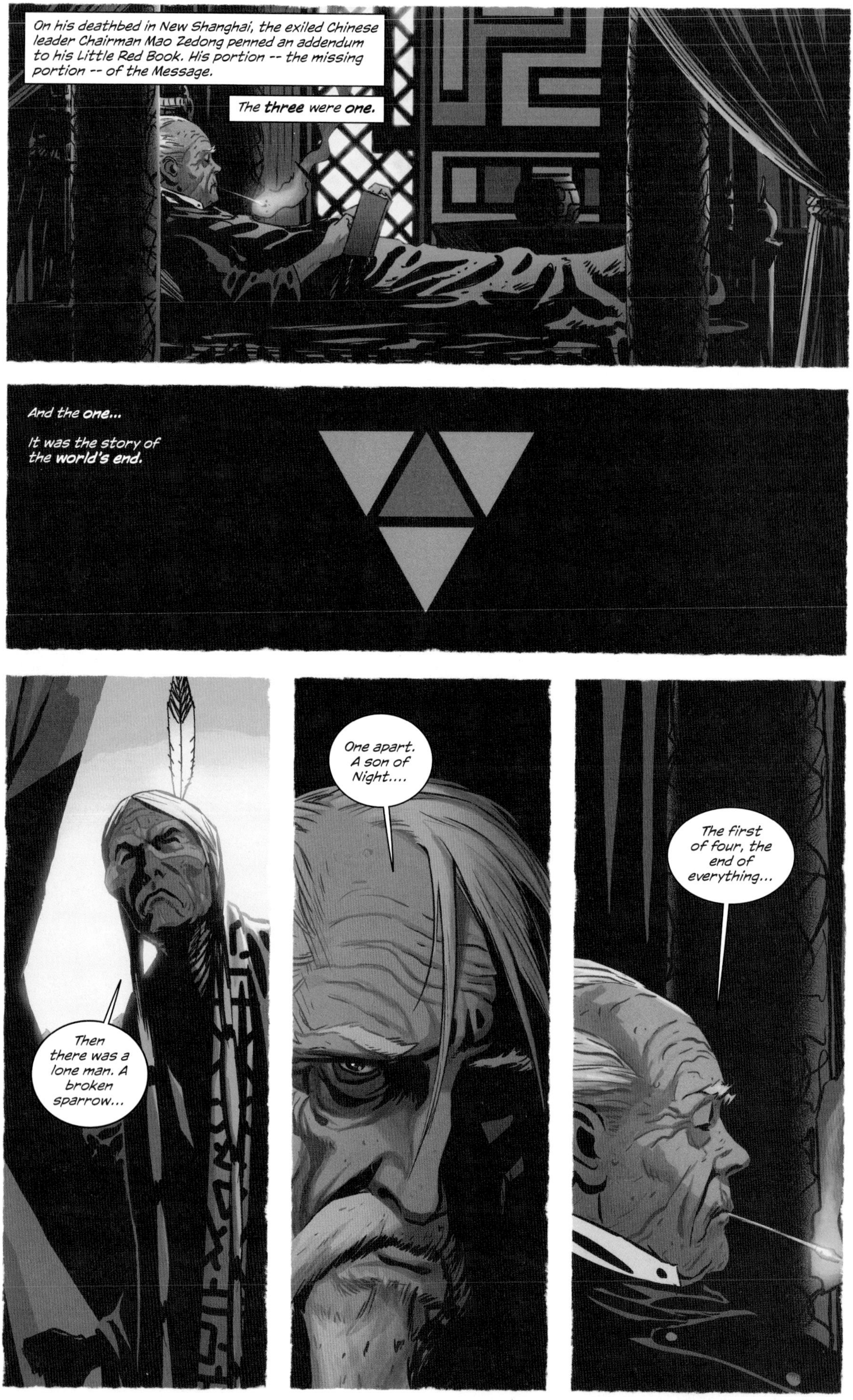

On his deathbed in New Shanghai, the exiled Chinese leader Chairman Mao Zedong penned an addendum to his Little Red Book. His portion -- the missing portion -- of the Message.
The **three** were **one.**
And the **one...**
It was the story of the **world's end.**
Then there was a lone man. A broken sparrow...
One apart. A son of Night....
The first of four, the end of everything...

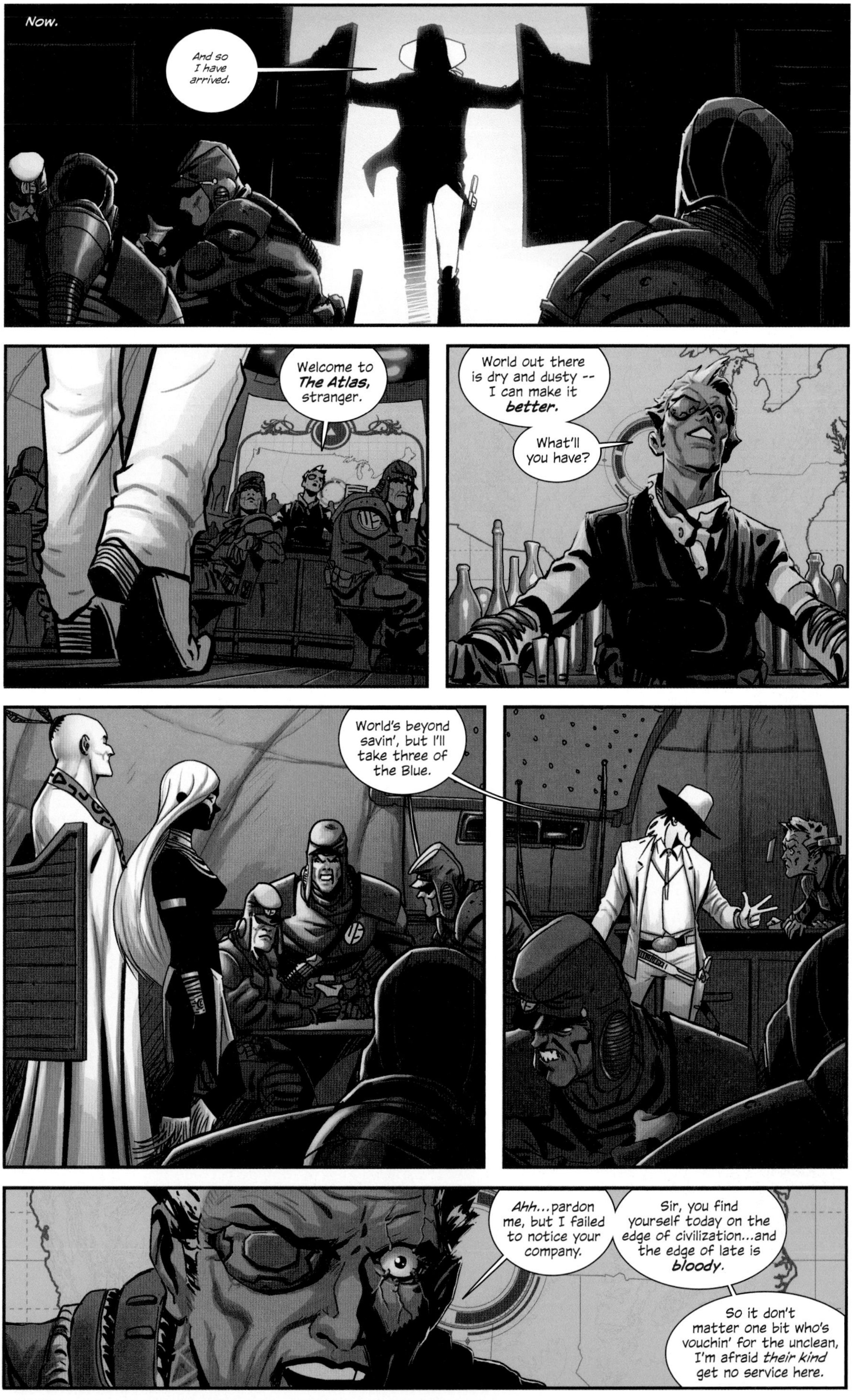
Now.
And so I have arrived.
Welcome to *The Atlas,* stranger.
World out there is dry and dusty -- I can make it *better.*
What'll you have?
World's beyond savin', but I'll take three of the Blue.
Ahh...pardon me, but I failed to notice your company.
Sir, you find yourself today on the edge of civilization...and the edge of late is *bloody*.
So it don't matter one bit who's vouchin' for the unclean, I'm afraid *their kind* get no service here.

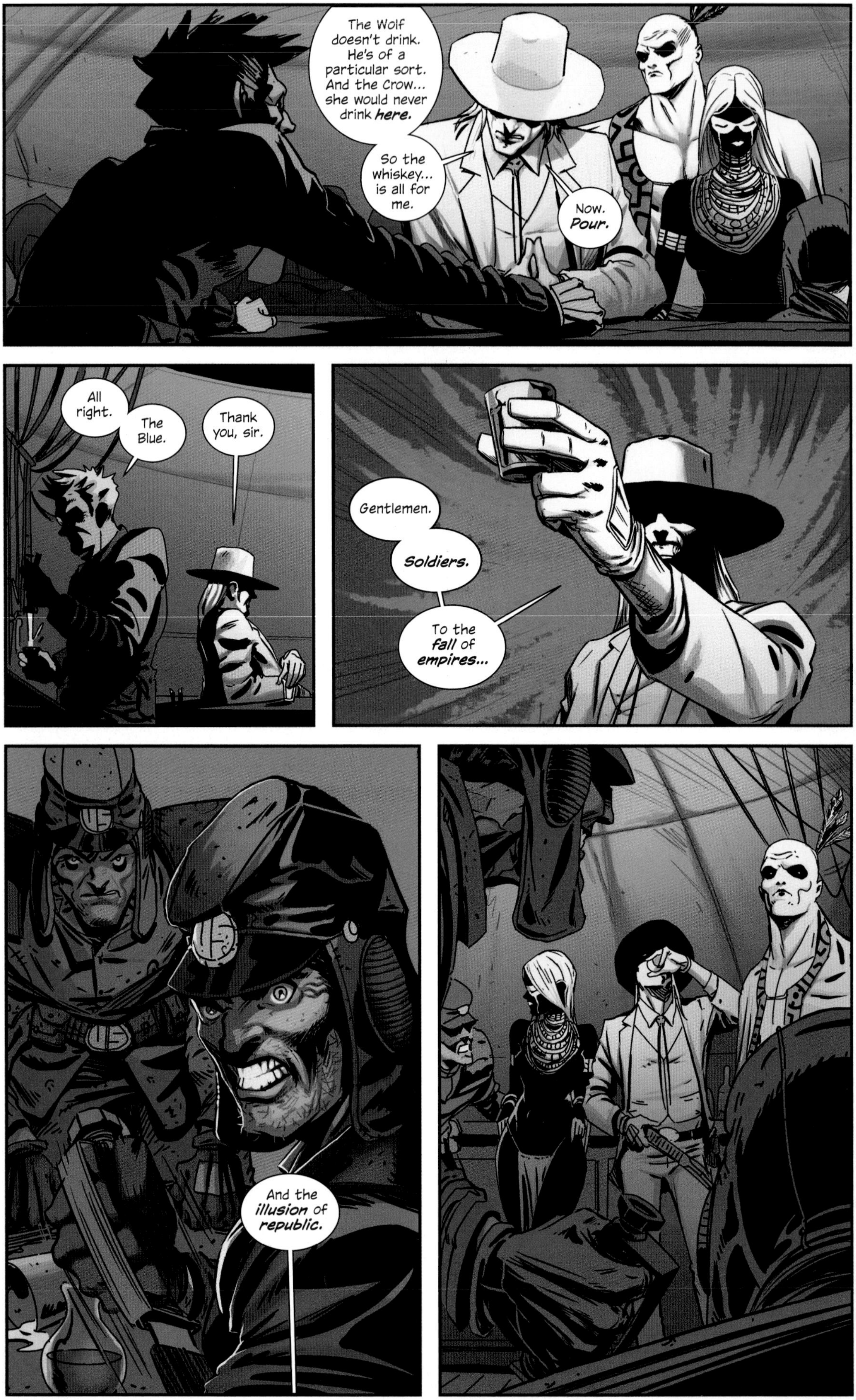
The Wolf doesn't drink. He's of a particular sort. And the Crow... she would never drink *here.*
So the whiskey... is all for me.
Now. *Pour.*
All right.
The Blue.
Thank you, sir.
Gentlemen.
Soldiers.
To the *fall* of *empires...*
And the *illusion* of *republic.*

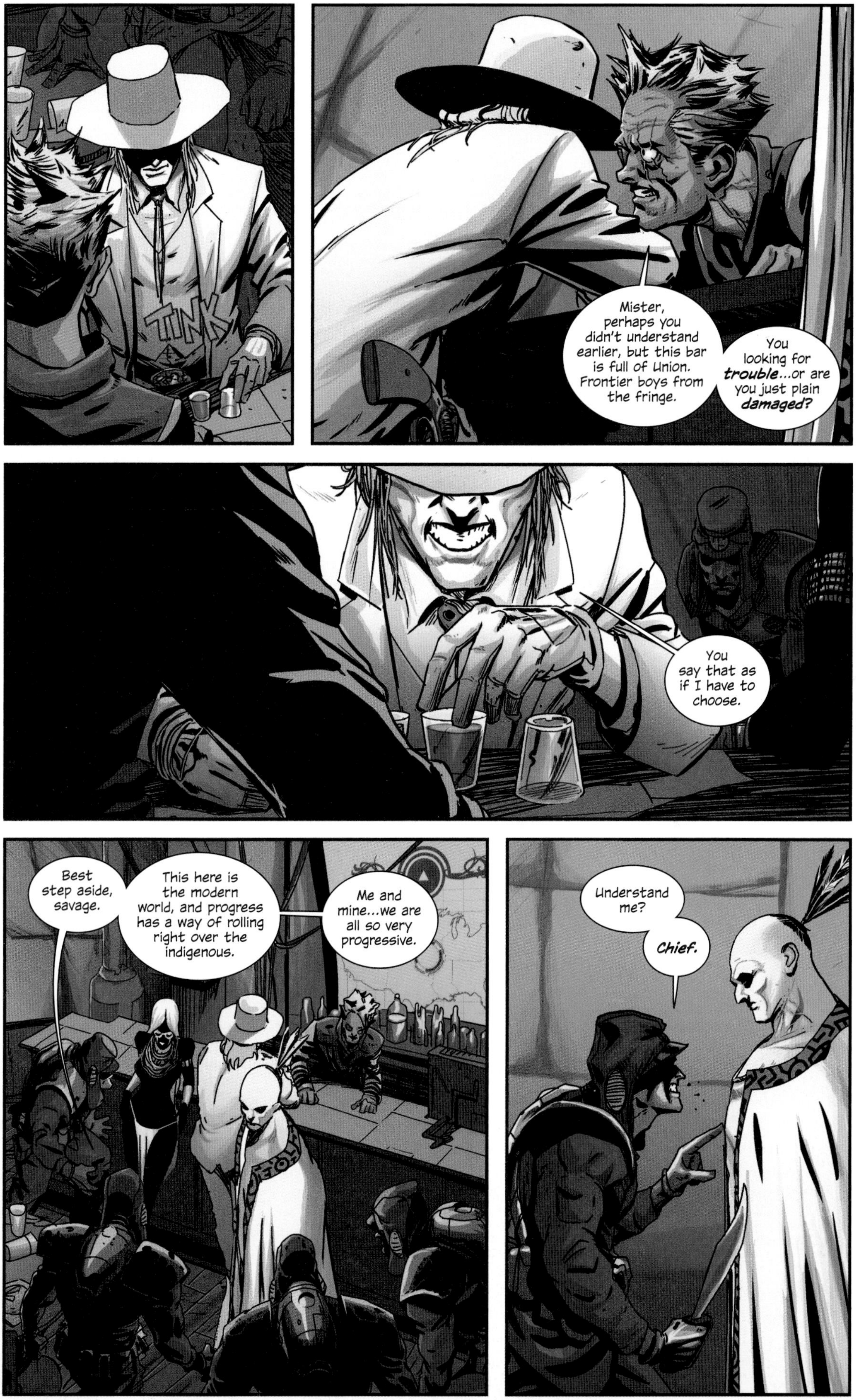
TINK
Mister, perhaps you didn't understand earlier, but this bar is full of Union. Frontier boys from the fringe.
You looking for *trouble*...or are you just plain *damaged?*
You say that as if I have to choose.
Best step aside, savage.
This here is the modern world, and progress has a way of rolling right over the indigenous.
Me and mine...we are all so very progressive.
Understand me?
Chief.

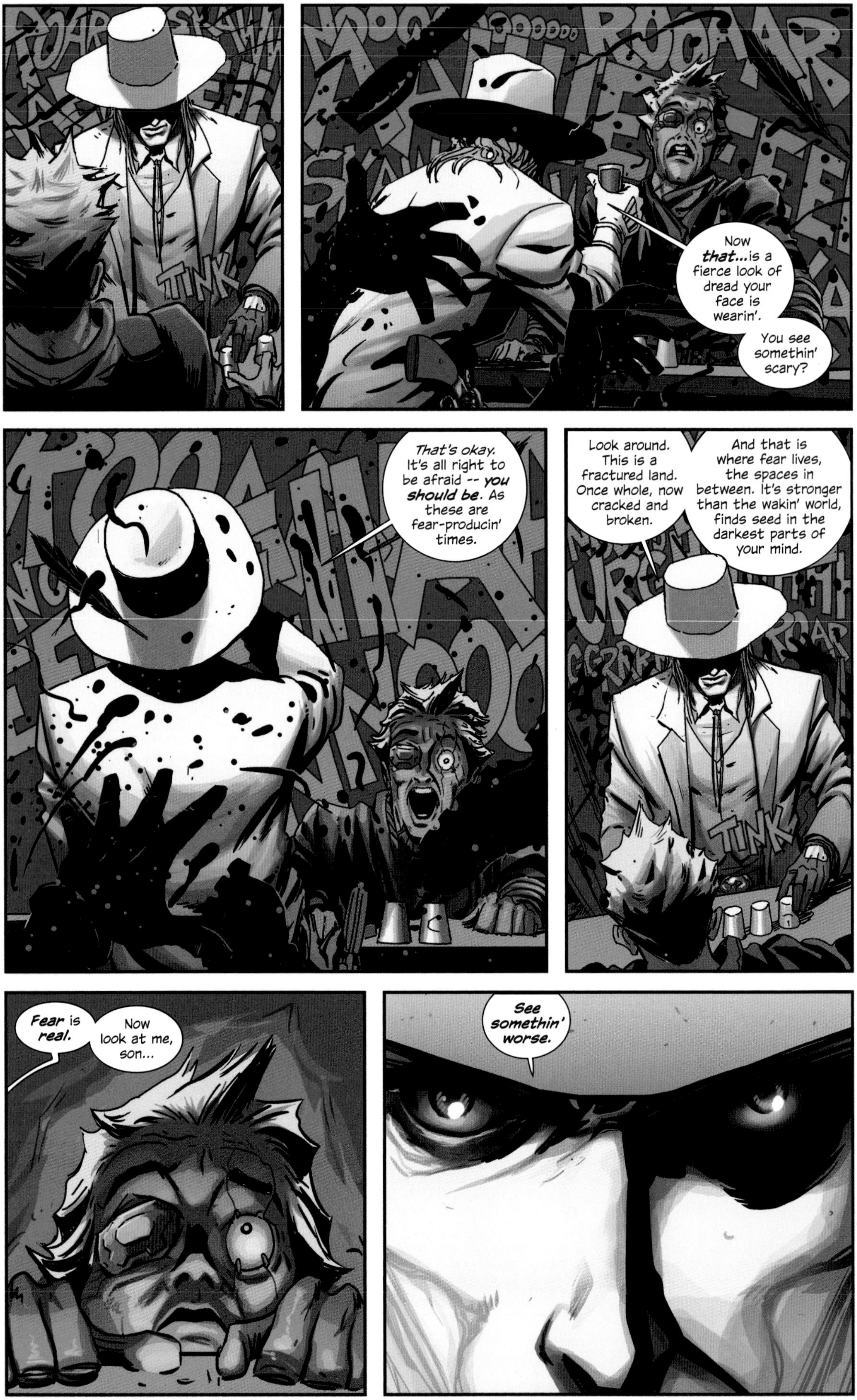
TINK
Now *that...*is a fierce look of dread your face is wearin'.
You see somethin' scary?
That's okay. It's all right to be afraid -- ***you should be***. As these are fear-producin' times.
Look around. This is a fractured land. Once whole, now cracked and broken.
And that is where fear lives, the spaces in between. It's stronger than the wakin' world, finds seed in the darkest parts of your mind.
TINK
Fear is ***real.***
Now look at me, son...
See somethin' worse.

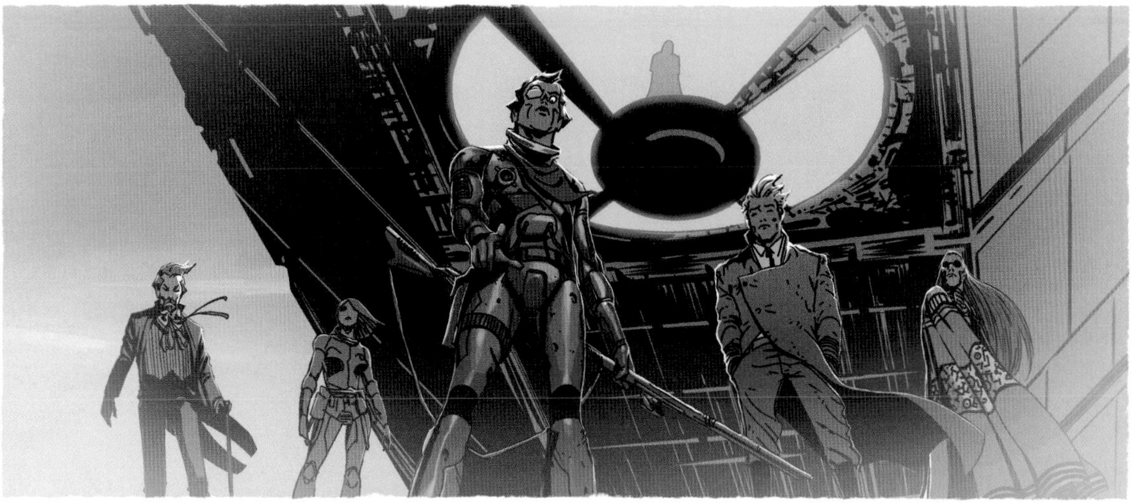

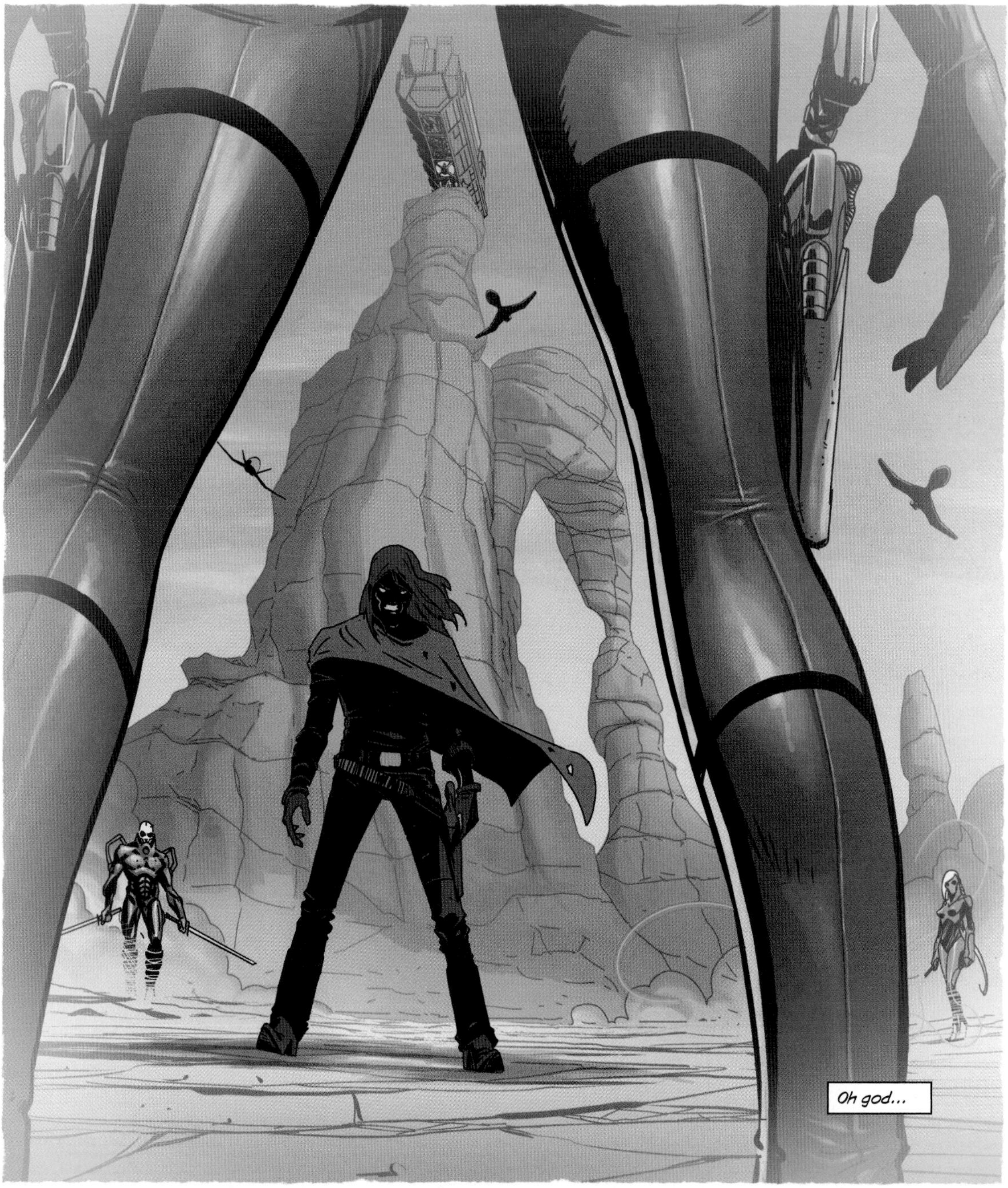
Oh god...

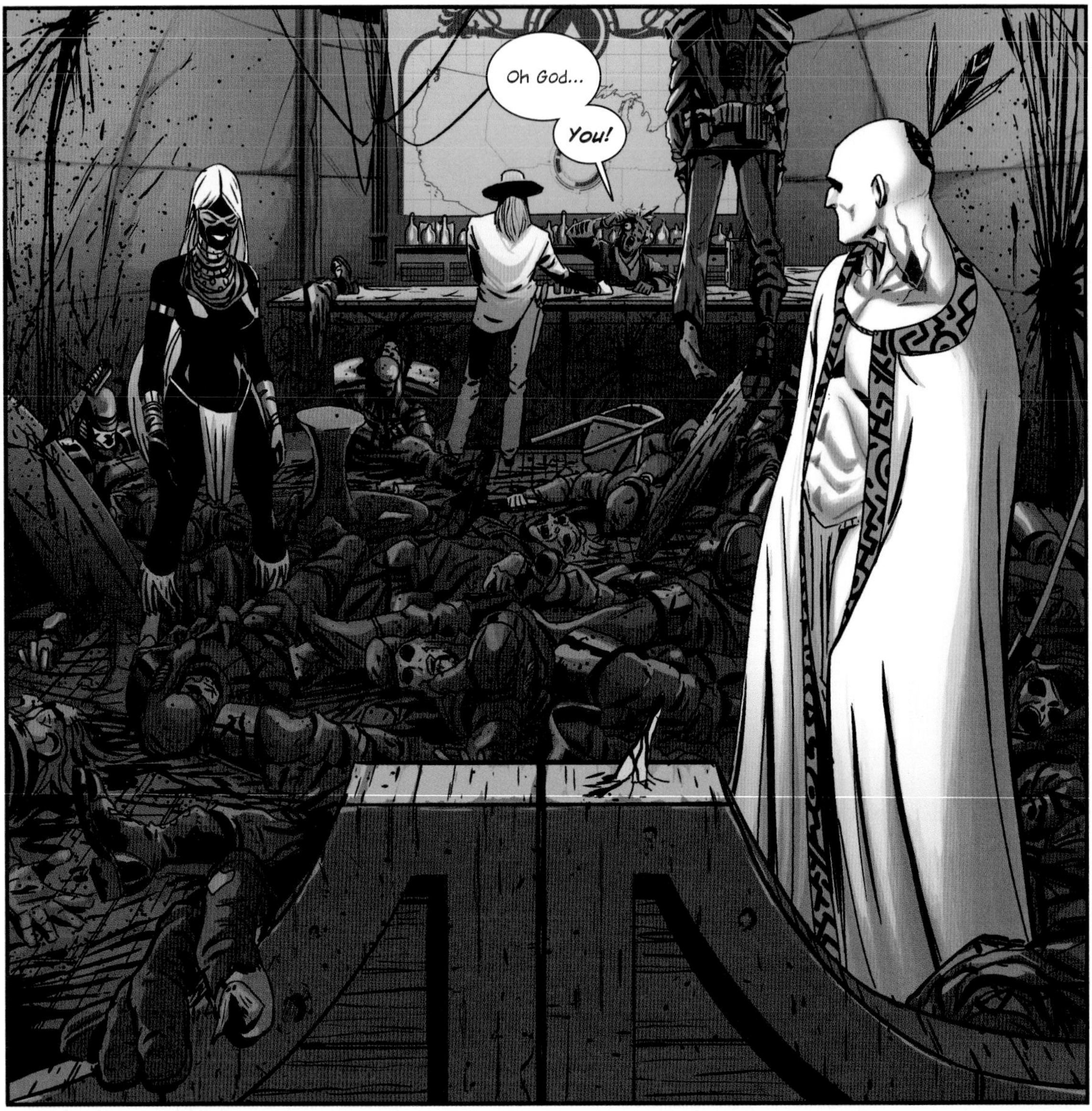
Oh God...
You!

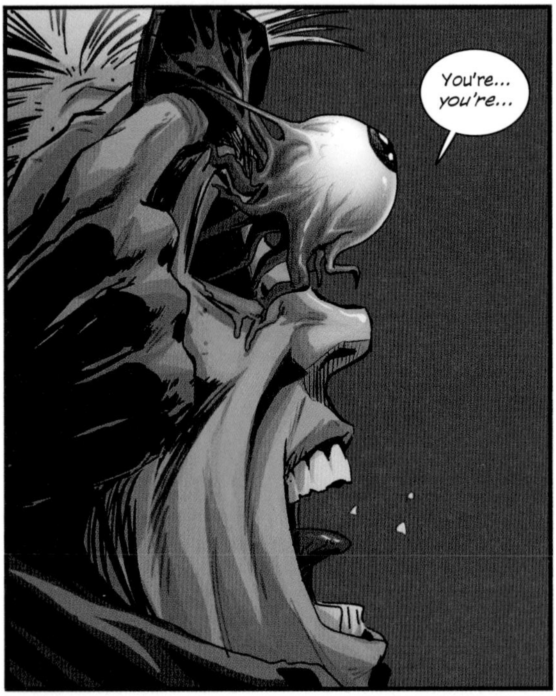
You're... you're...

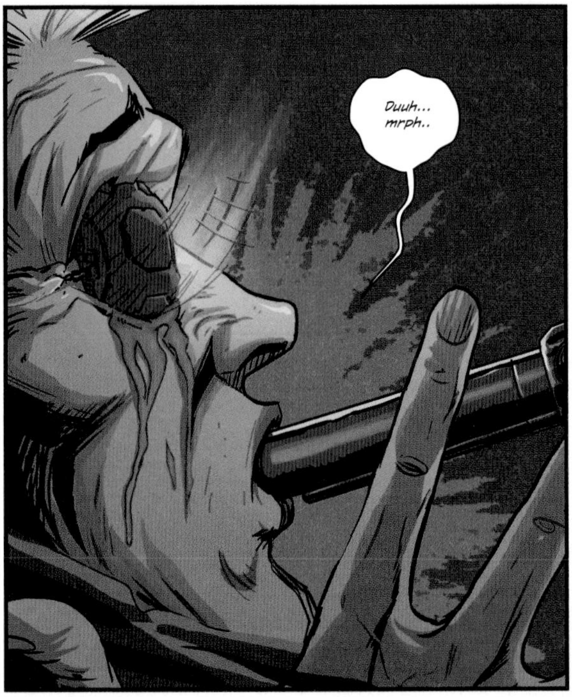
Duuh... mrph..

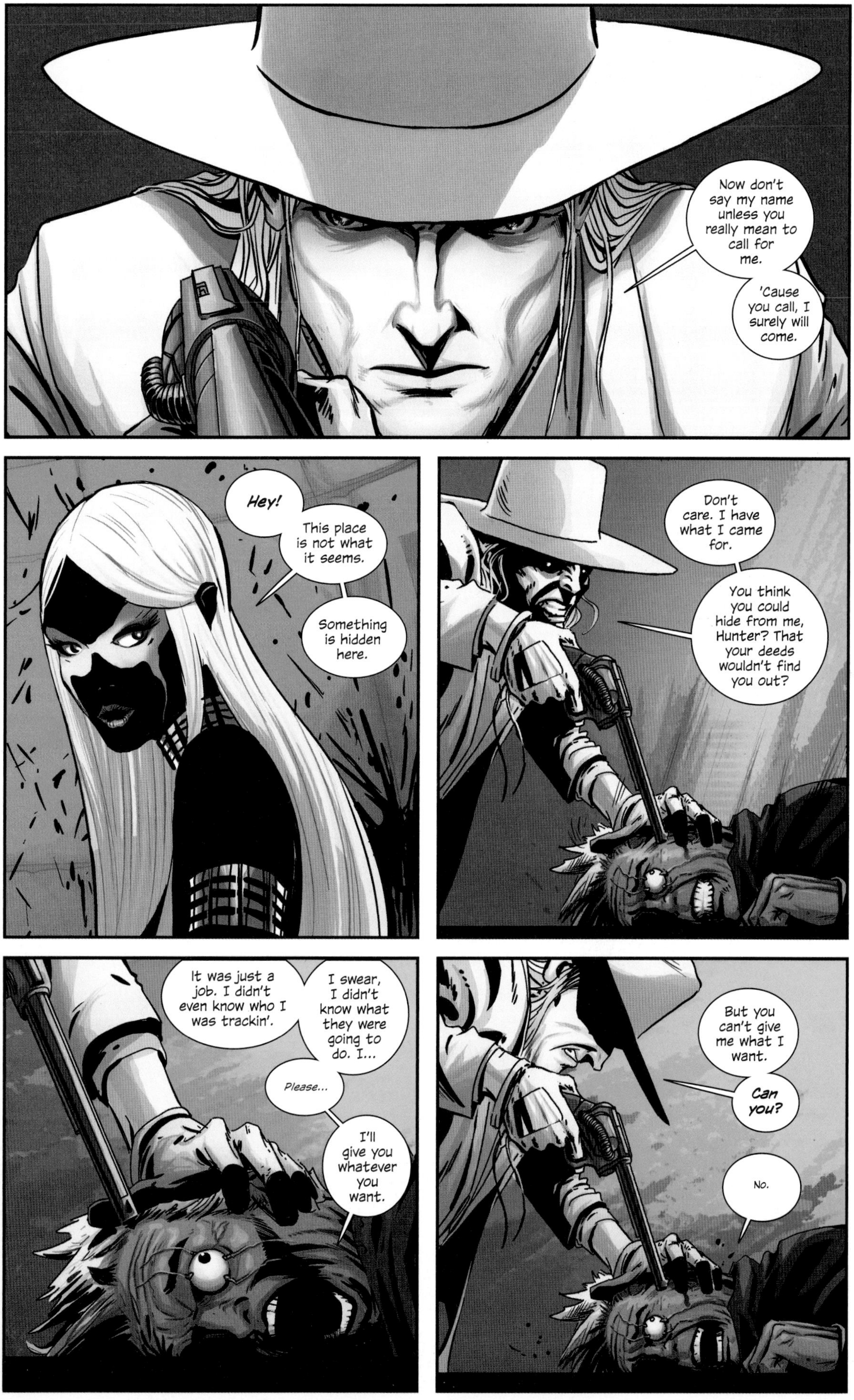
Now don't say my name unless you really mean to call for me.
'Cause you call, I surely will come.
Hey!
This place is not what it seems.
Something is hidden here.
Don't care. I have what I came for.
You think you could hide from me, Hunter? That your deeds wouldn't find you out?
It was just a job. I didn't even know who I was trackin'.
I swear, I didn't know what they were going to do. I...
Please...
I'll give you whatever you want.
But you can't give me what I want.
Can you?
No.

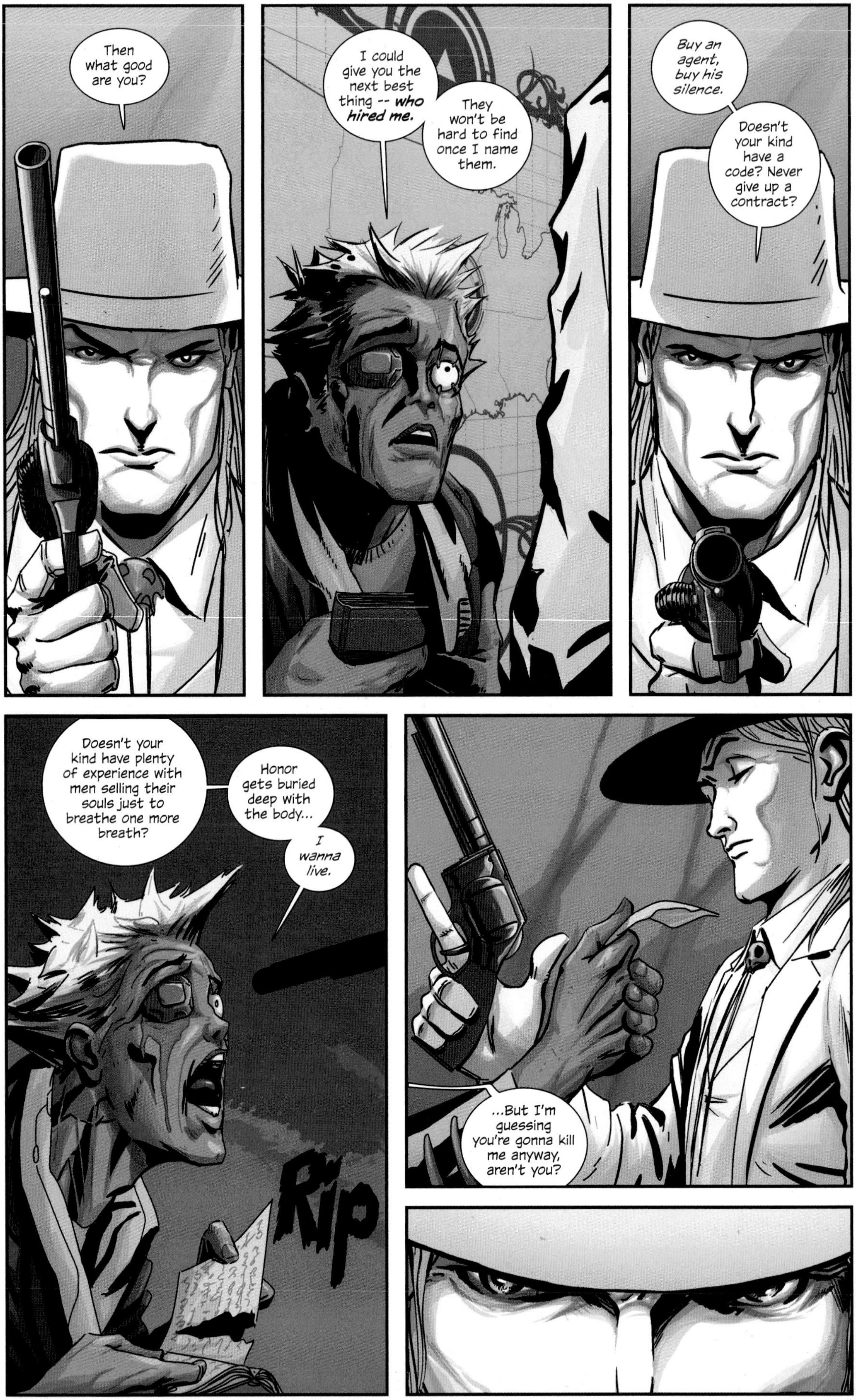
Then what good are you?
I could give you the next best thing -- **who hired me.**
They won't be hard to find once I name them.
Buy an agent, buy his silence.
Doesn't your kind have a code? Never give up a contract?
Doesn't your kind have plenty of experience with men selling their souls just to breathe one more breath?
Honor gets buried deep with the body...
I wanna live.
Rip
...But I'm guessing you're gonna kill me anyway, aren't you?

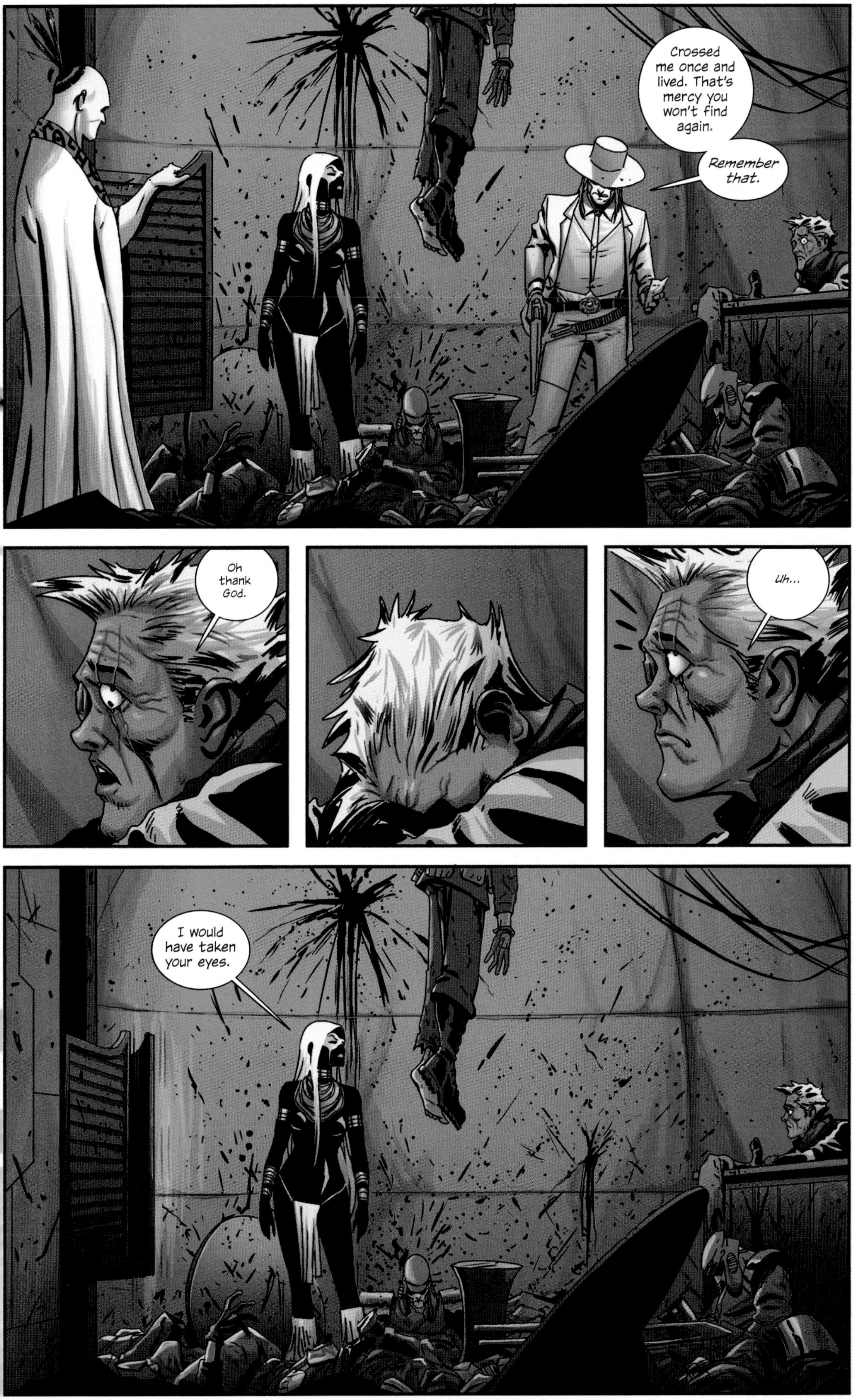
Crossed me once and lived. That's mercy you won't find again.
Remember that.
Oh thank God.
Uh...
I would have taken your eyes.

Not good.

The list smokey?

Solid. But look at the first name.

Feh! Ain't walking the *White Tower*.

Nothing there but lies and the lying mouths that produce them.

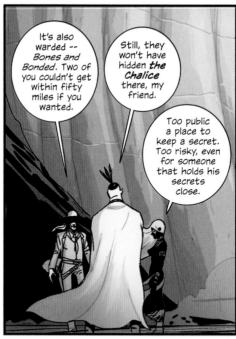

It's also warded -- *Bones and Bonded*. Two of you couldn't get within fifty miles if you wanted.

Still, they won't have hidden *the Chalice* there, my friend.

Too public a place to keep a secret. Too risky, even for someone that holds his secrets close.

I know.

Suppose I'll have to think of some other reason for my bein' there.

I recognized one other name on the list, but that's all. Find me the others.

I'll see you on the second day.

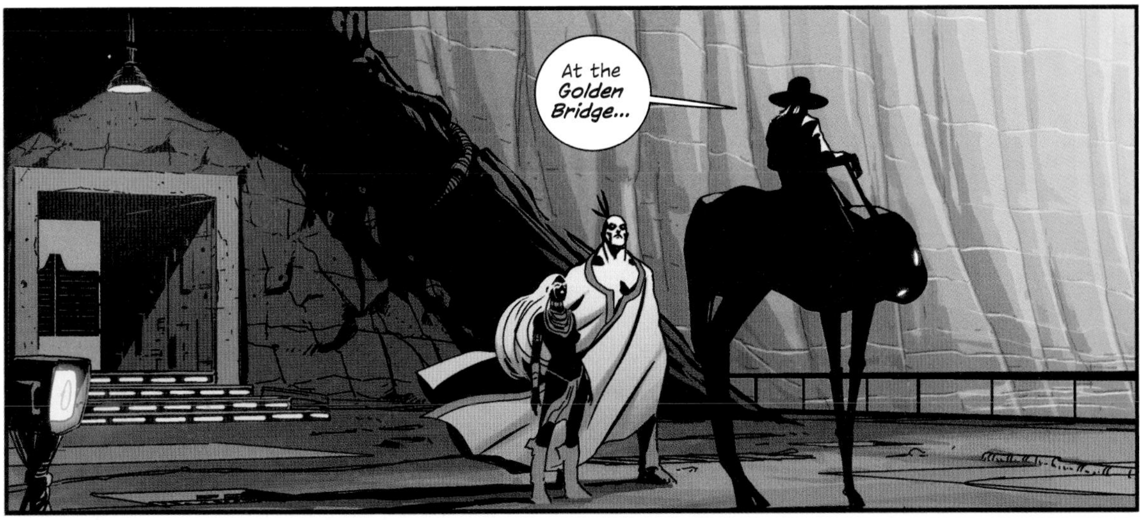
At the Golden Bridge...

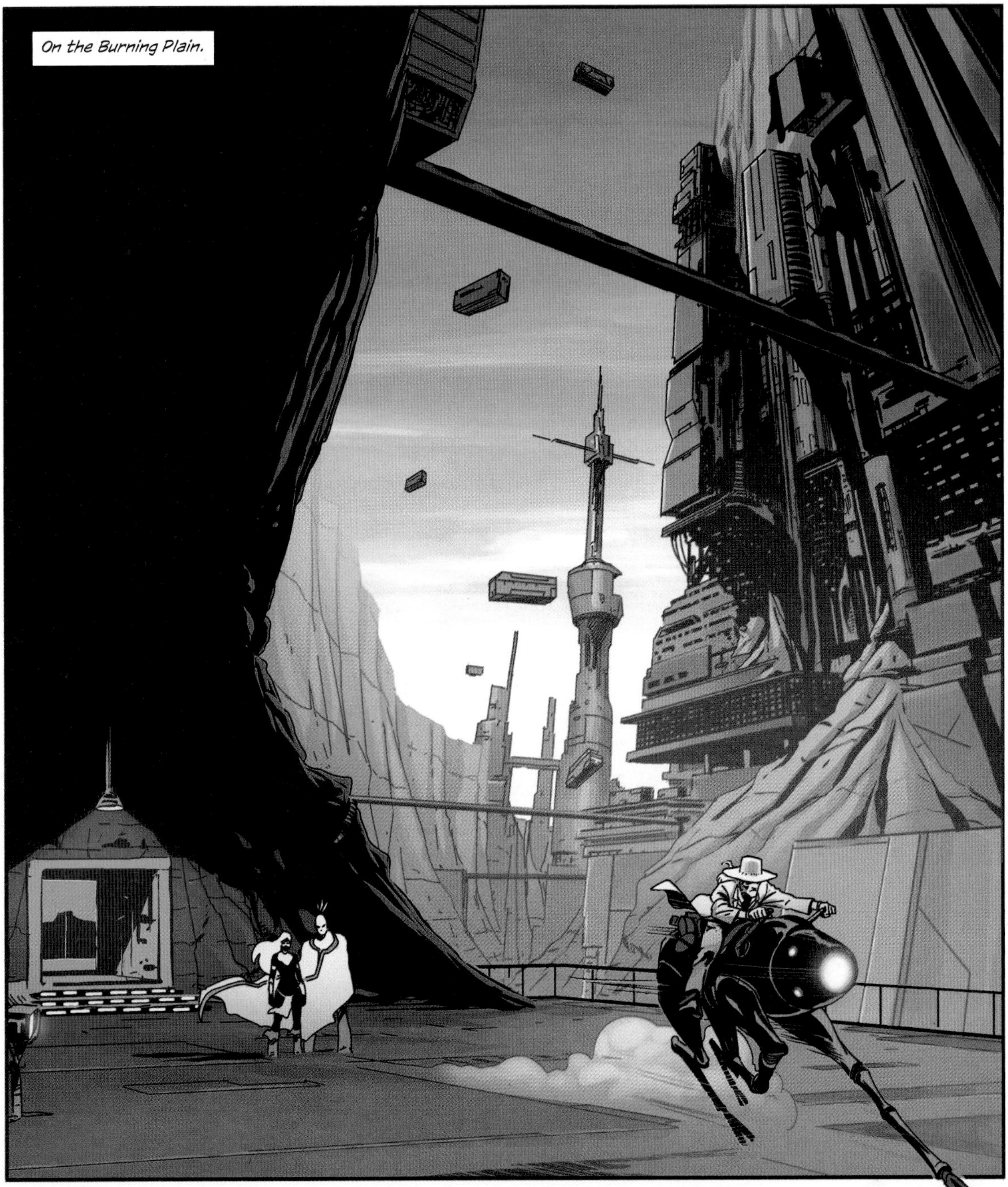
On the Burning Plain.

2064

THE APOCALYPSE: YEAR ONE

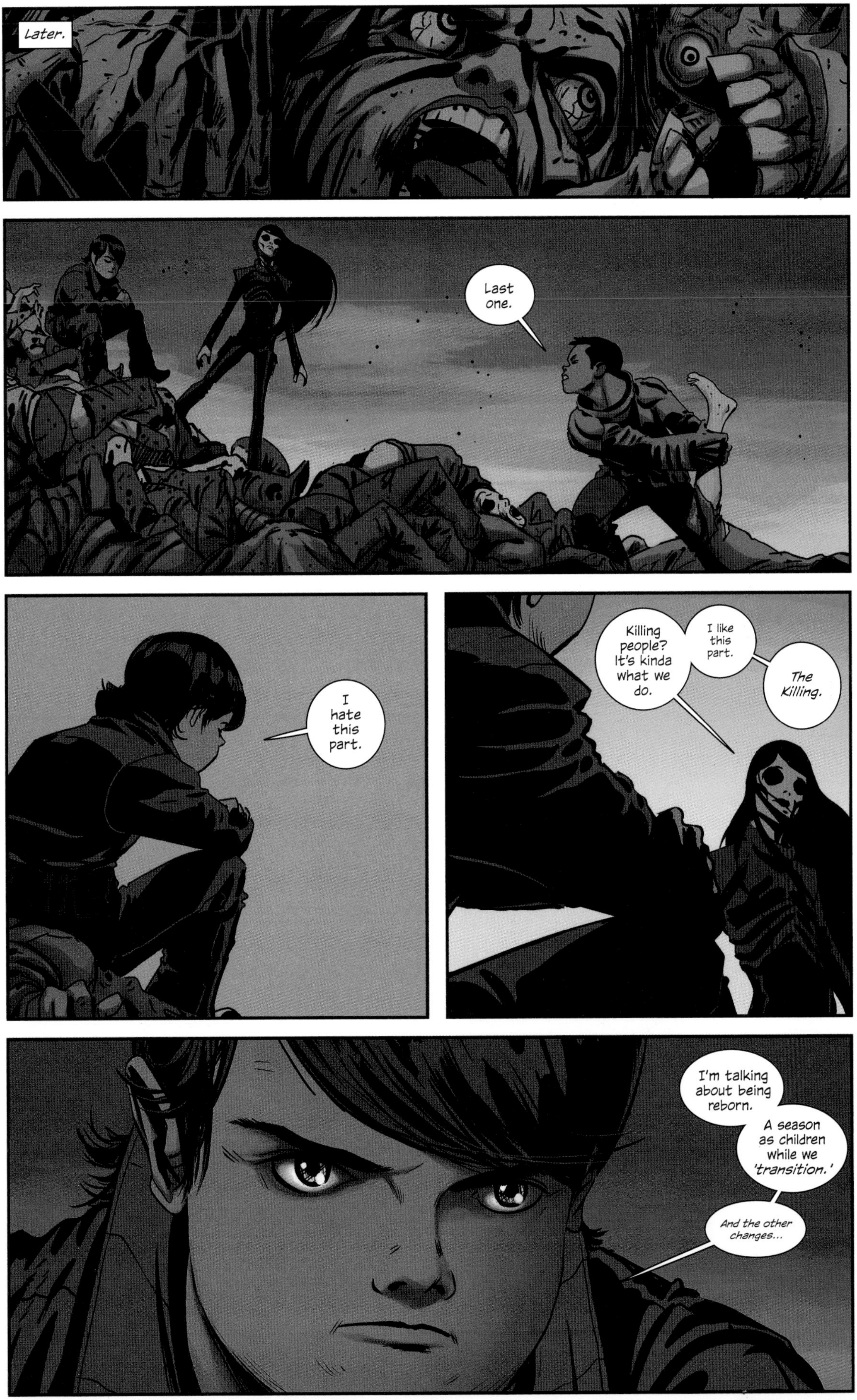
Later.
Last one.
I hate this part.
Killing people? It's kinda what we do.
I like this part.
The Killing.
I'm talking about being reborn.
A season as children while we 'transition.'
And the other changes...

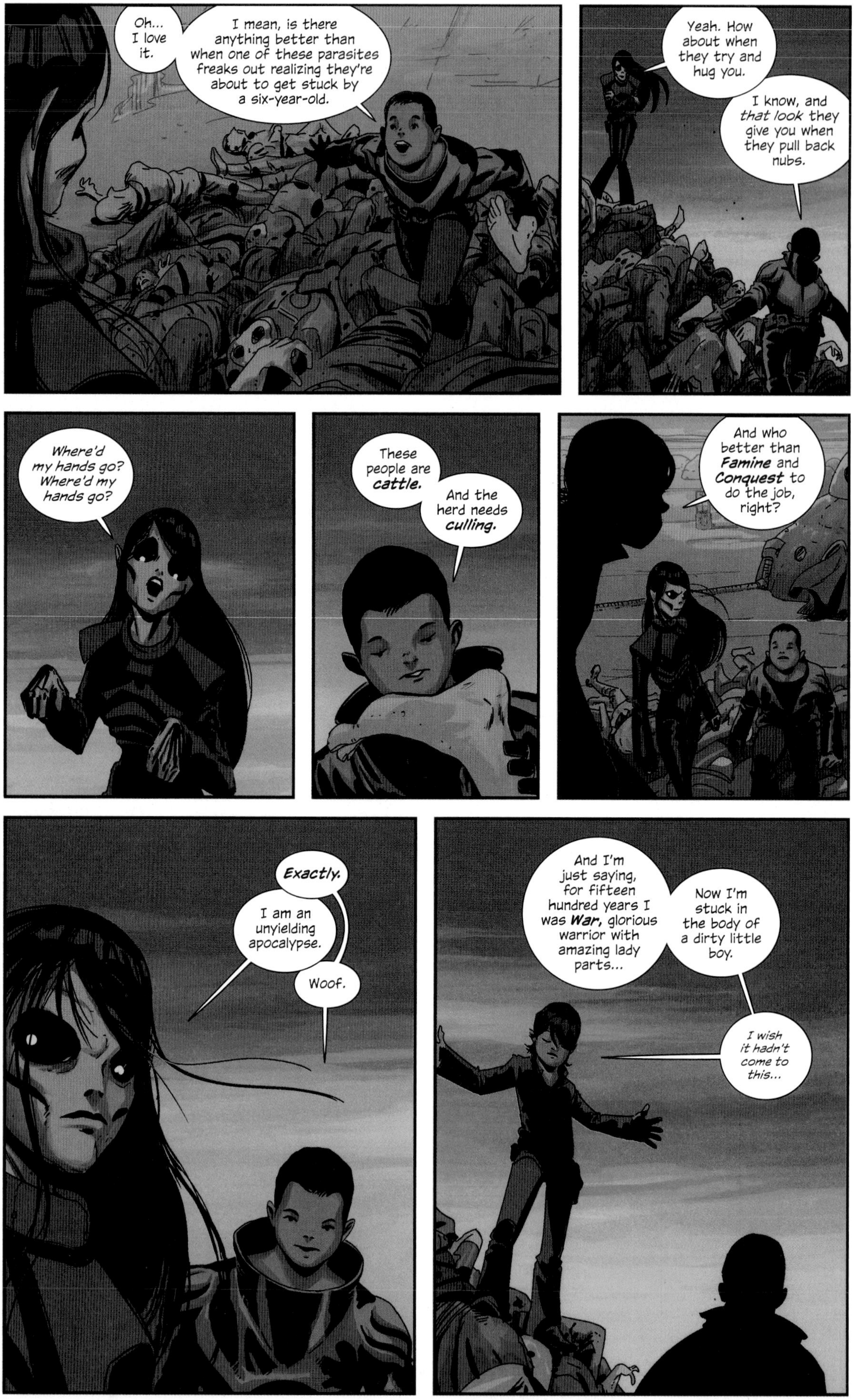
Oh... I love it.
I mean, is there anything better than when one of these parasites freaks out realizing they're about to get stuck by a six-year-old.
Yeah. How about when they try and hug you.
I know, and *that look* they give you when they pull back nubs.
Where'd my hands go? Where'd my hands go?
These people are ***cattle.***
And the herd needs ***culling.***
And who better than ***Famine*** and ***Conquest*** to do the job, right?
Exactly.
I am an unyielding apocalypse.
Woof.
And I'm just saying, for fifteen hundred years I was ***War,*** glorious warrior with amazing lady parts...
Now I'm stuck in the body of a dirty little boy.
I wish it hadn't come to this...

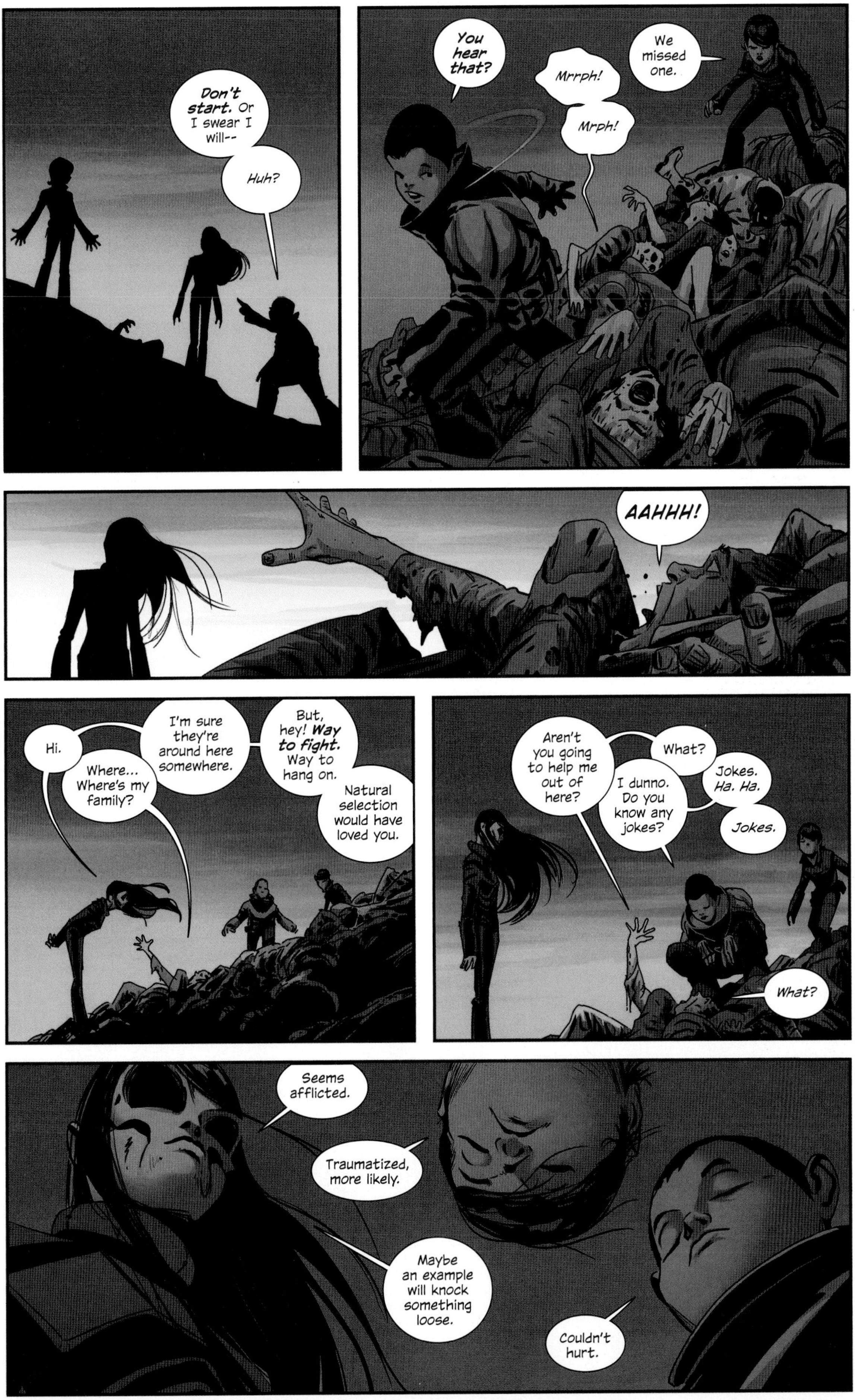
Don't start. Or I swear I will--
Huh?
You hear that?
Mrrph!
Mrph!
We missed one.
AAHHH!
Hi.
Where... Where's my family?
I'm sure they're around here somewhere.
But, hey! Way to fight. Way to hang on.
Natural selection would have loved you.
Aren't you going to help me out of here?
What?
I dunno. Do you know any jokes?
Jokes. Ha. Ha.
Jokes.
What?
Seems afflicted.
Traumatized, more likely.
Maybe an example will knock something loose.
Couldn't hurt.

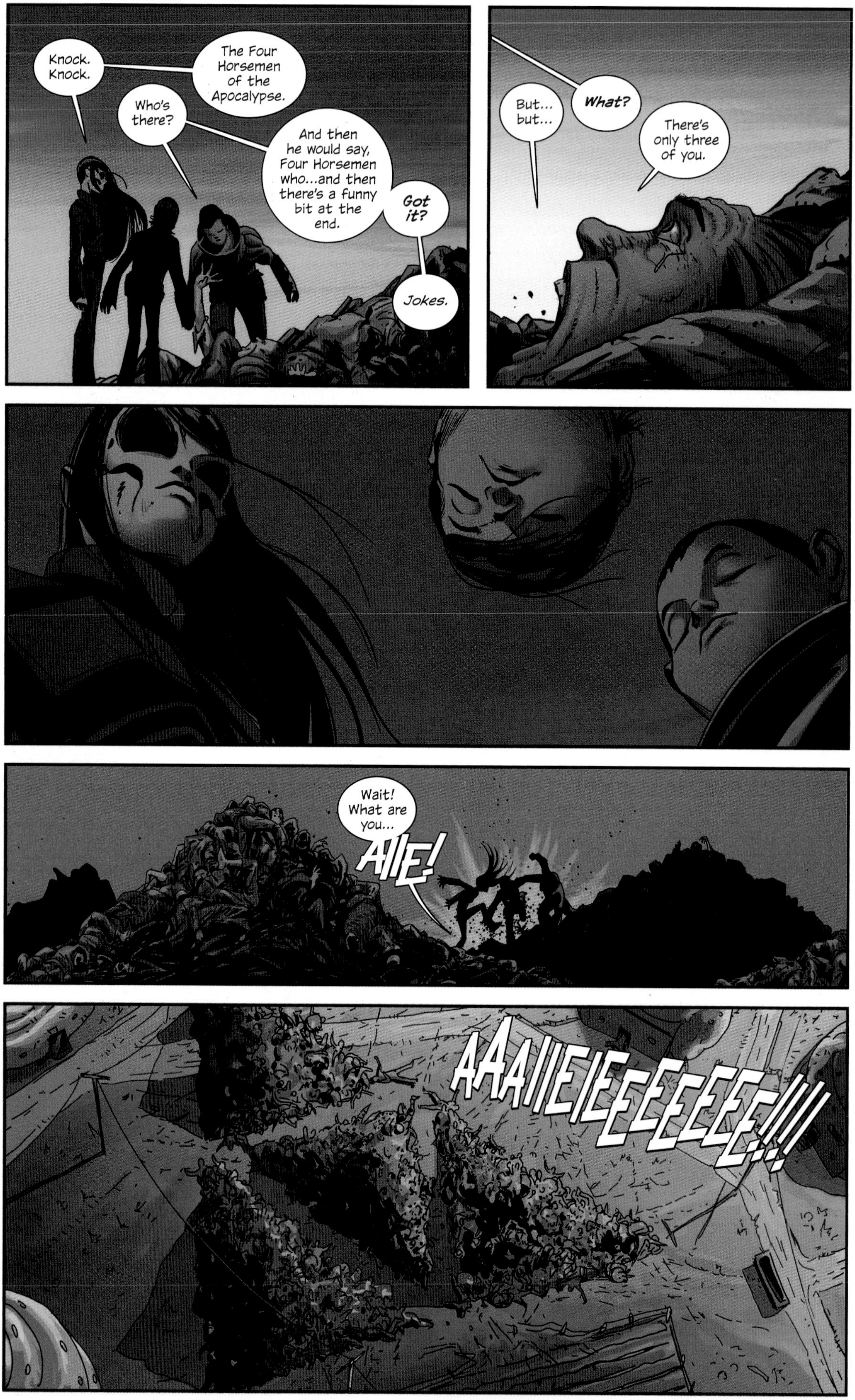

Knock. Knock.
Who's there?
The Four Horsemen of the Apocalypse.
And then he would say, Four Horsemen who...and then there's a funny bit at the end.
Got it?
Jokes.
What?
But... but...
There's only three of you.
Wait! What are you...
AIIE!
AAAIIEIEEEEEEE..!!!

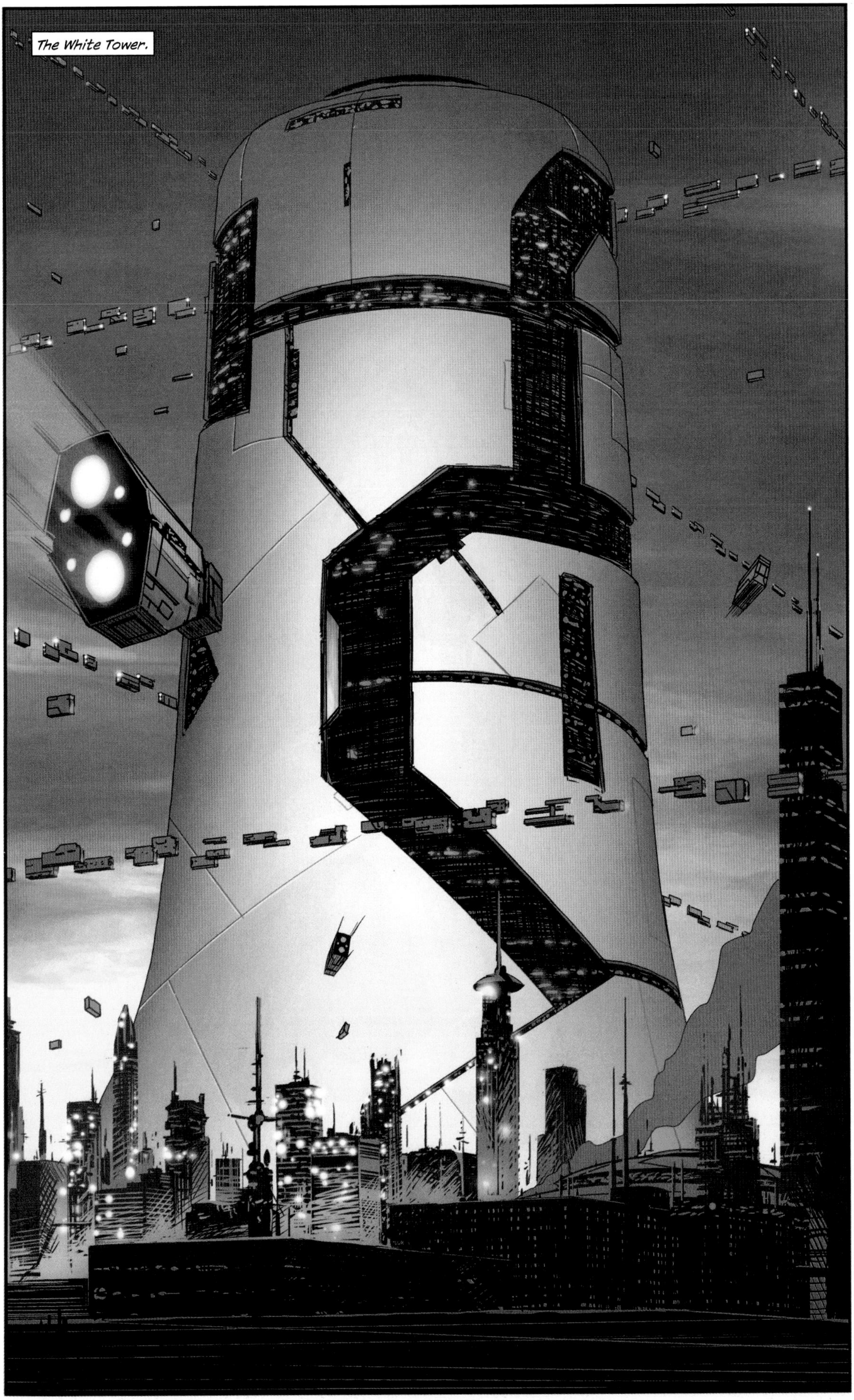
The White Tower.

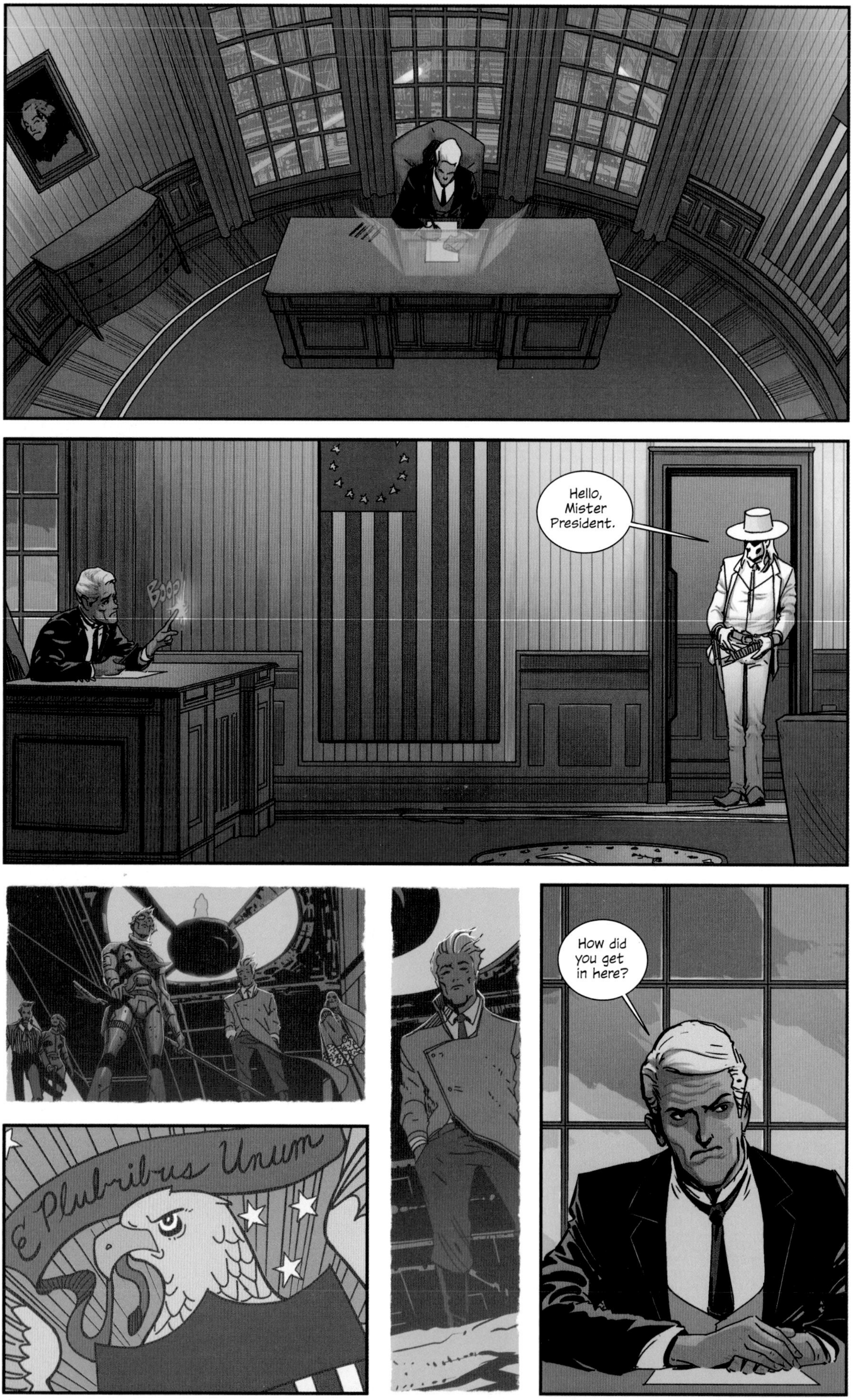
Hello, Mister President.
BOOP!
How did you get in here?
E Plubribus Unum

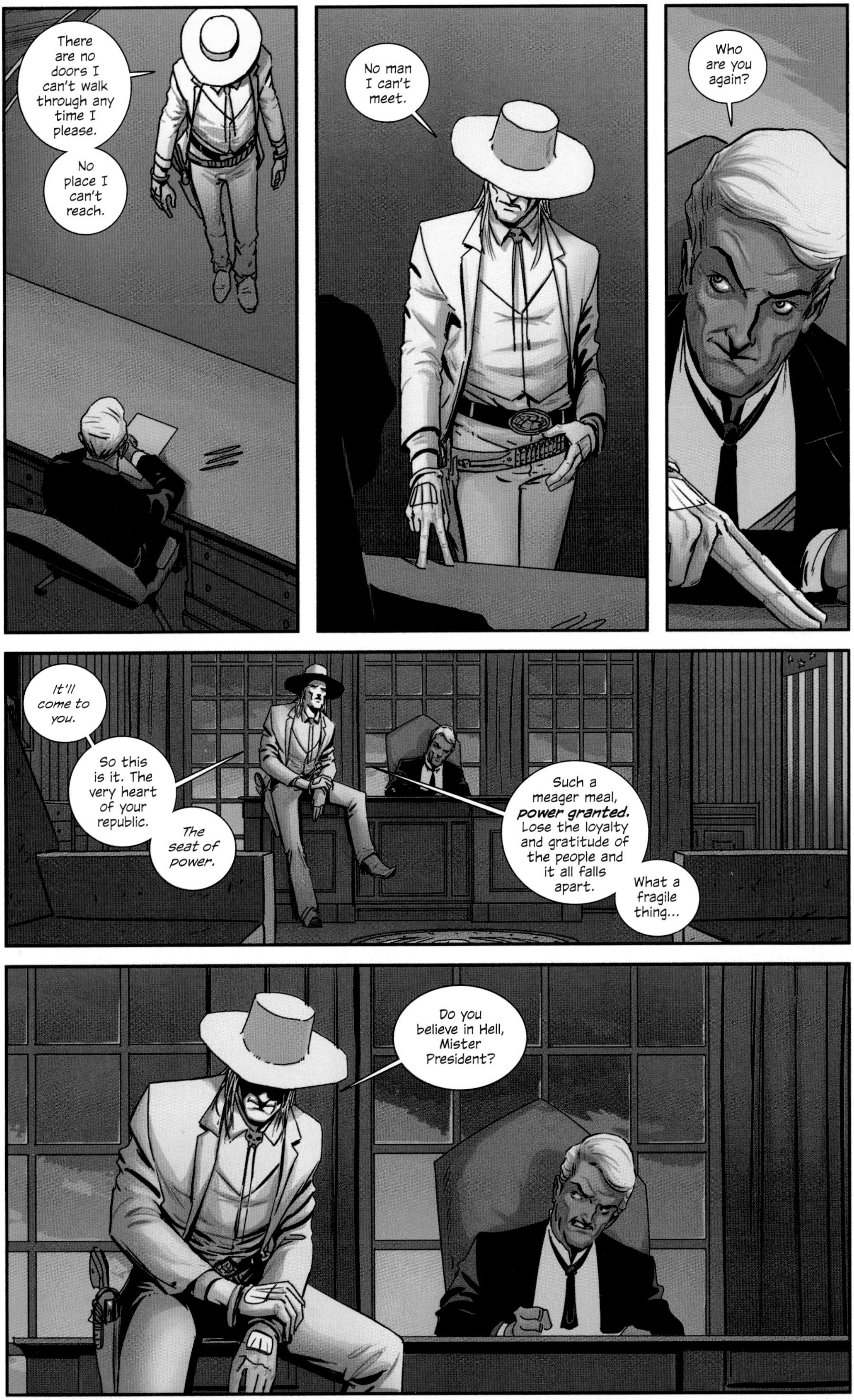
There are no doors I can't walk through any time I please.
No place I can't reach.
No man I can't meet.
Who are you again?
It'll come to you.
So this is it. The very heart of your republic.
The seat of power.
Such a meager meal, **power granted.** Lose the loyalty and gratitude of the people and it all falls apart.
What a fragile thing...
Do you believe in Hell, Mister President?

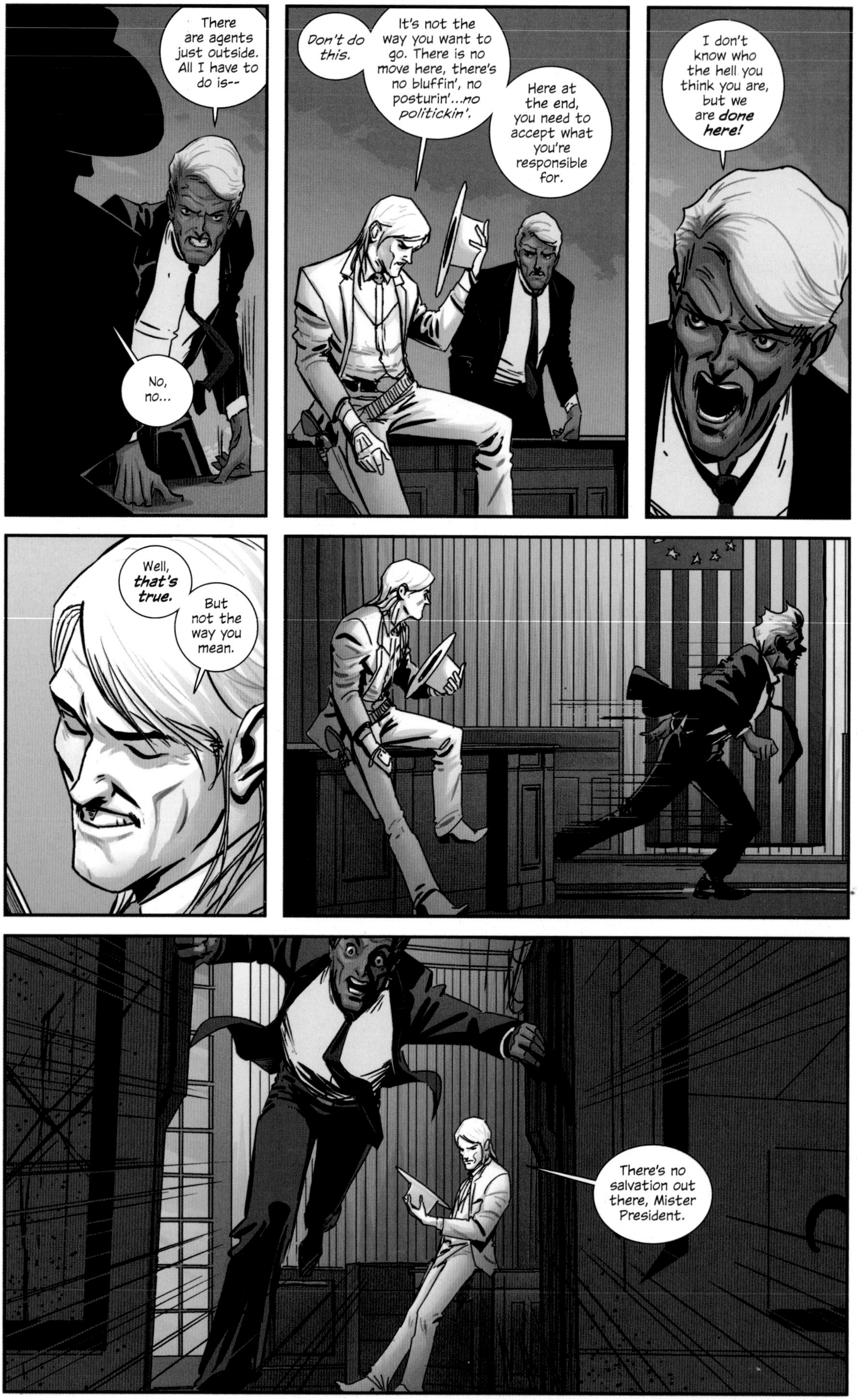
There are agents just outside. All I have to do is--
No, no...
Don't do this.
It's not the way you want to go. There is no move here, there's no bluffin', no posturin'...no politickin'.
Here at the end, you need to accept what you're responsible for.
I don't know who the hell you think you are, but we are done here!
Well, that's true.
But not the way you mean.
There's no salvation out there, Mister President.

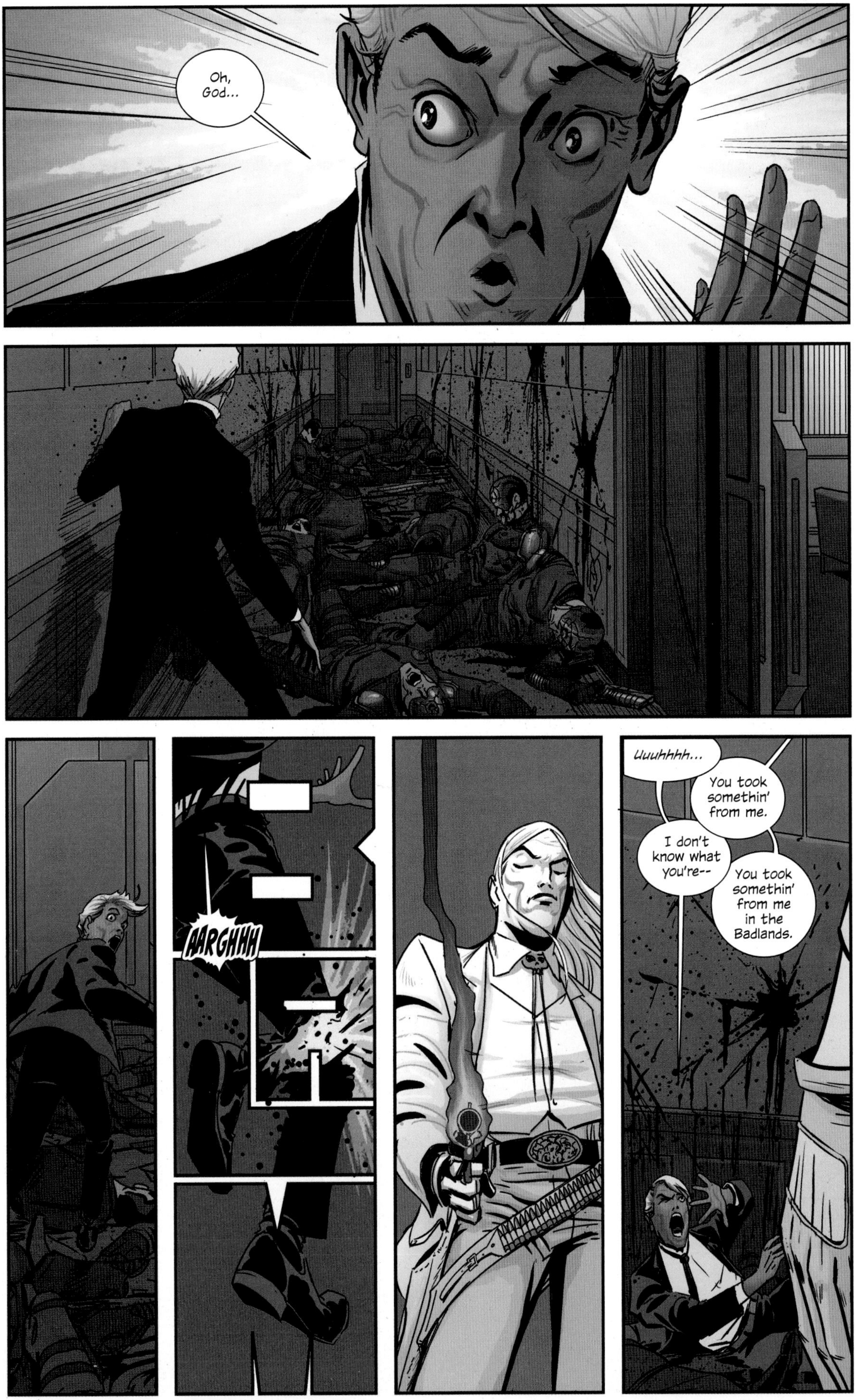
Oh, God...
AARGHHH
Uuuhhhh...
You took somethin' from me.
I don't know what you're--
You took somethin' from me in the Badlands.

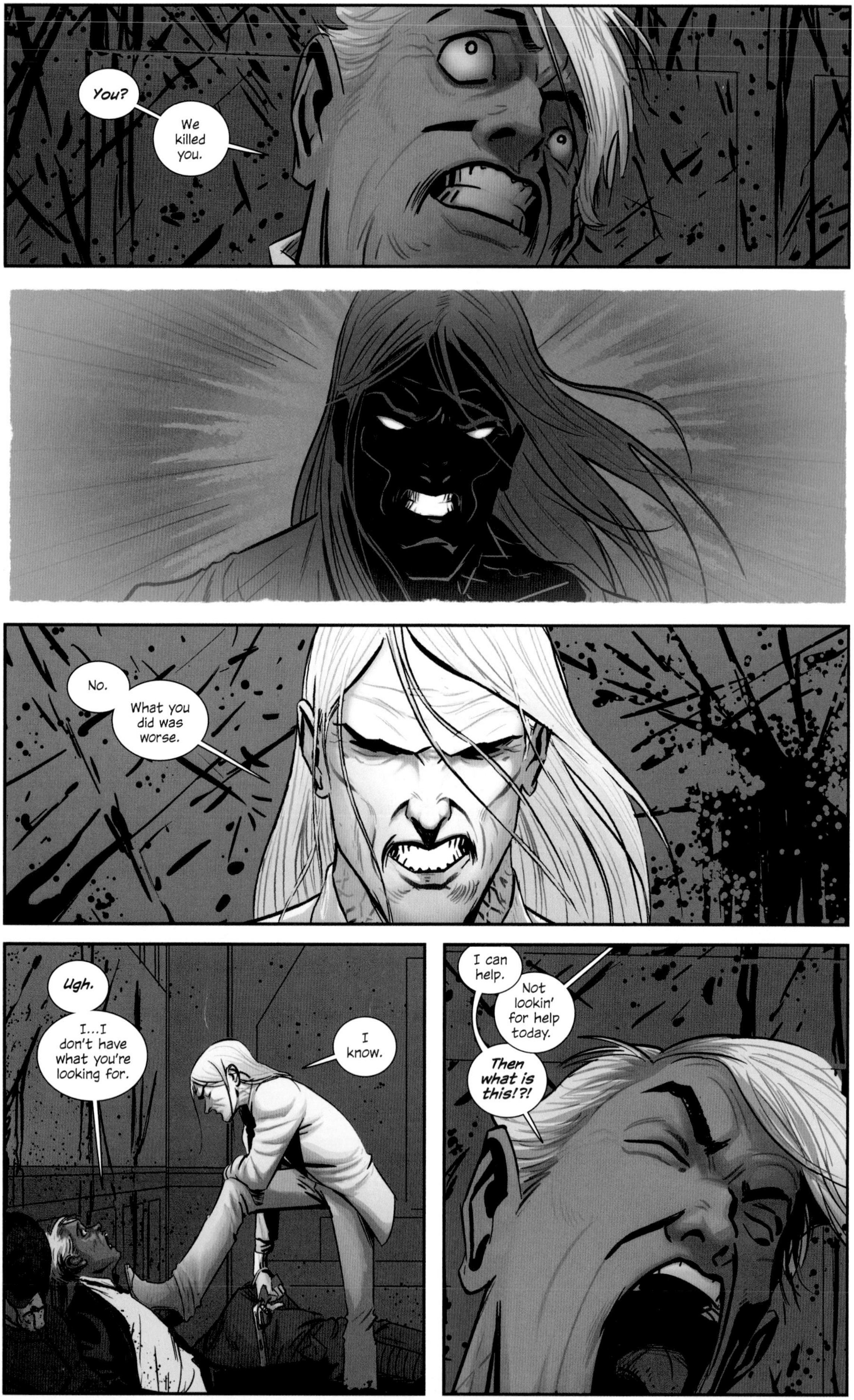
You?
We killed you.
No.
What you did was worse.
Ugh.
I...I don't have what you're looking for.
I know.
I can help.
Not lookin' for help today.
Then what is this!?!

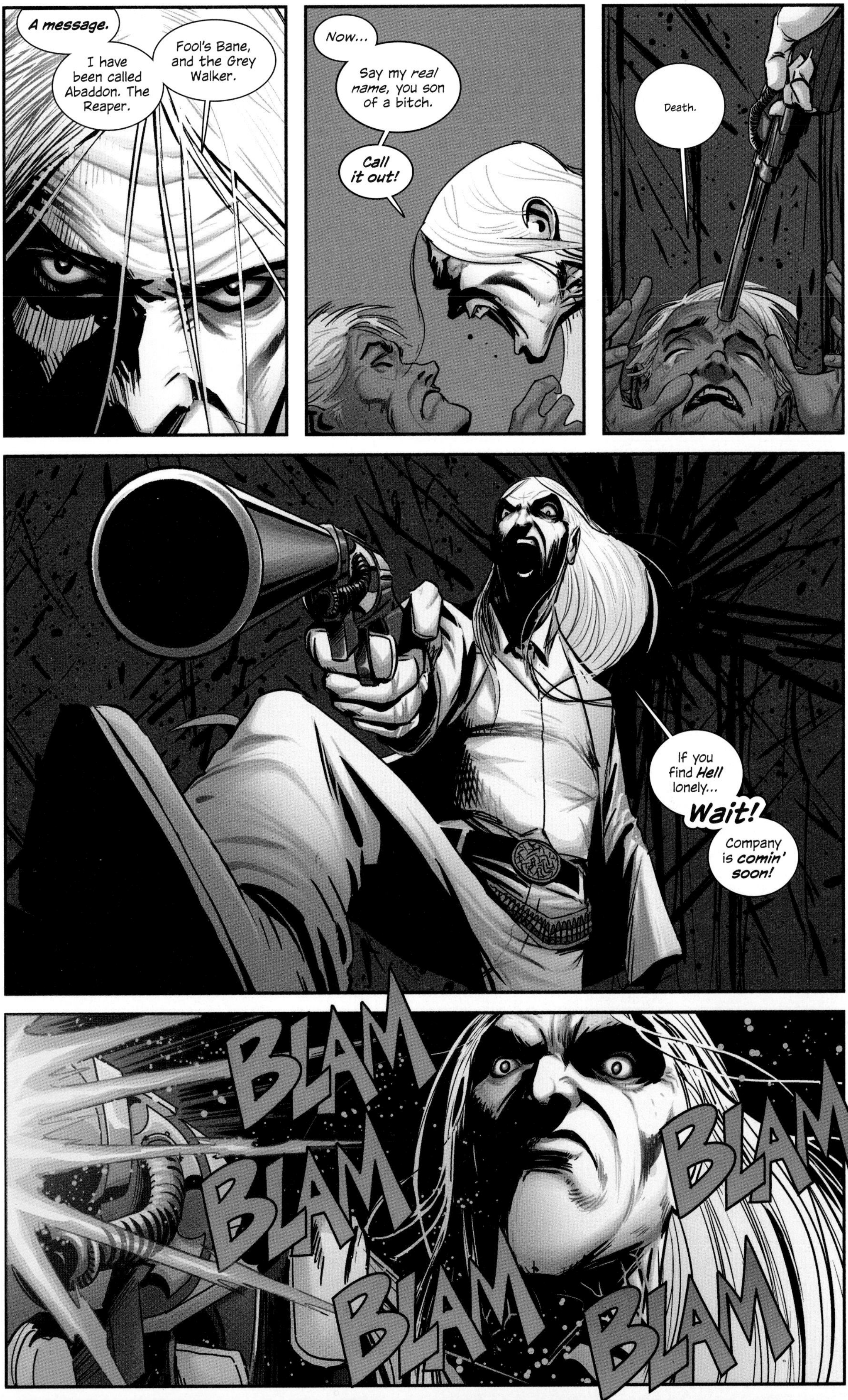
A message.
I have been called Abaddon. The Reaper.
Fool's Bane, and the Grey Walker.
Now...
Say my *real name*, you son of a bitch.
Call it out!
Death.
If you find *Hell* lonely...
Wait!
Company is *comin'* soon!
BLAM
BLAM
BLAM
BLAM
BLAM

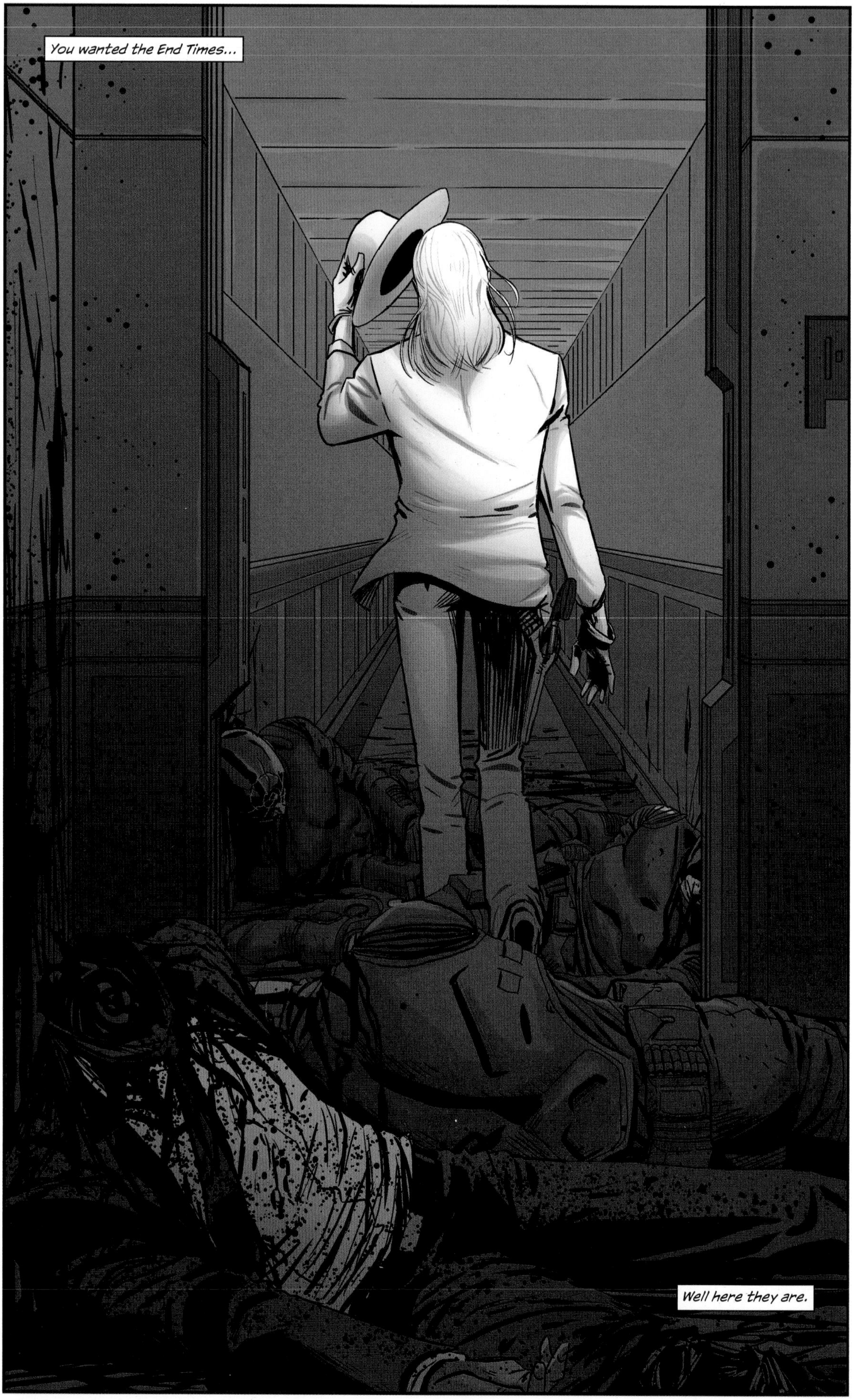
You wanted the End Times...
Well here they are.

TWELVE HOURS AGO, **THE PRESIDENT** WAS **MURDERED,** AND THE WORLD NOW AWAITS WORD OF THE NEW ONE.

ALL EYES ARE ON **THE WHITE TOWER**.

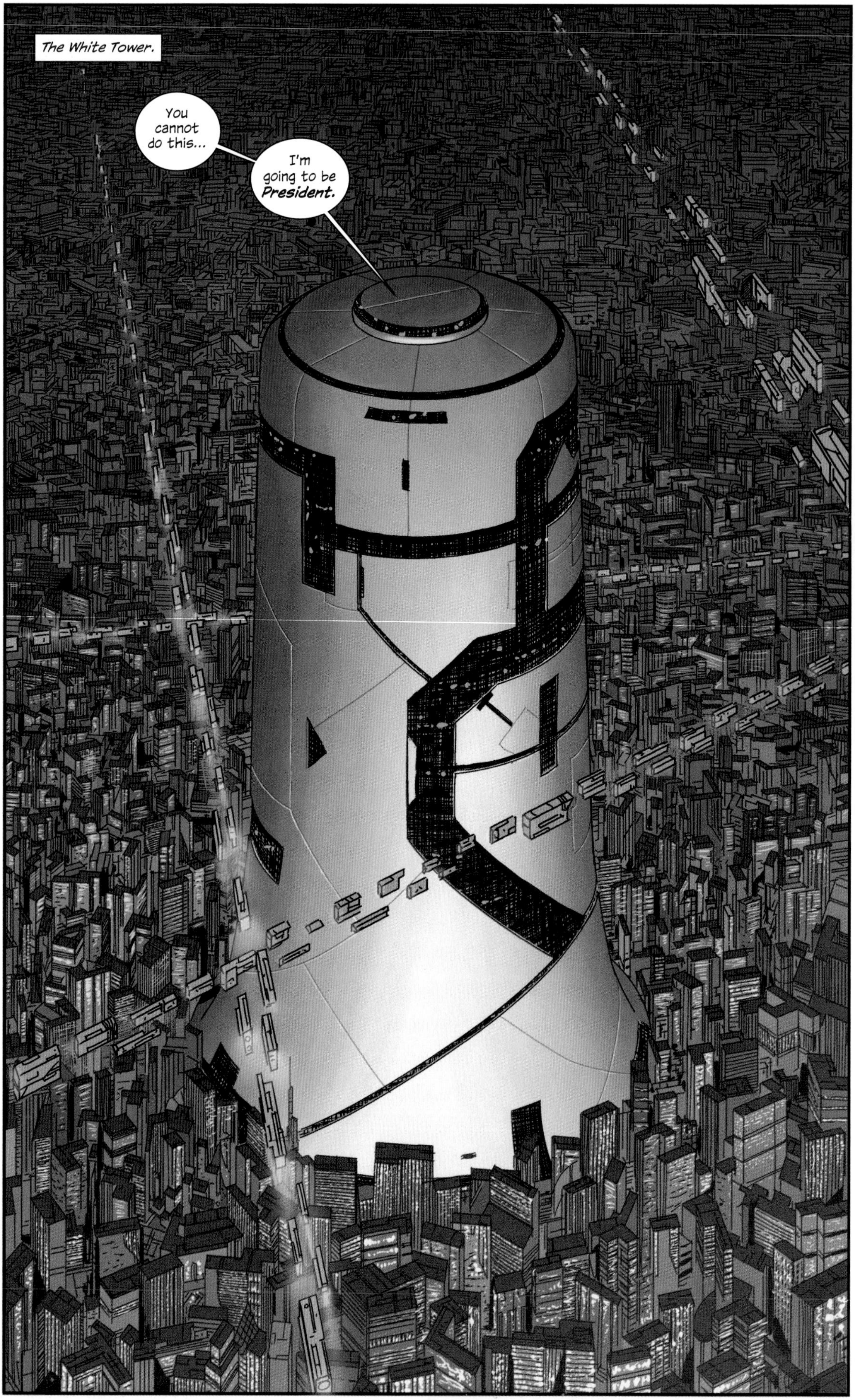
The White Tower.
You cannot do this...
I'm going to be President.

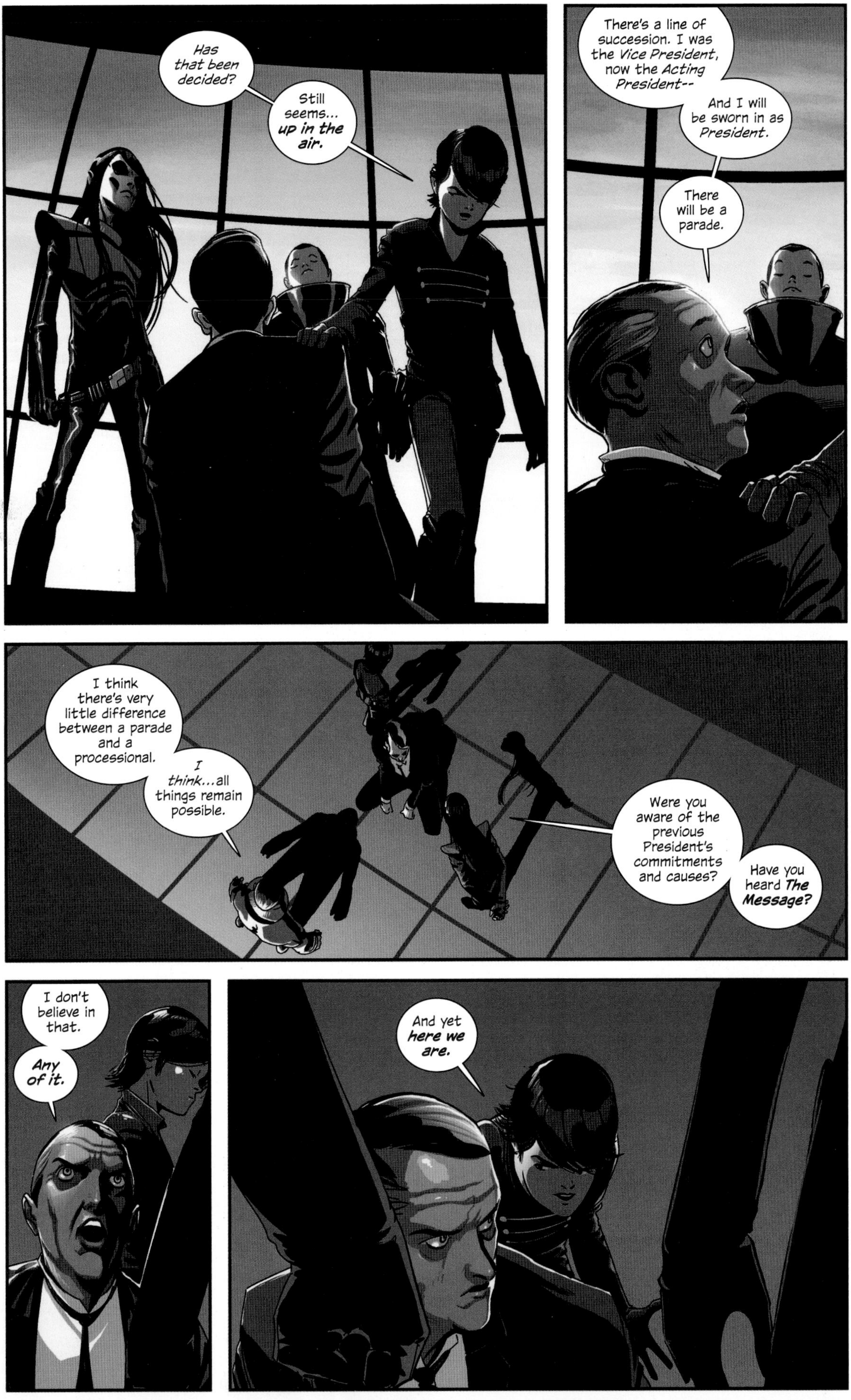
Has that been decided?
Still seems... up in the air.
There's a line of succession. I was the Vice President, now the Acting President--
And I will be sworn in as President.
There will be a parade.
I think there's very little difference between a parade and a processional.
I think...all things remain possible.
Were you aware of the previous President's commitments and causes?
Have you heard The Message?
I don't believe in that.
Any of it.
And yet here we are.

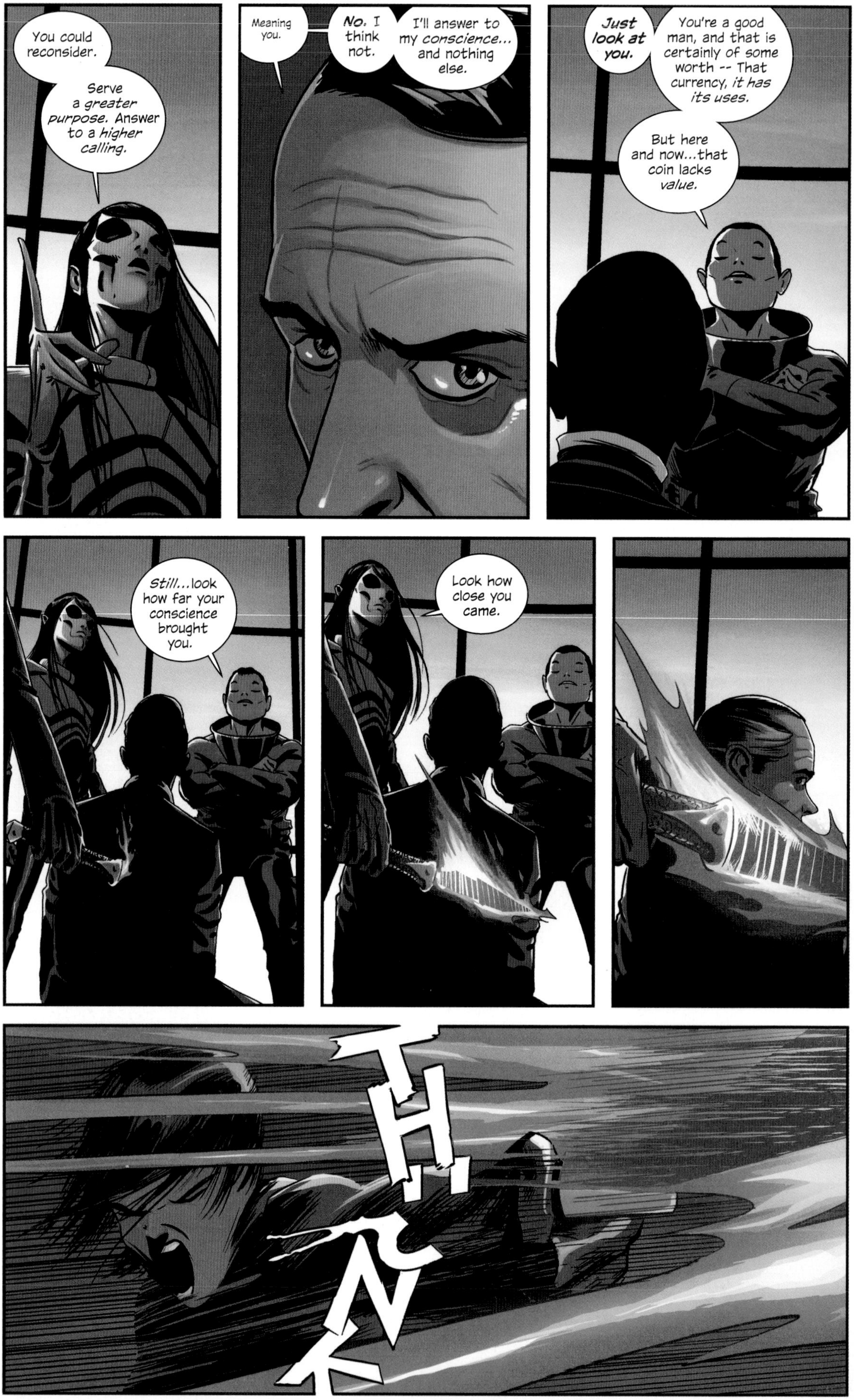
You could reconsider.
Serve a *greater purpose.* Answer to a *higher calling.*
Meaning you.
No. I think not.
I'll answer to my *conscience...* and nothing else.
Just look at you.
You're a good man, and that is certainly of some worth -- That currency, *it has its uses.*
But here and now...that coin lacks *value.*
*Still...*look how far your conscience brought you.
Look how close you came.
THUNK

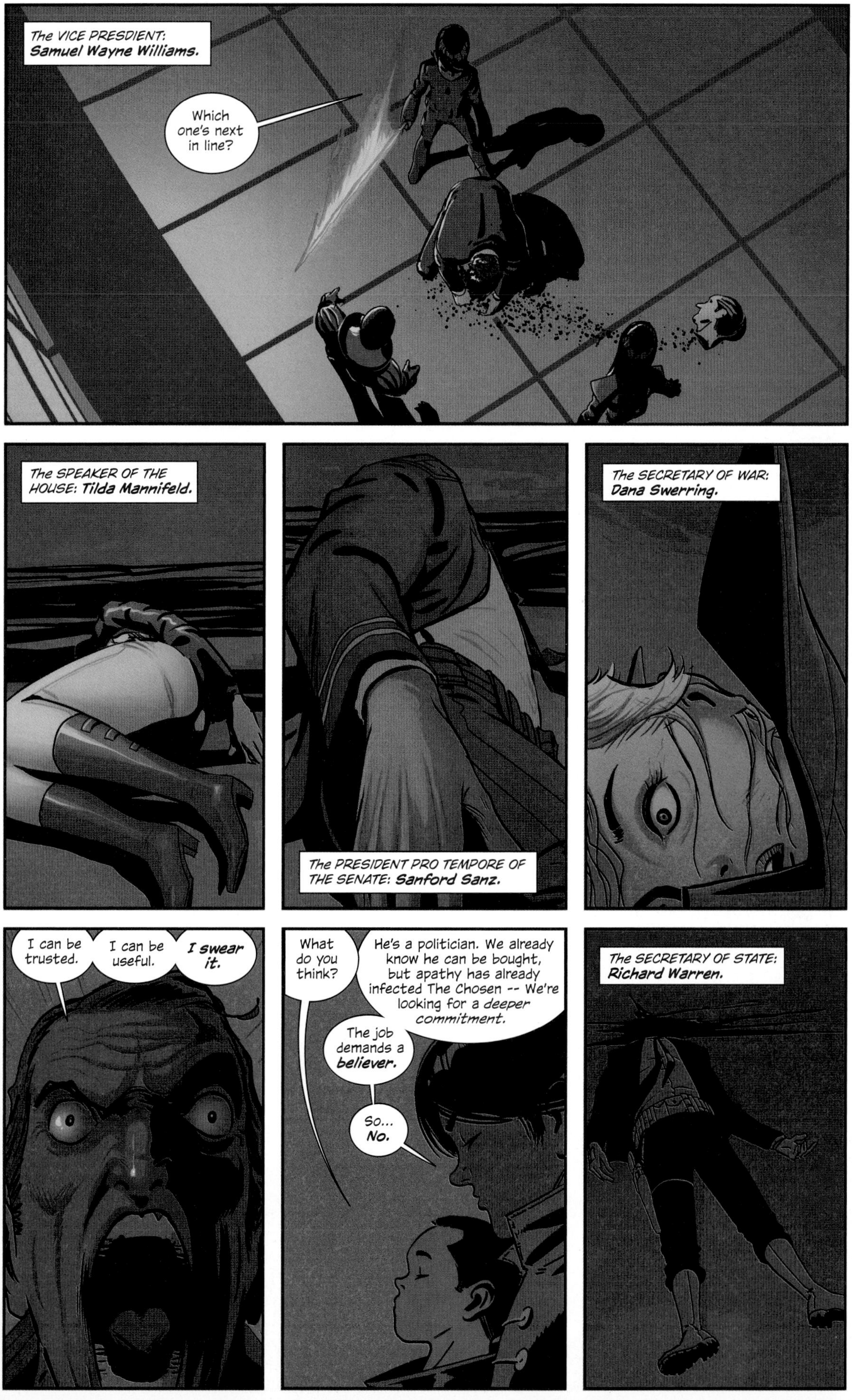
The VICE PRESIDENT: Samuel Wayne Williams.
Which one's next in line?
The SPEAKER OF THE HOUSE: Tilda Mannifeld.
The PRESIDENT PRO TEMPORE OF THE SENATE: Sanford Sanz.
The SECRETARY OF WAR: Dana Swerring.
I can be trusted.
I can be useful.
I swear it.
What do you think?
He's a politician. We already know he can be bought, but apathy has already infected The Chosen -- We're looking for a deeper commitment.
The job demands a believer.
So... No.
The SECRETARY OF STATE: Richard Warren.

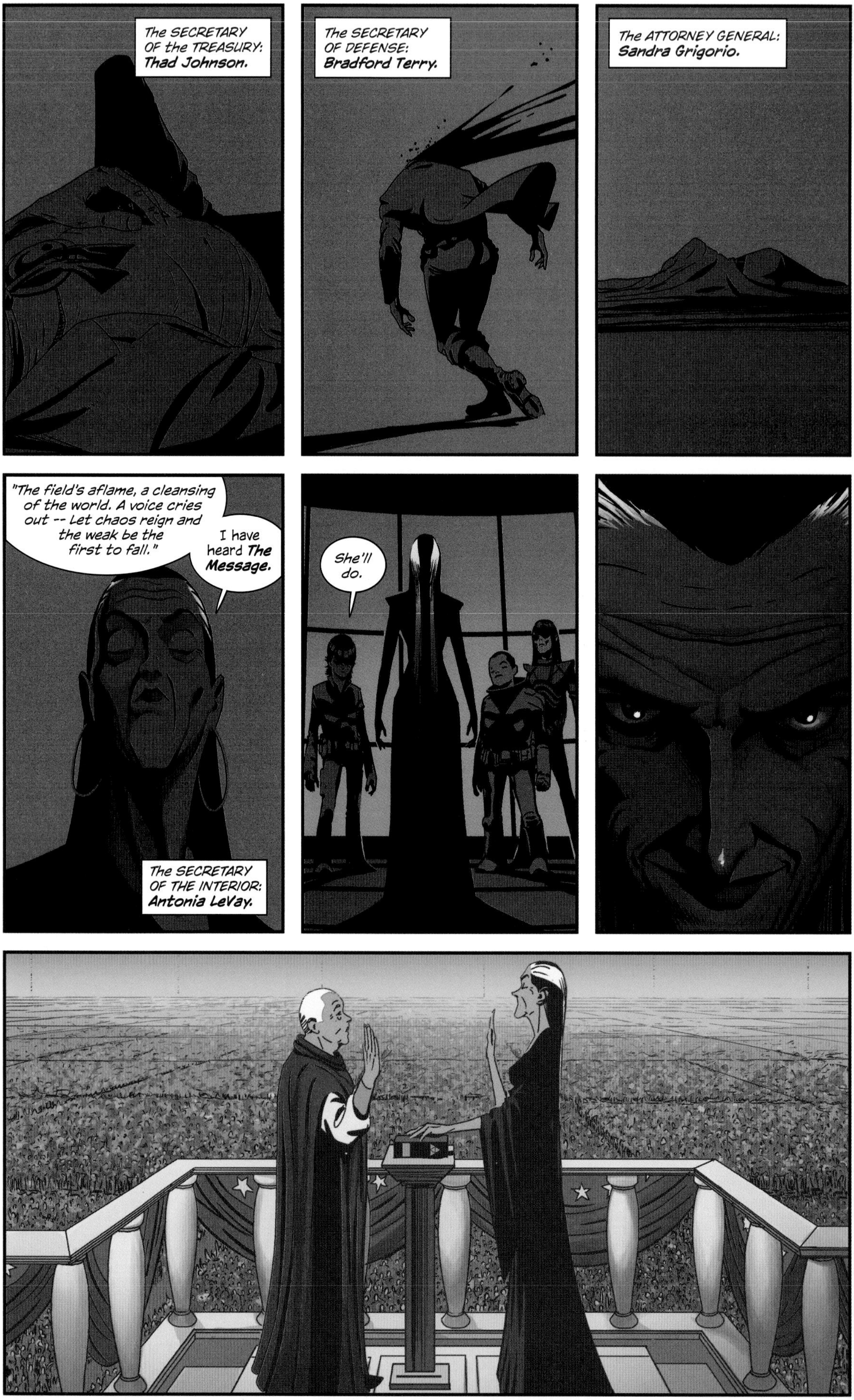
The SECRETARY OF the TREASURY: Thad Johnson.
The SECRETARY OF DEFENSE: Bradford Terry.
The ATTORNEY GENERAL: Sandra Grigorio.
"The field's aflame, a cleansing of the world. A voice cries out -- Let chaos reign and the weak be the first to fall."
I have heard The Message.
The SECRETARY OF THE INTERIOR: Antonia LeVay.
She'll do.

OF **THE THIRD**, BUT NOT OF **THE THREE.** A LOTUS, THE DEATH AND RESURRECTION OF LOVE.

A **CUP**, OF A **CUP**. A **CHALICE**, OF A **CHALICE**.

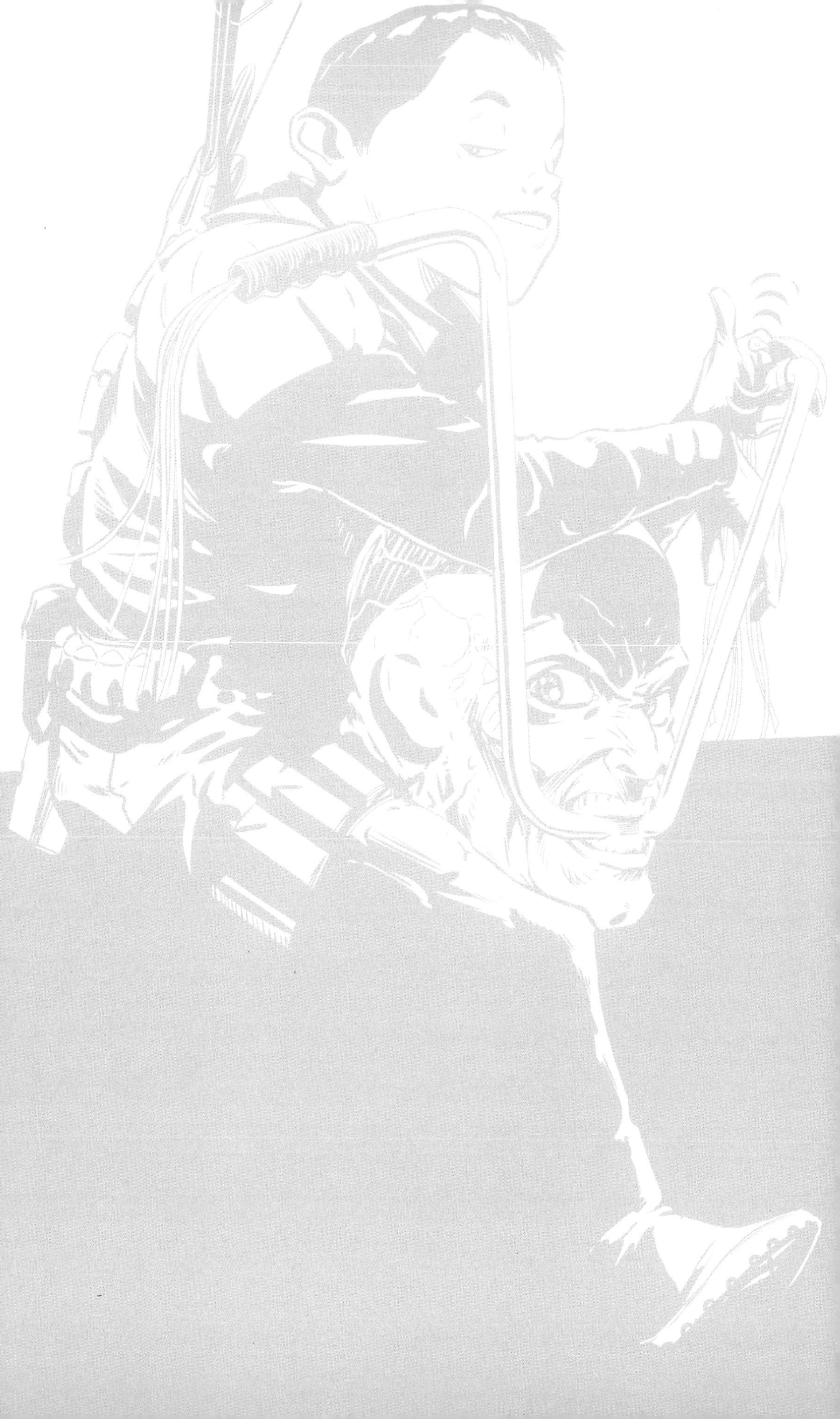

TWO: ABOVE ALL,
FEW ARE **CHOSEN**

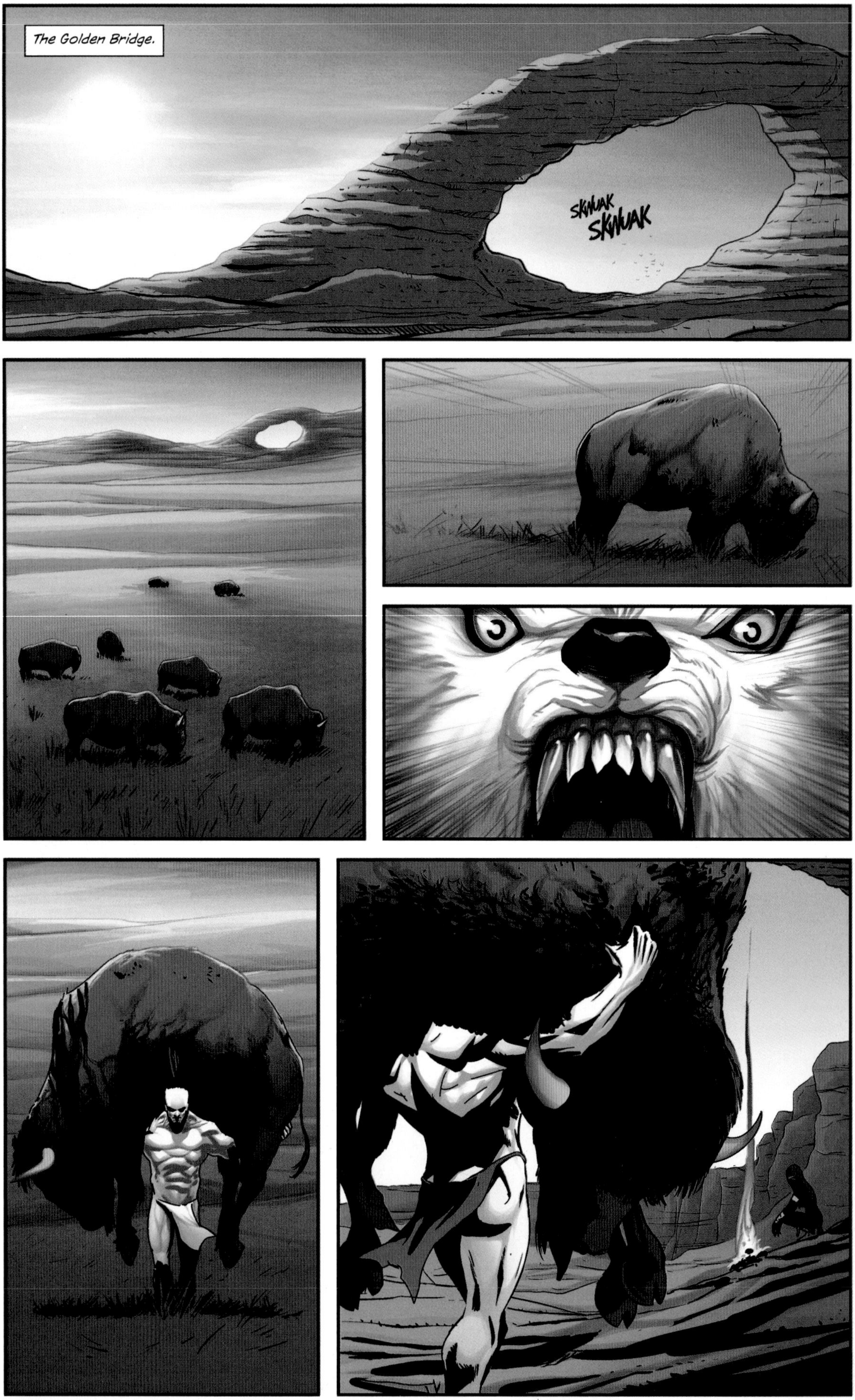
The Golden Bridge.
SKWUAK
SKWUAK

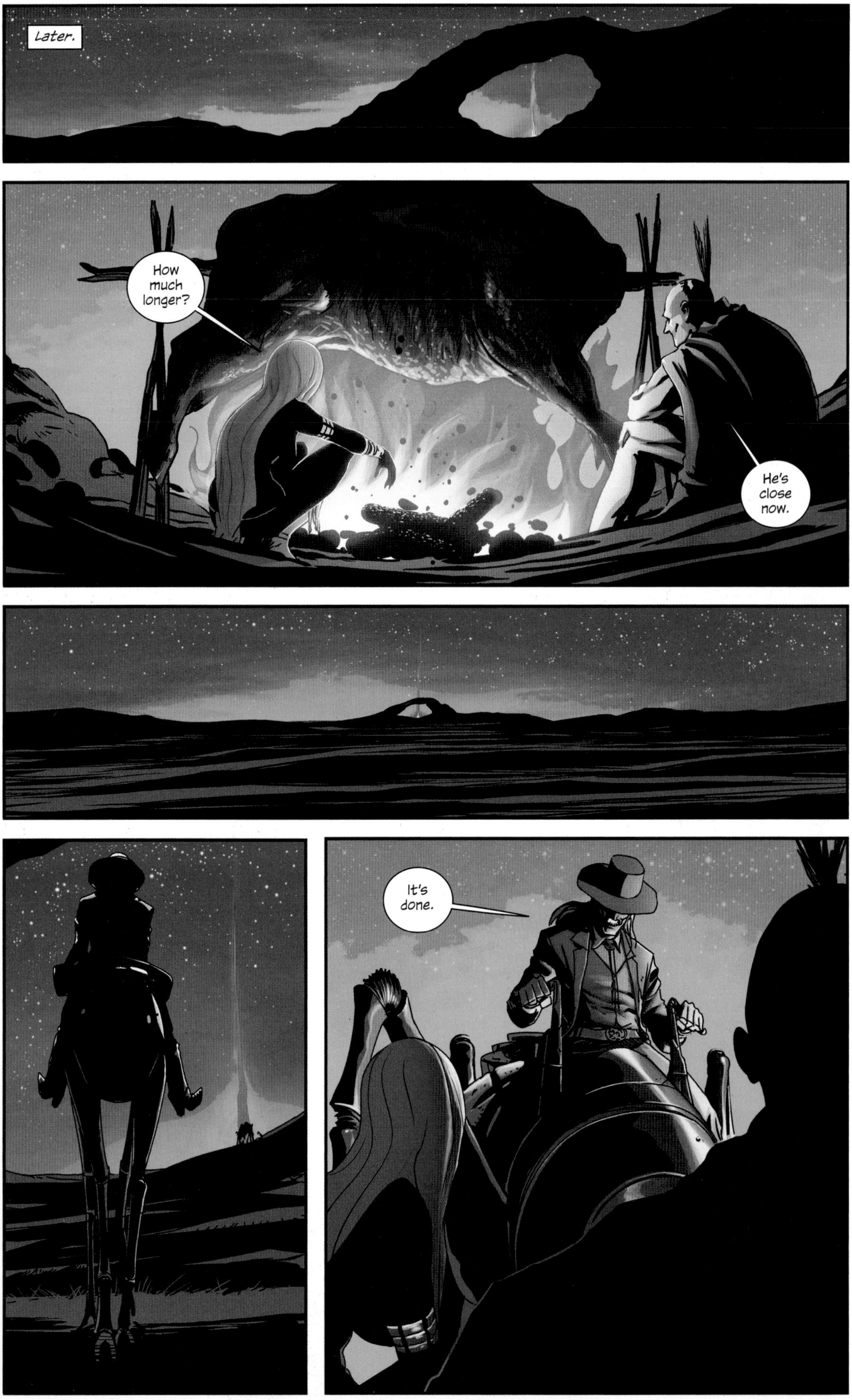
Later.
How much longer?
He's close now.
It's done.

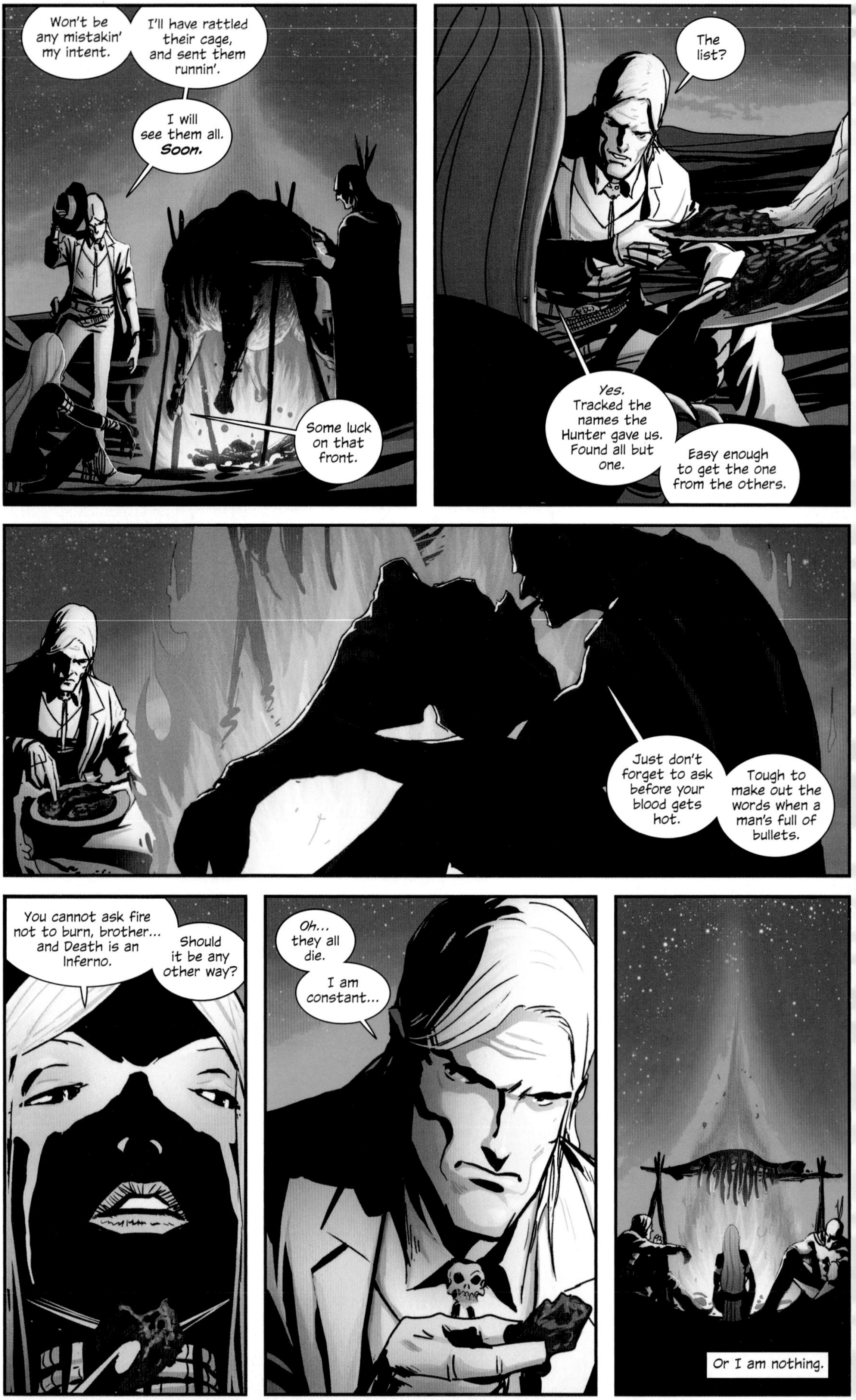
Won't be any mistakin' my intent.
I'll have rattled their cage, and sent them runnin'.
I will see them all. **Soon.**
Some luck on that front.
The list?
Yes. Tracked the names the Hunter gave us. Found all but one.
Easy enough to get the one from the others.
Just don't forget to ask before your blood gets hot.
Tough to make out the words when a man's full of bullets.
You cannot ask fire not to burn, brother... and Death is an Inferno.
Should it be any other way?
Oh... they all die.
I am constant...
Or I am nothing.

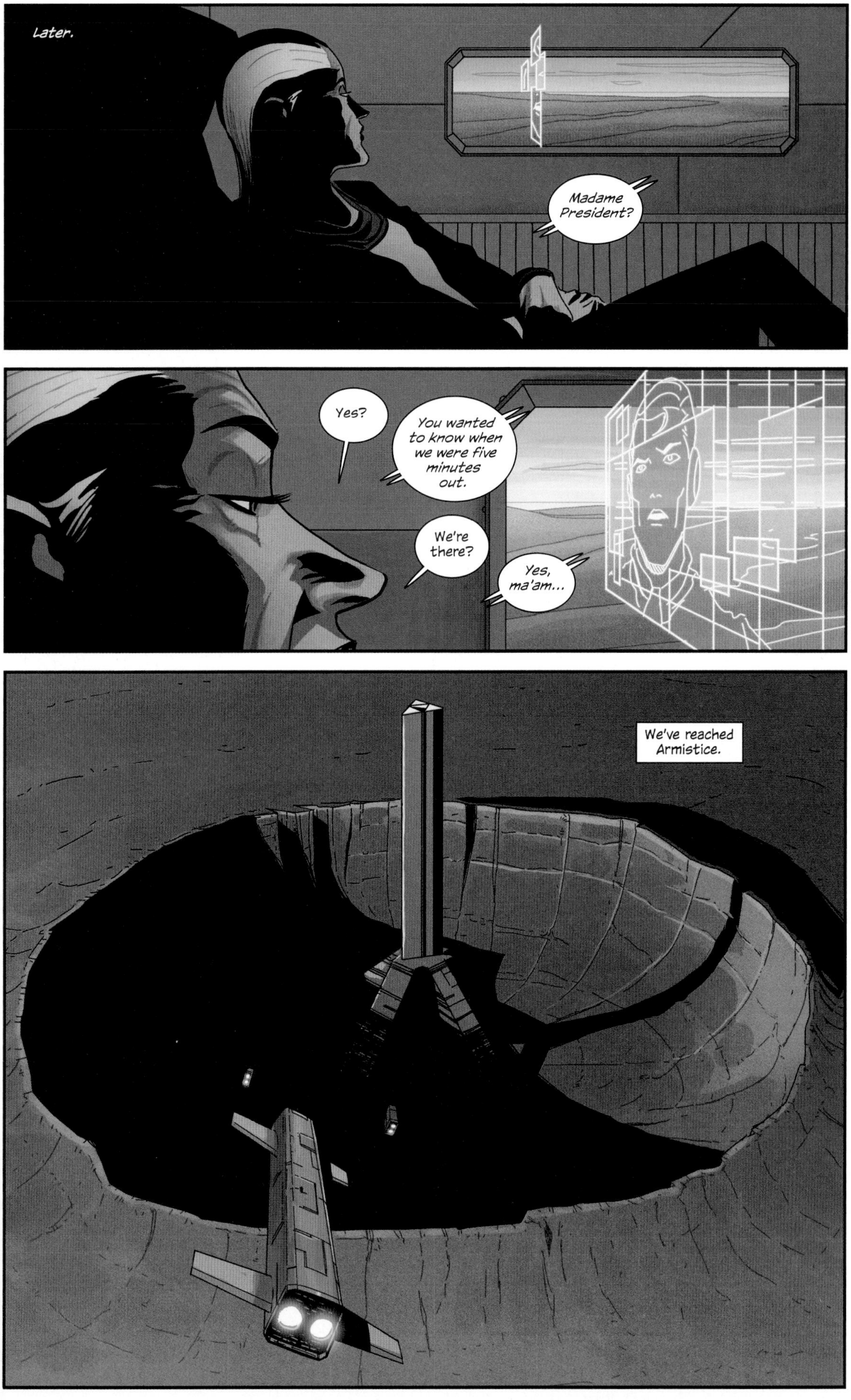
Later.
Madame President?
Yes?
You wanted to know when we were five minutes out.
We're there?
Yes, ma'am...
We've reached Armistice.

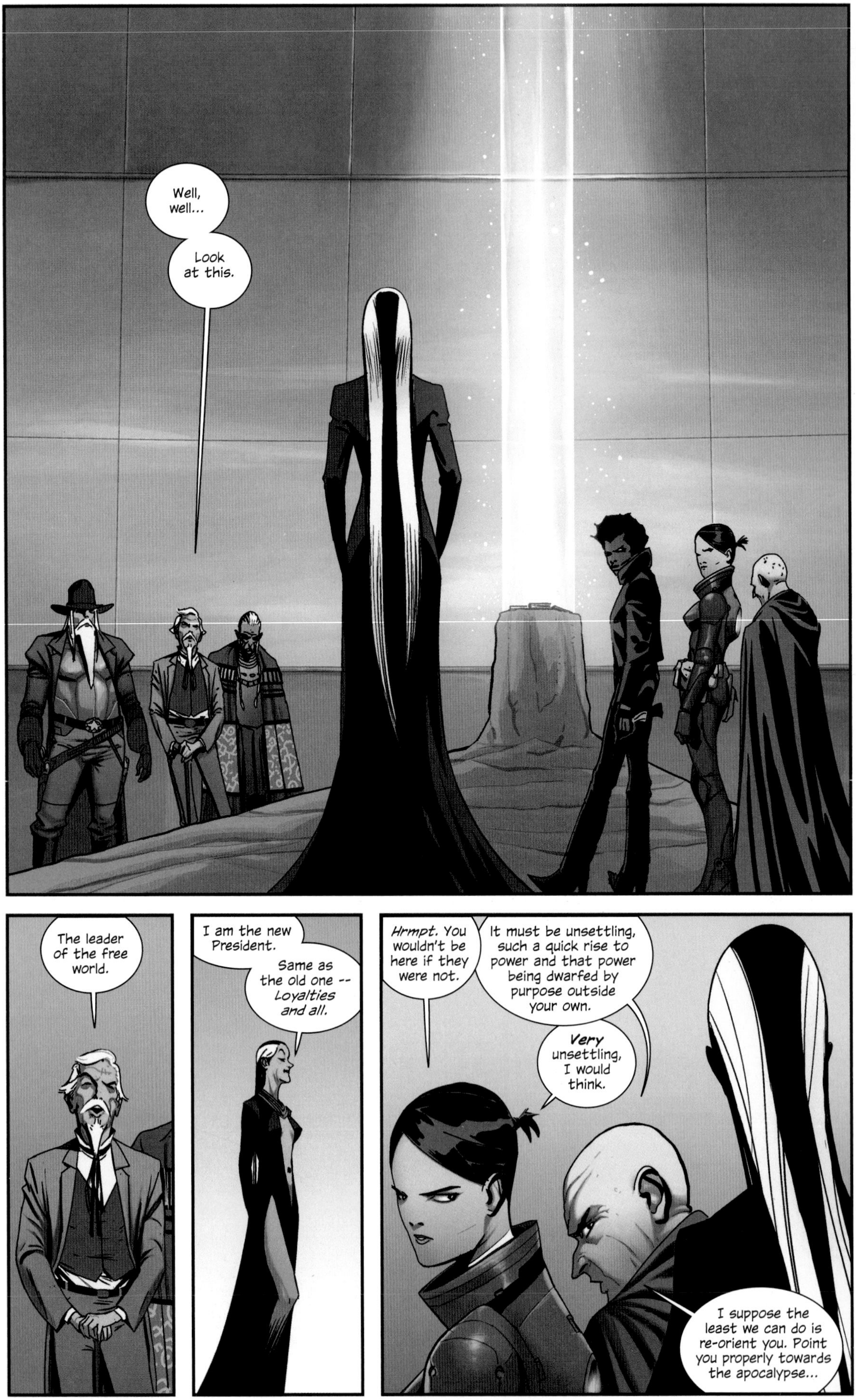
Well, well...
Look at this.
The leader of the free world.
I am the new President.
Same as the old one -- *Loyalties and all.*
Hrmpt. You wouldn't be here if they were not.
It must be unsettling, such a quick rise to power and that power being dwarfed by purpose outside your own.
Very unsettling, I would think.
I suppose the least we can do is re-orient you. Point you properly towards the apocalypse...

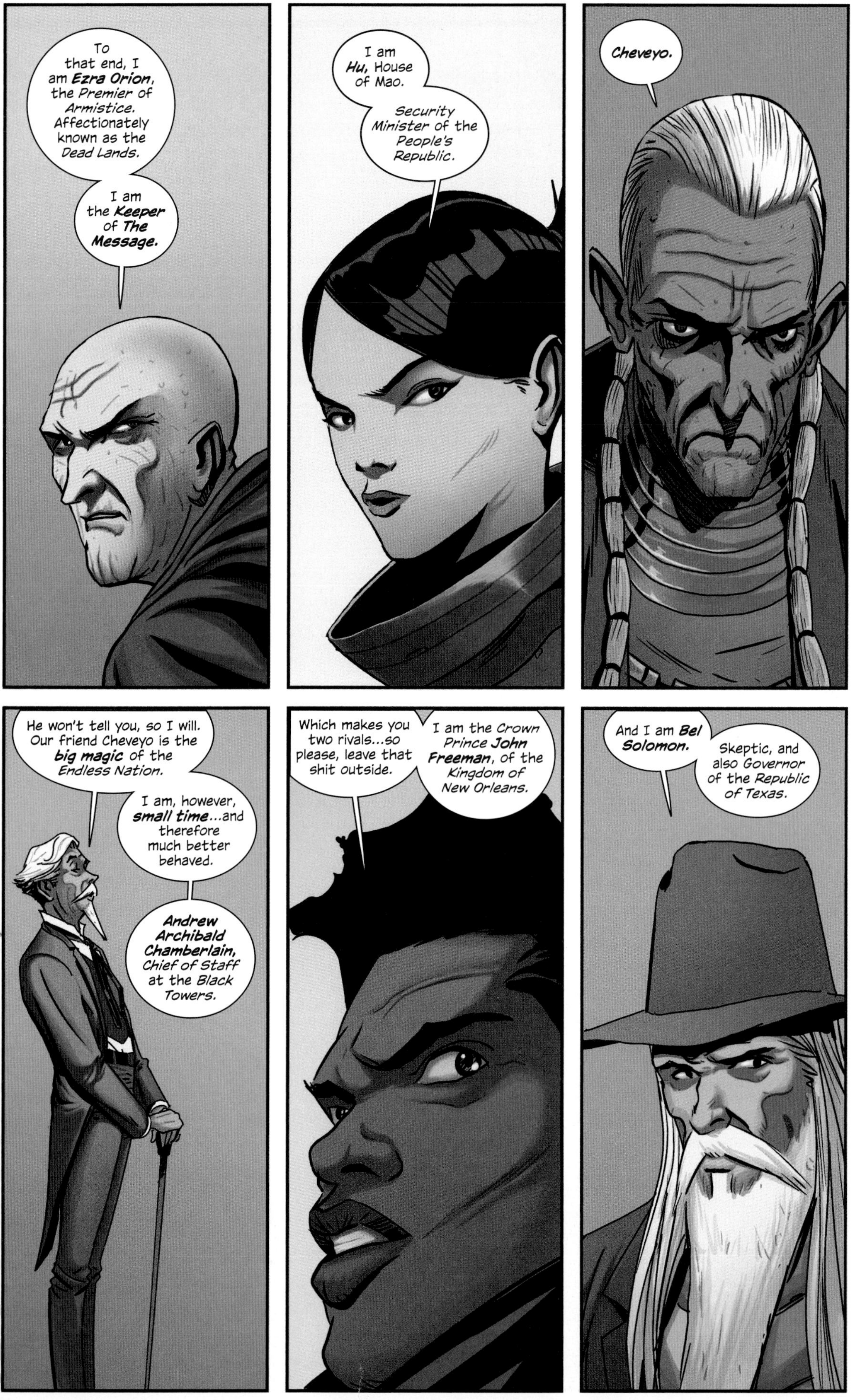
To that end, I am Ezra Orion, the Premier of Armistice. Affectionately known as the Dead Lands.
I am the Keeper of The Message.
I am Hu, House of Mao.
Security Minister of the People's Republic.
Cheveyo.
He won't tell you, so I will. Our friend Cheveyo is the big magic of the Endless Nation.
I am, however, small time...and therefore much better behaved.
Andrew Archibald Chamberlain, Chief of Staff at the Black Towers.
Which makes you two rivals...so please, leave that shit outside.
I am the Crown Prince John Freeman, of the Kingdom of New Orleans.
And I am Bel Solomon.
Skeptic, and also Governor of the Republic of Texas.

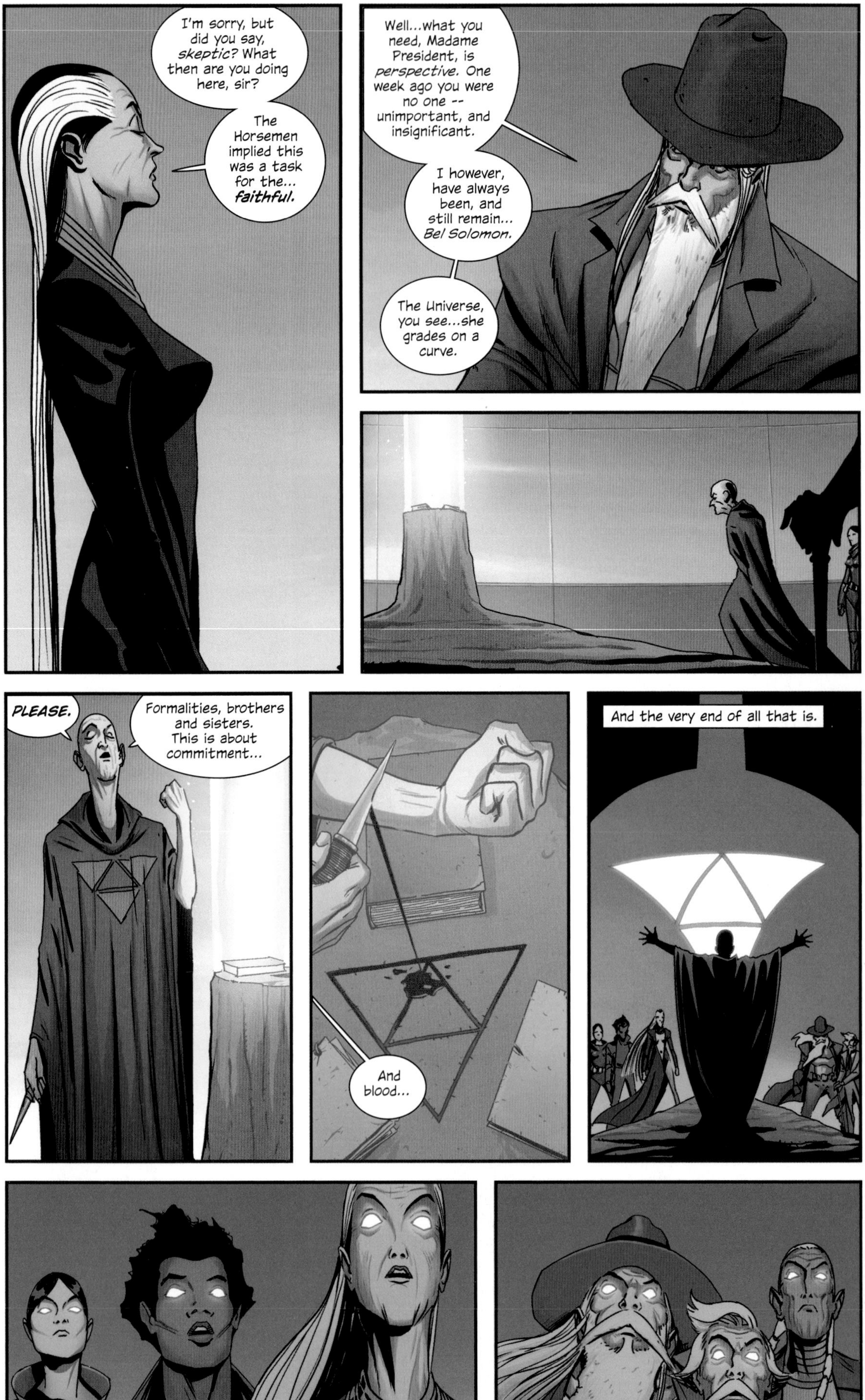
I'm sorry, but did you say, *skeptic*? What then are you doing here, sir?
The Horsemen implied this was a task for the... ***faithful.***
Well...what you need, Madame President, is *perspective.* One week ago you were no one -- unimportant, and insignificant.
I however, have always been, and still remain... *Bel Solomon.*
The Universe, you see...she grades on a curve.
PLEASE.
Formalities, brothers and sisters. This is about commitment...
And blood...
And the very end of all that is.

So you see now... The waking world, and what must happen.

I believed... but I never imagined.

Most men cannot. Which is why we have **The Message,** to keep us from getting lost on the path.

But that's providence... what are we going to do about *our* problem?

The message is not vague regarding the Horseman -- If you believe the apocrypha, it is very clear.

Maybe we cut the cord... and Mister Bones gets back to business.

Yes, but we all know what the man **wants...**

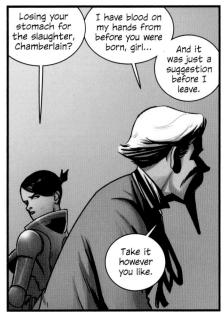

Losing your stomach for the slaughter, Chamberlain?

I have blood on my hands from before you were born, girl...

And it was just a suggestion before I leave.

Take it however you like.

Not staying for the feast?

I came when called. We all met the new President. *I saw her, she saw me...*

And now I have pressing business back home.

But eat well, for it may very well be your last meal. He is coming, people...

Coming for us all.

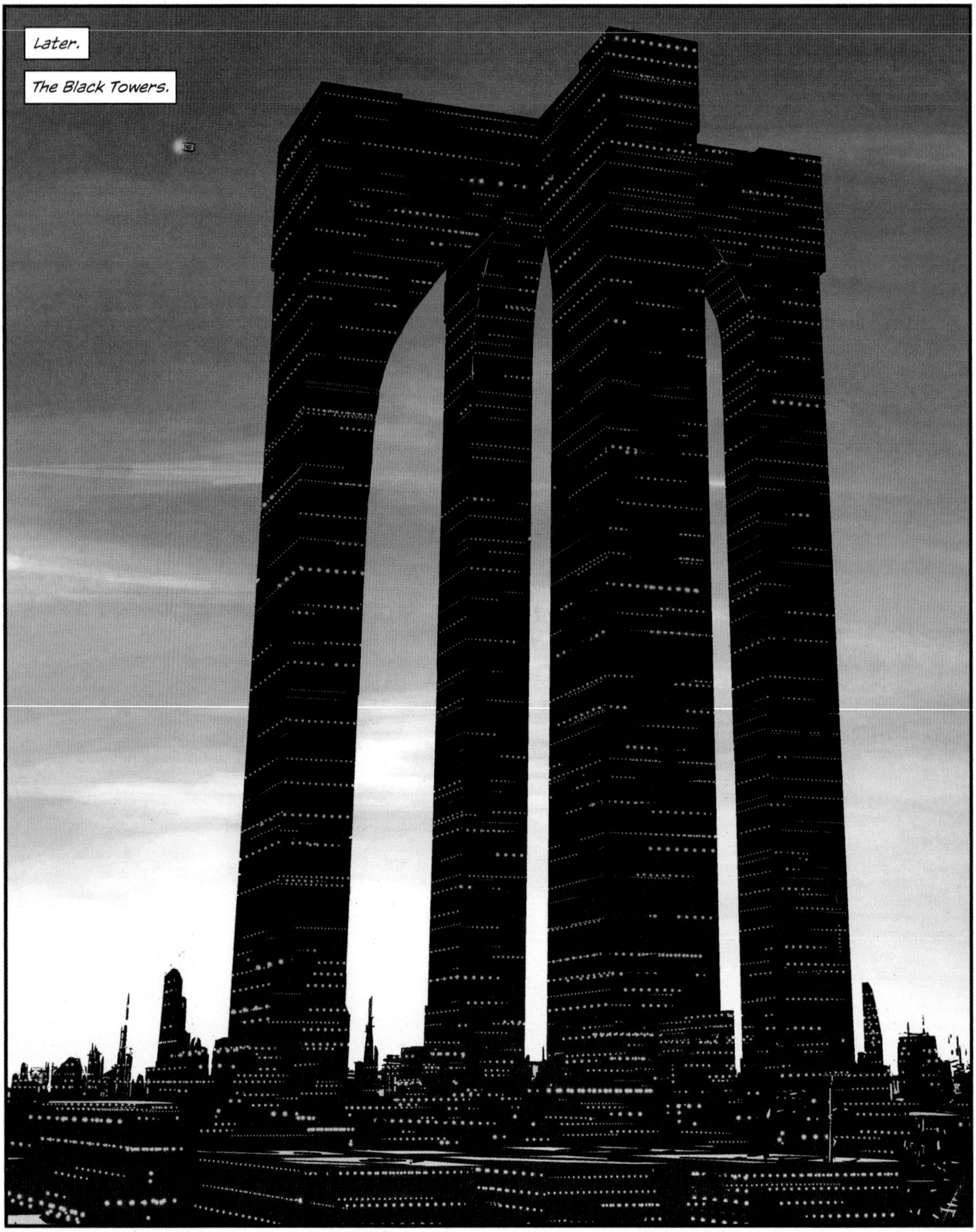
Later.
The Black Towers.

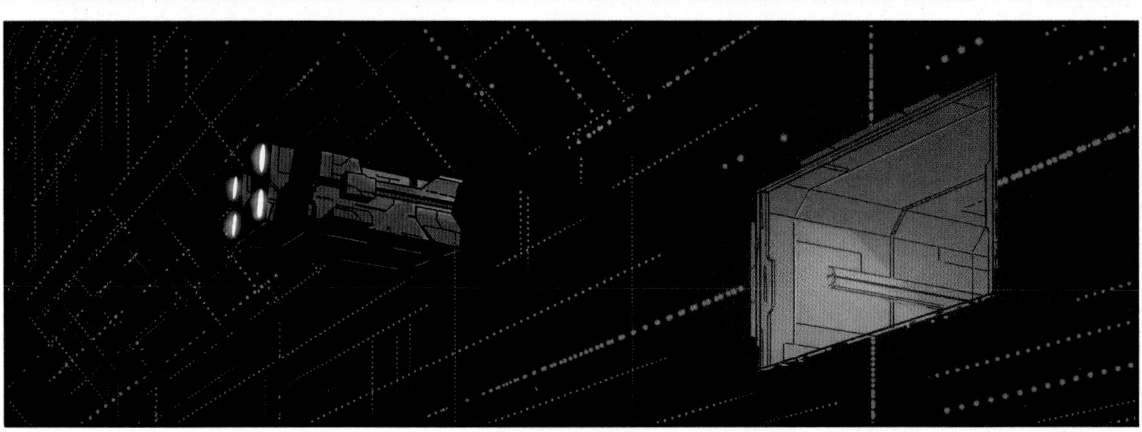

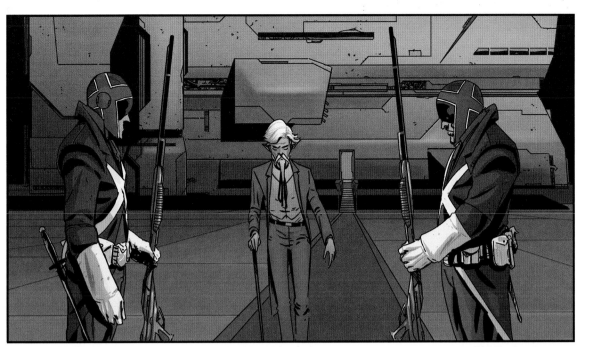

A. Archibald
Chamberlain
Chief of Staff

!

Ah. Well... sooner than expected, but *inevitable.*

After all, I hear Death waits for no man.

Inevitable. I like that.

And aren't you somethin' special? All nice and gracious, sayin' what I need to hear.

Sayin' the words...

Sayin' my name.

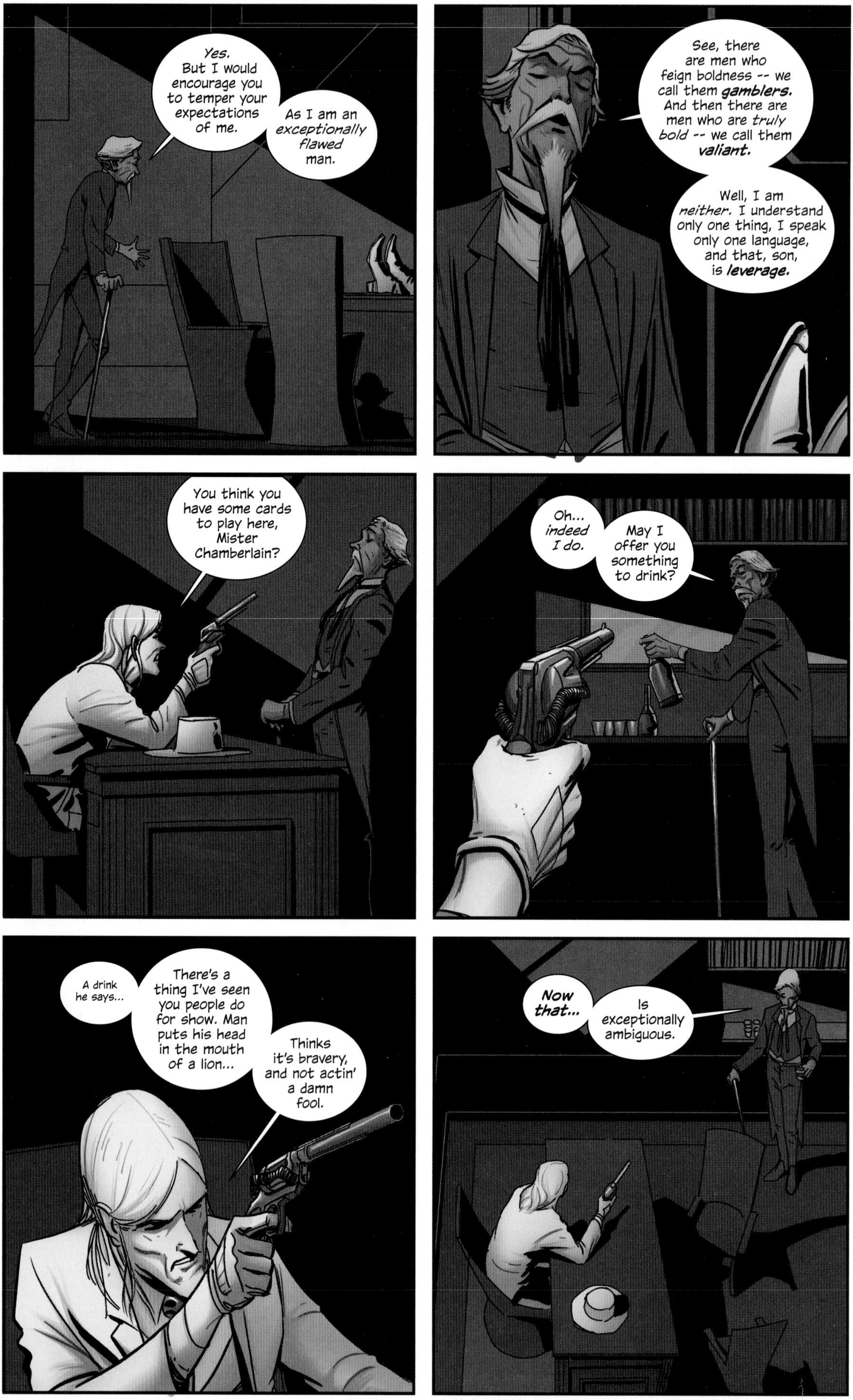
Yes. But I would encourage you to temper your expectations of me.
As I am an exceptionally flawed man.
See, there are men who feign boldness -- we call them gamblers. And then there are men who are truly bold -- we call them valiant.
Well, I am neither. I understand only one thing, I speak only one language, and that, son, is leverage.
You think you have some cards to play here, Mister Chamberlain?
Oh... indeed I do.
May I offer you something to drink?
A drink he says...
There's a thing I've seen you people do for show. Man puts his head in the mouth of a lion...
Thinks it's bravery, and not actin' a damn fool.
Now that...
Is exceptionally ambiguous.

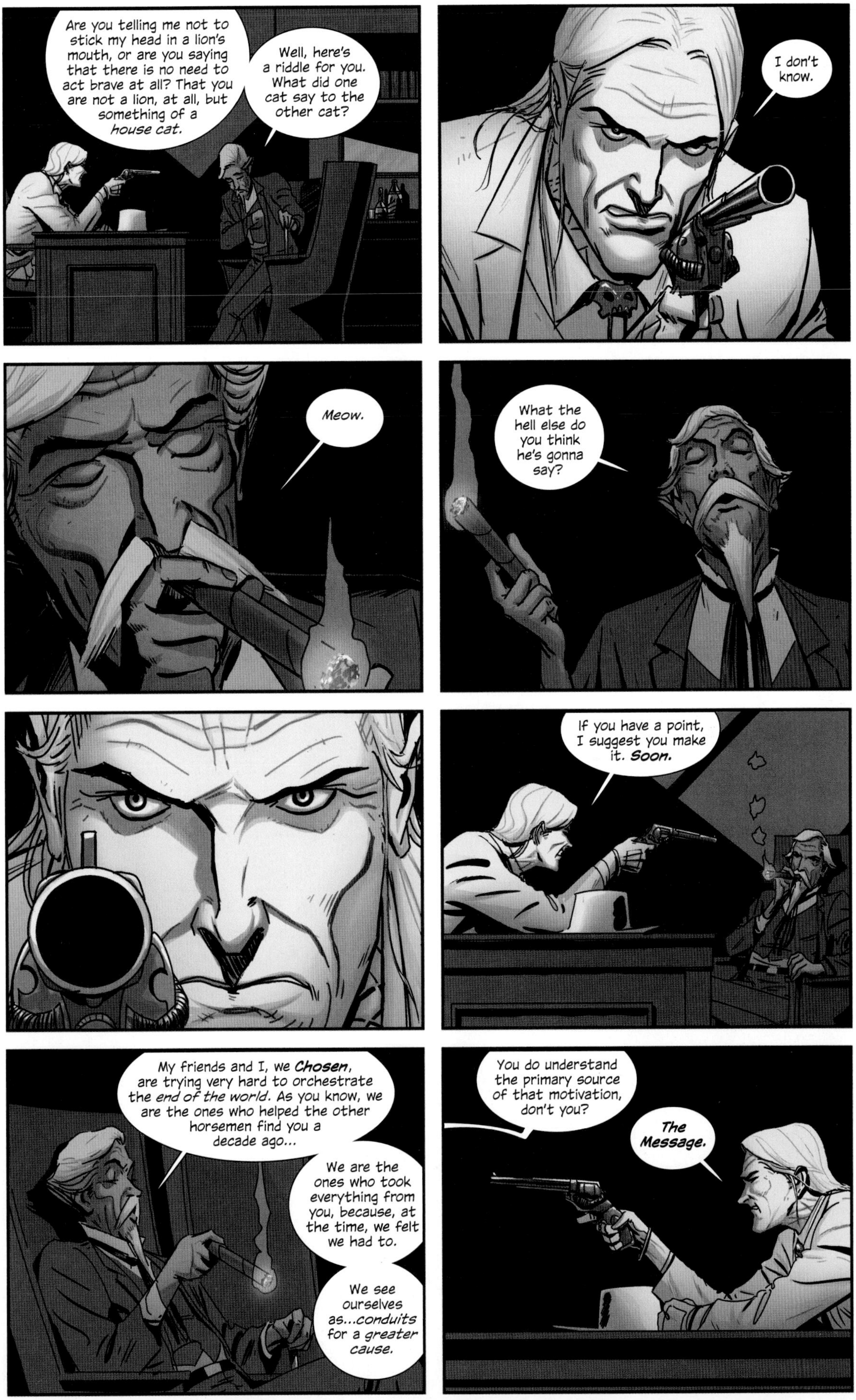

Are you telling me not to stick my head in a lion's mouth, or are you saying that there is no need to act brave at all? That you are not a lion, at all, but something of a *house cat.*
Well, here's a riddle for you. What did one cat say to the other cat?
I don't know.
Meow.
What the hell else do you think he's gonna say?
If you have a point, I suggest you make it. ***Soon.***
My friends and I, we ***Chosen***, are trying very hard to orchestrate the *end of the world.* As you know, we are the ones who helped the other horsemen find you a decade ago...
We are the ones who took everything from you, because, at the time, we felt we had to.
We see ourselves as...*conduits* for a *greater cause.*
You do understand the primary source of that motivation, don't you?
The Message.

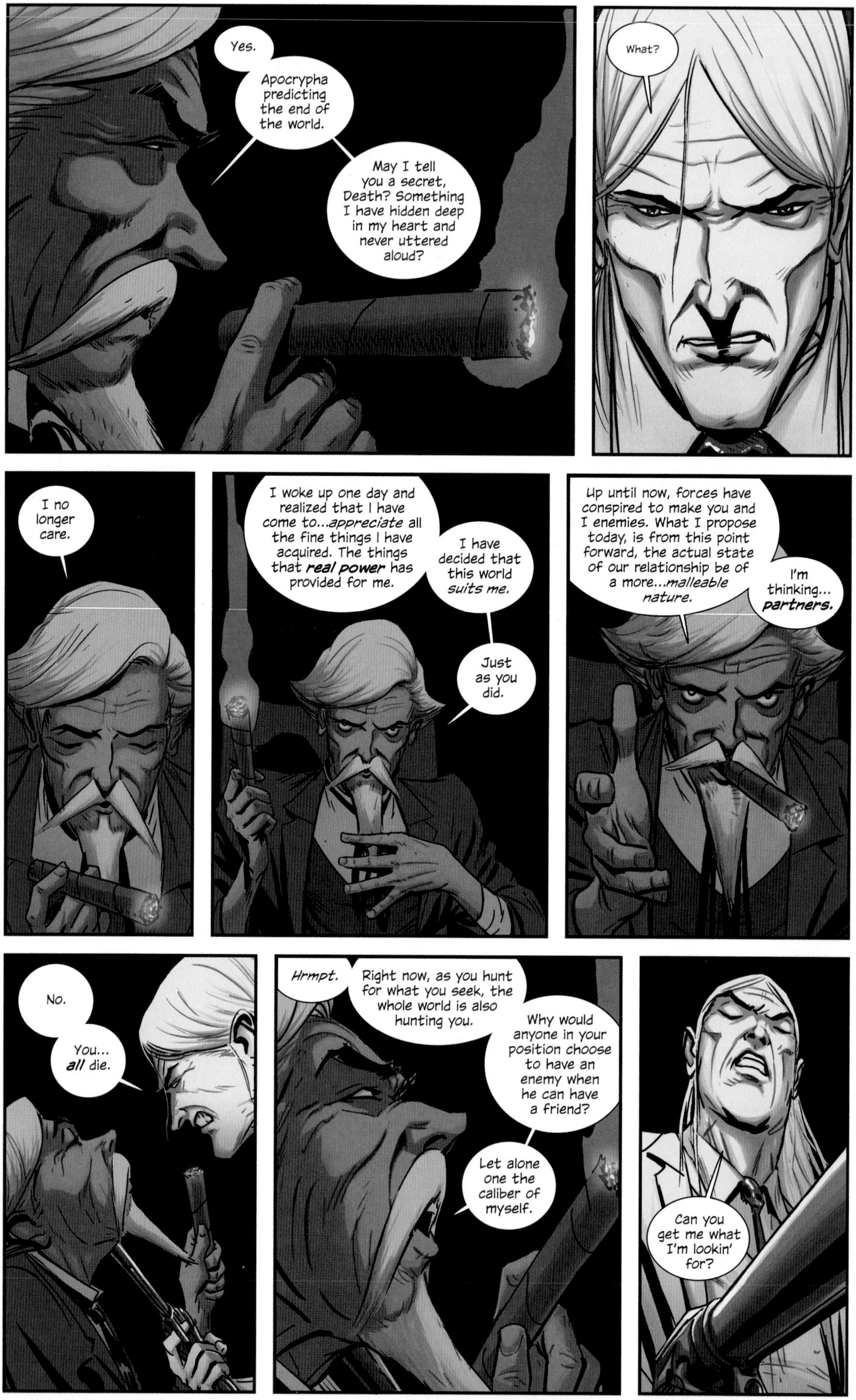
Yes.
Apocrypha predicting the end of the world.
May I tell you a secret, Death? Something I have hidden deep in my heart and never uttered aloud?
What?
I no longer care.
I woke up one day and realized that I have come to...*appreciate* all the fine things I have acquired. The things that ***real power*** has provided for me.
I have decided that this world *suits me.*
Just as you did.
Up until now, forces have conspired to make you and I enemies. What I propose today, is from this point forward, the actual state of our relationship be of a more...*malleable nature.*
I'm thinking... ***partners.***
No.
You... ***all*** die.
Hrmpt.
Right now, as you hunt for what you seek, the whole world is also hunting you.
Why would anyone in your position choose to have an enemy when he can have a friend?
Let alone one the caliber of myself.
Can you get me what I'm lookin' for?

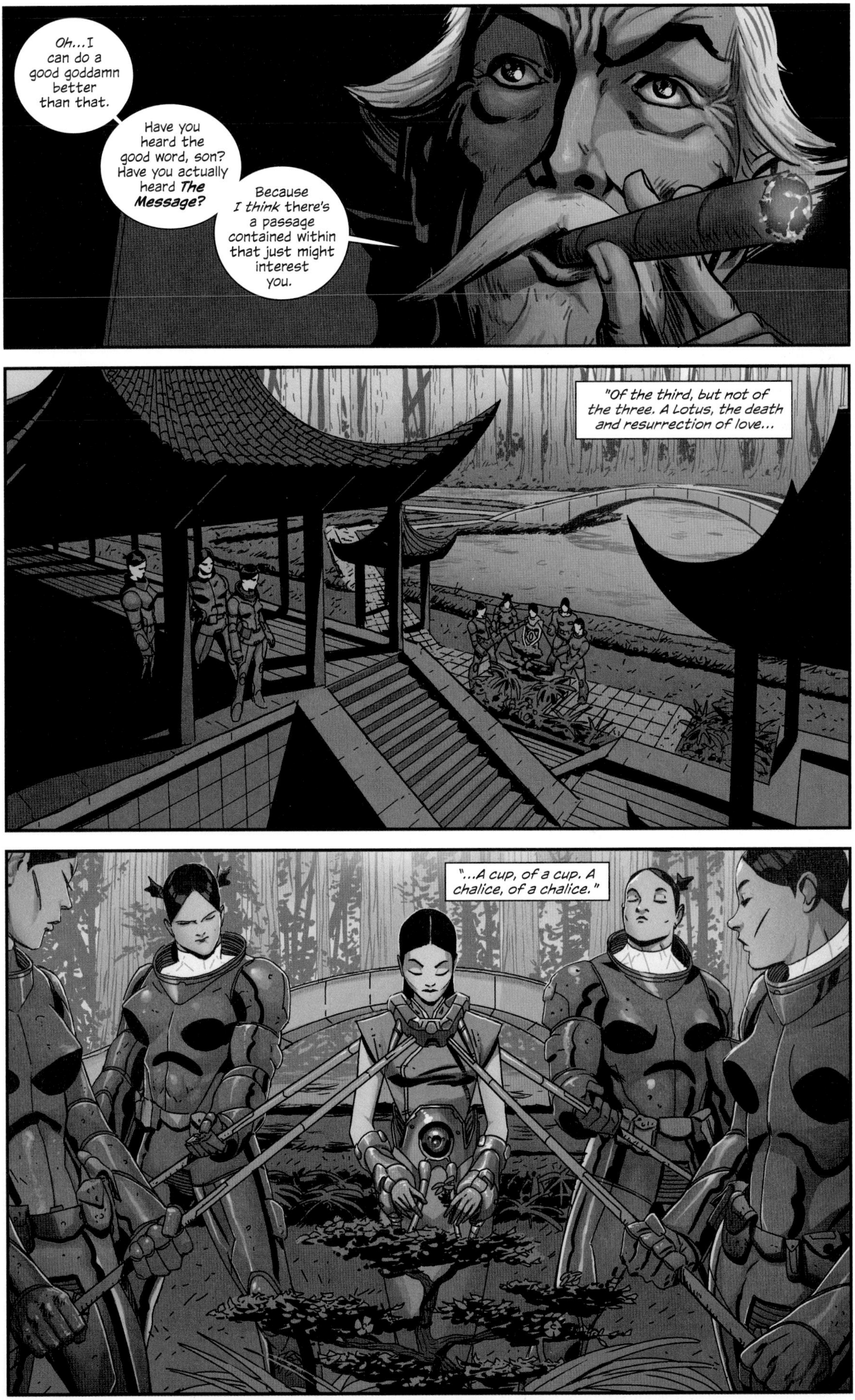
Oh...I can do a good goddamn better than that.
Have you heard the good word, son? Have you actually heard The Message?
Because I think there's a passage contained within that just might interest you.
"Of the third, but not of the three. A Lotus, the death and resurrection of love...
"...A cup, of a cup. A chalice, of a chalice."

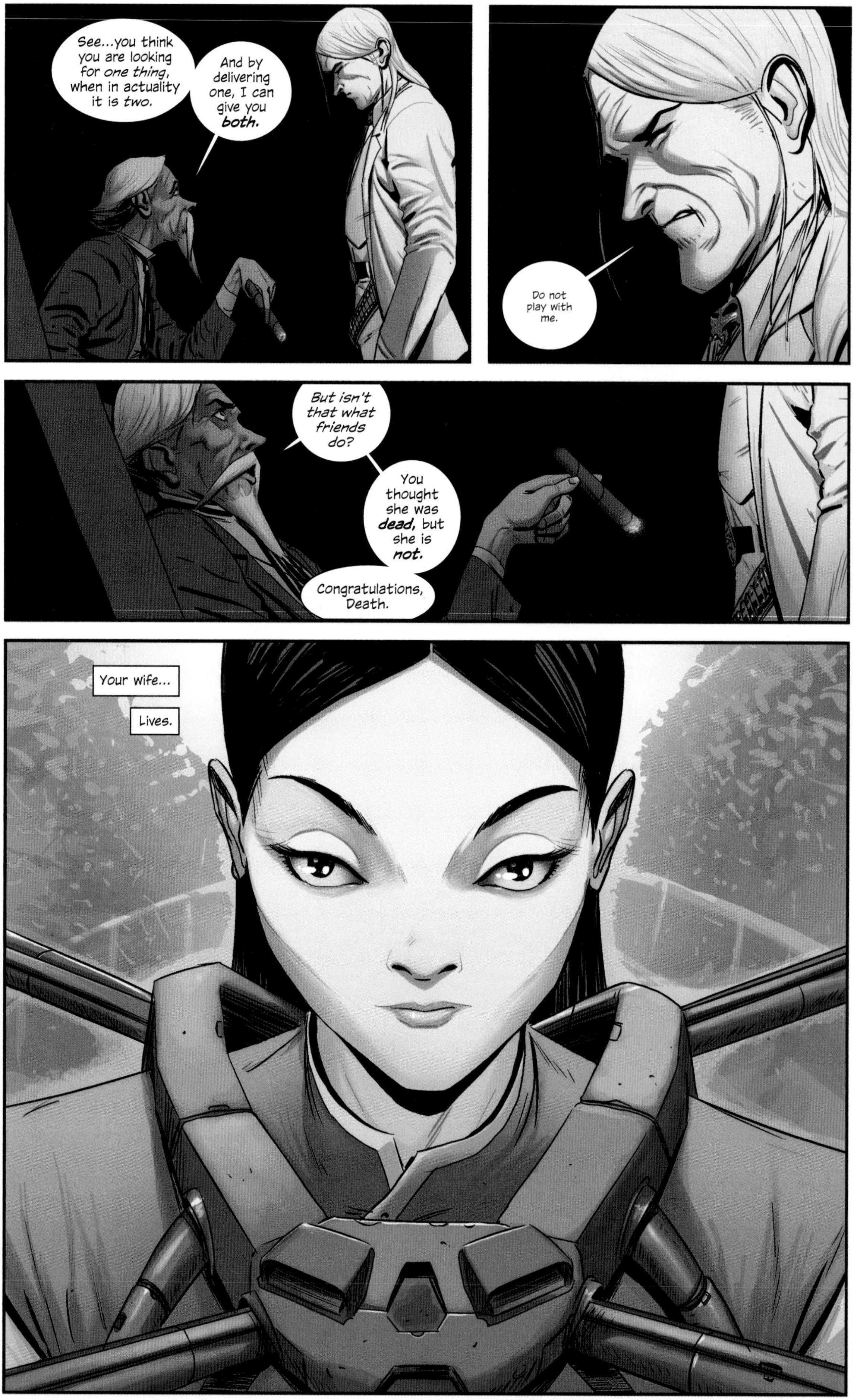
See...you think you are looking for *one thing*, when in actuality it is *two.*
And by delivering one, I can give you **both.**
Do not play with me.
But isn't that what friends do?
You thought she was ***dead,*** but she is ***not.***
Congratulations, Death.
Your wife...
Lives.

WHO IS THIS **WOMAN**,
THE ONE WHO **CONQUERED**
DEATH?

New Shanghai.

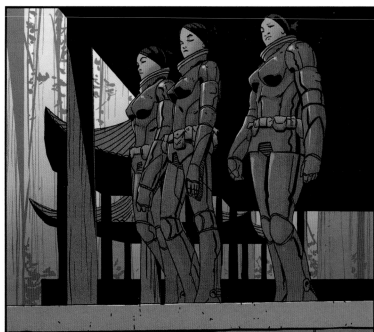

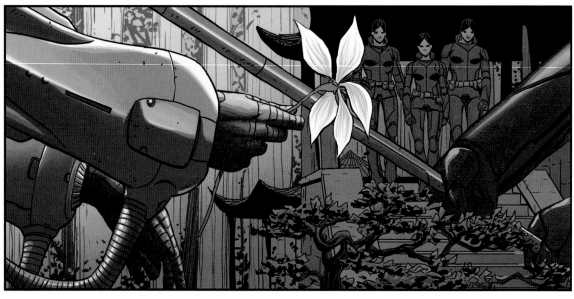

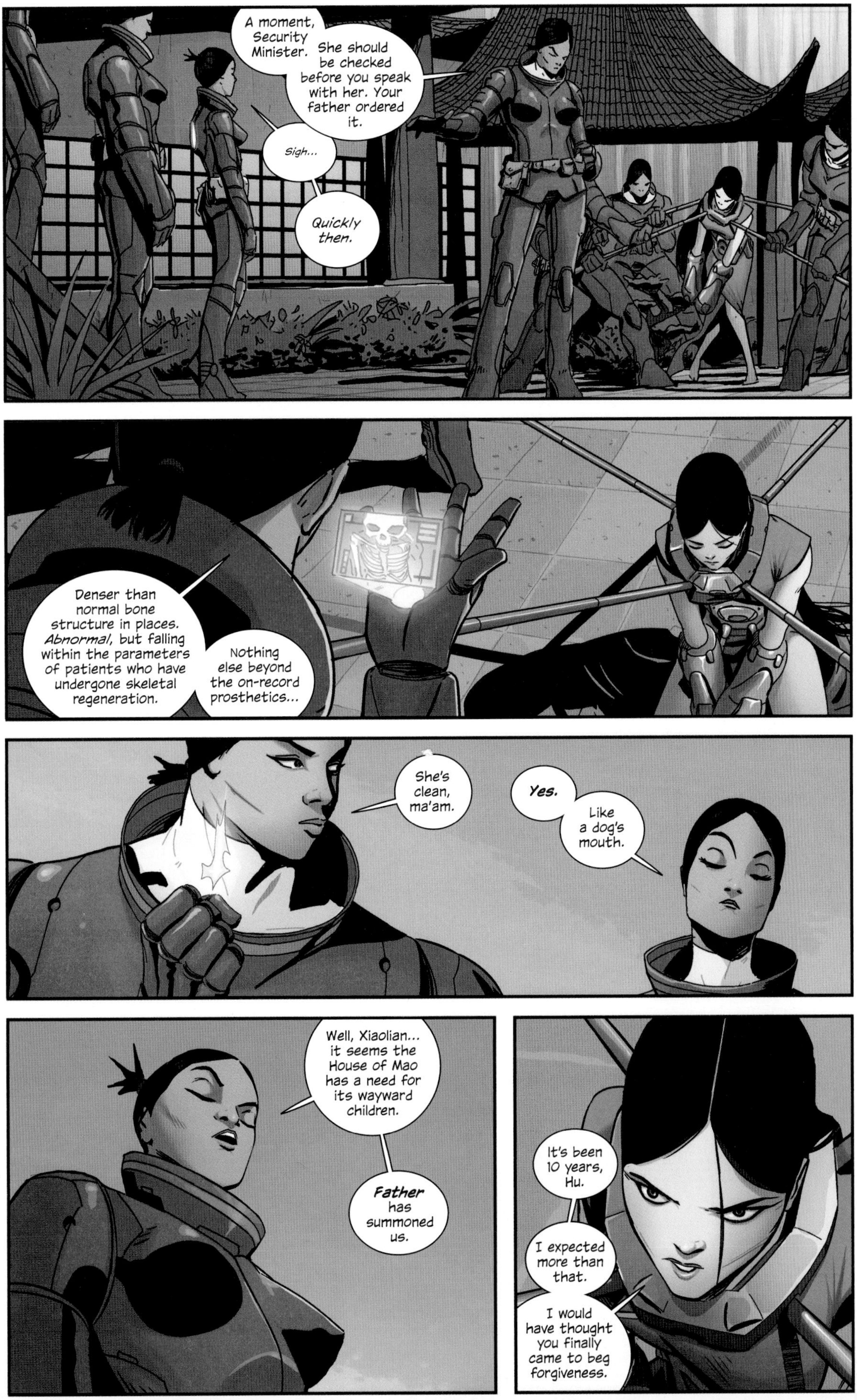
A moment, Security Minister.
She should be checked before you speak with her. Your father ordered it.
Sigh...
Quickly then.
Denser than normal bone structure in places. *Abnormal*, but falling within the parameters of patients who have undergone skeletal regeneration.
Nothing else beyond the on-record prosthetics...
She's clean, ma'am.
Yes.
Like a dog's mouth.
Well, Xiaolian... it seems the House of Mao has a need for its wayward children.
Father has summoned us.
It's been 10 years, Hu.
I expected more than that.
I would have thought you finally came to beg forgiveness.

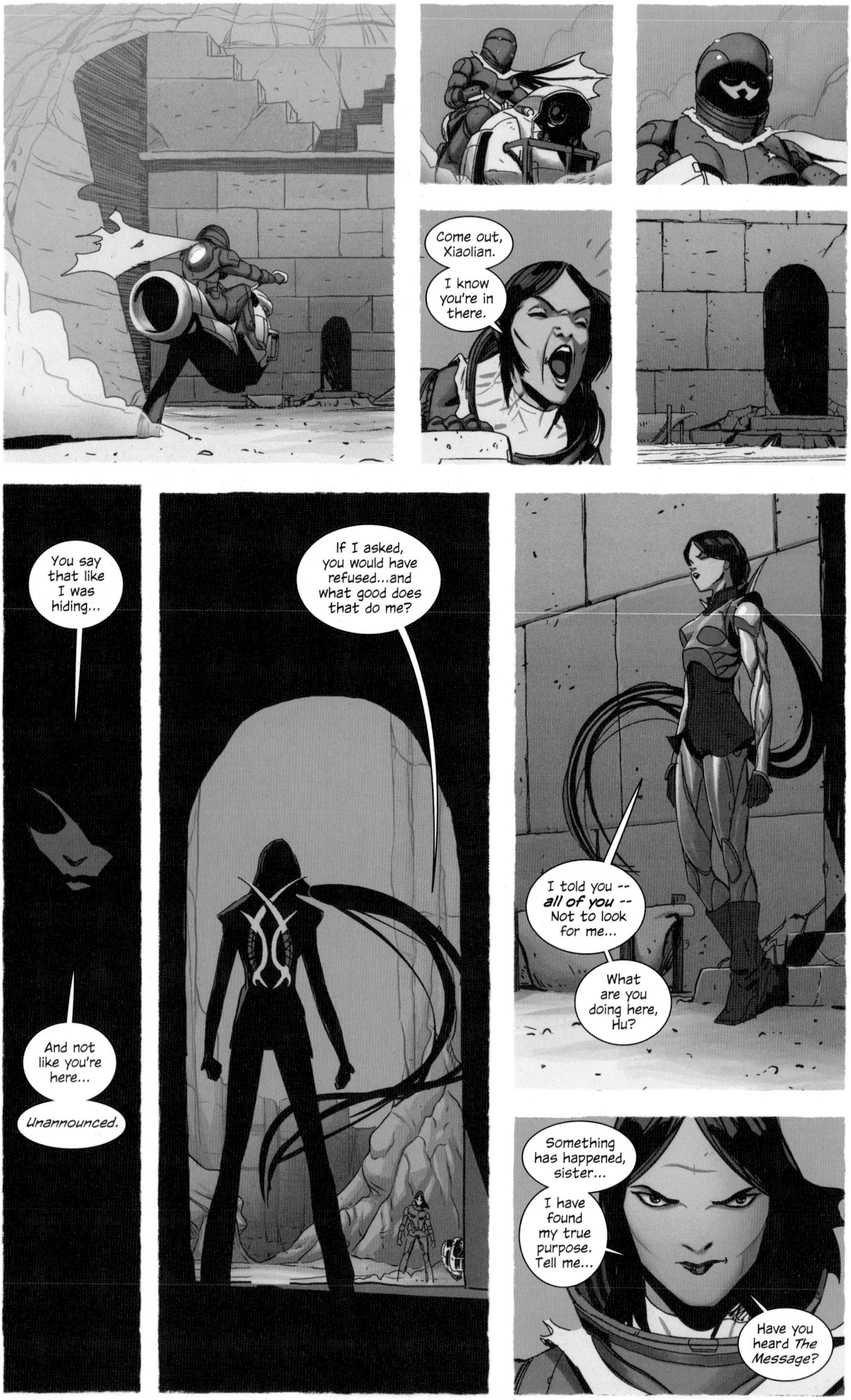
Come out, Xiaolian.
I know you're in there.
You say that like I was hiding...
And not like you're here...
Unannounced.
If I asked, you would have refused...and what good does that do me?
I told you -- **all of you** -- Not to look for me...
What are you doing here, Hu?
Something has happened, sister...
I have found my true purpose. Tell me...
Have you heard *The Message?*

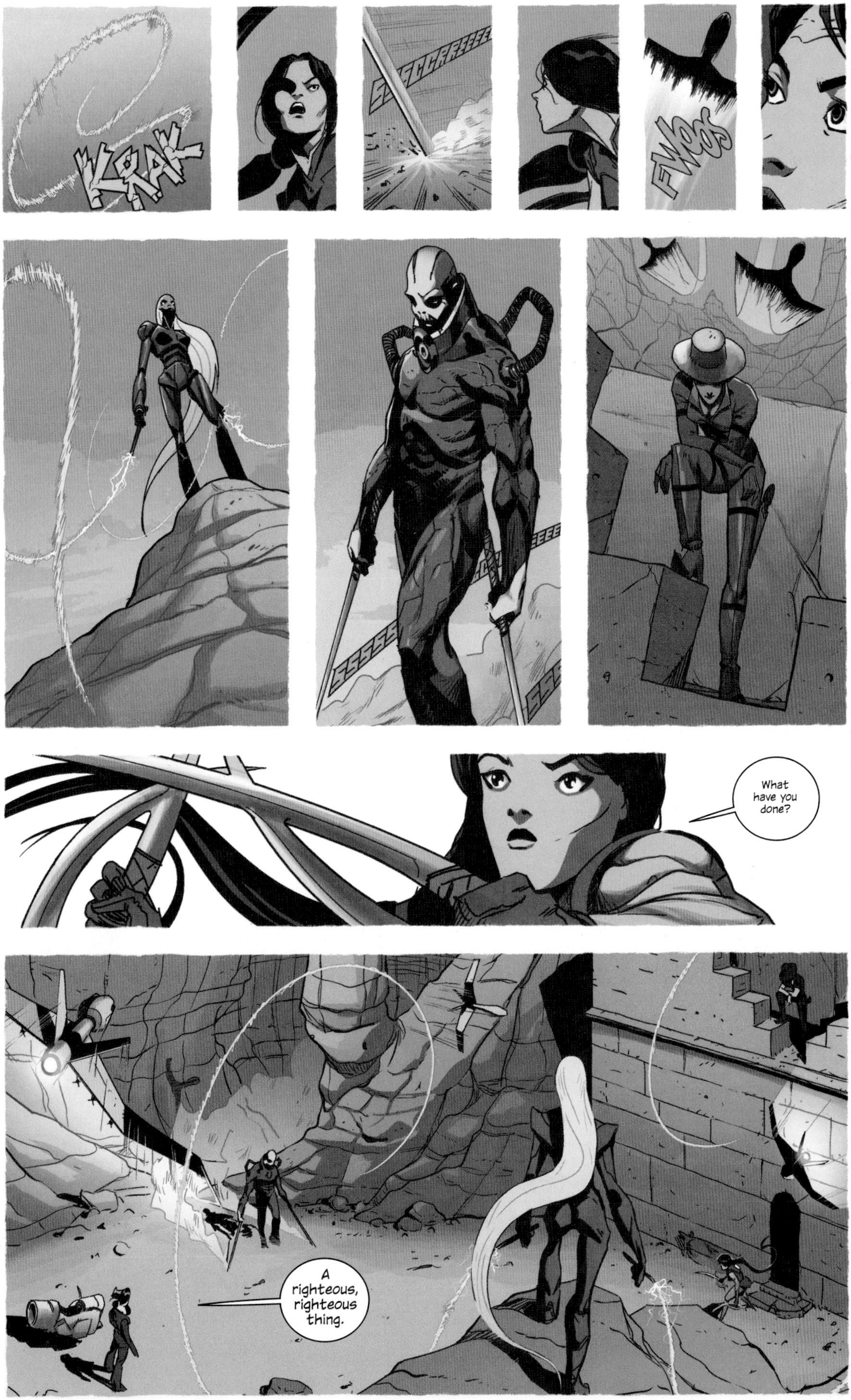
KRAK
FWOOS
What have you done?
A righteous, righteous thing.

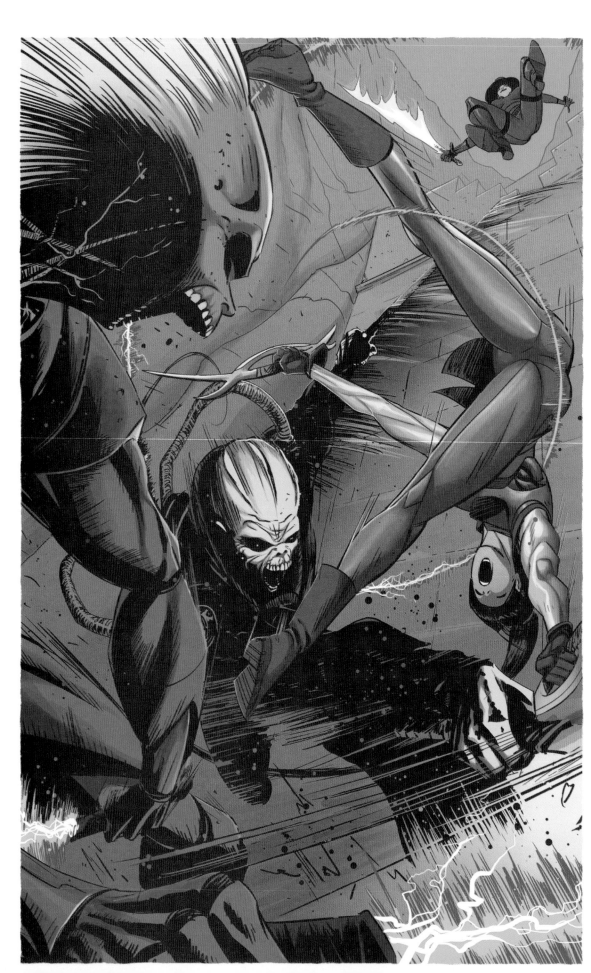

SHE LASTED **LONGER** THAN
YOU WILL.

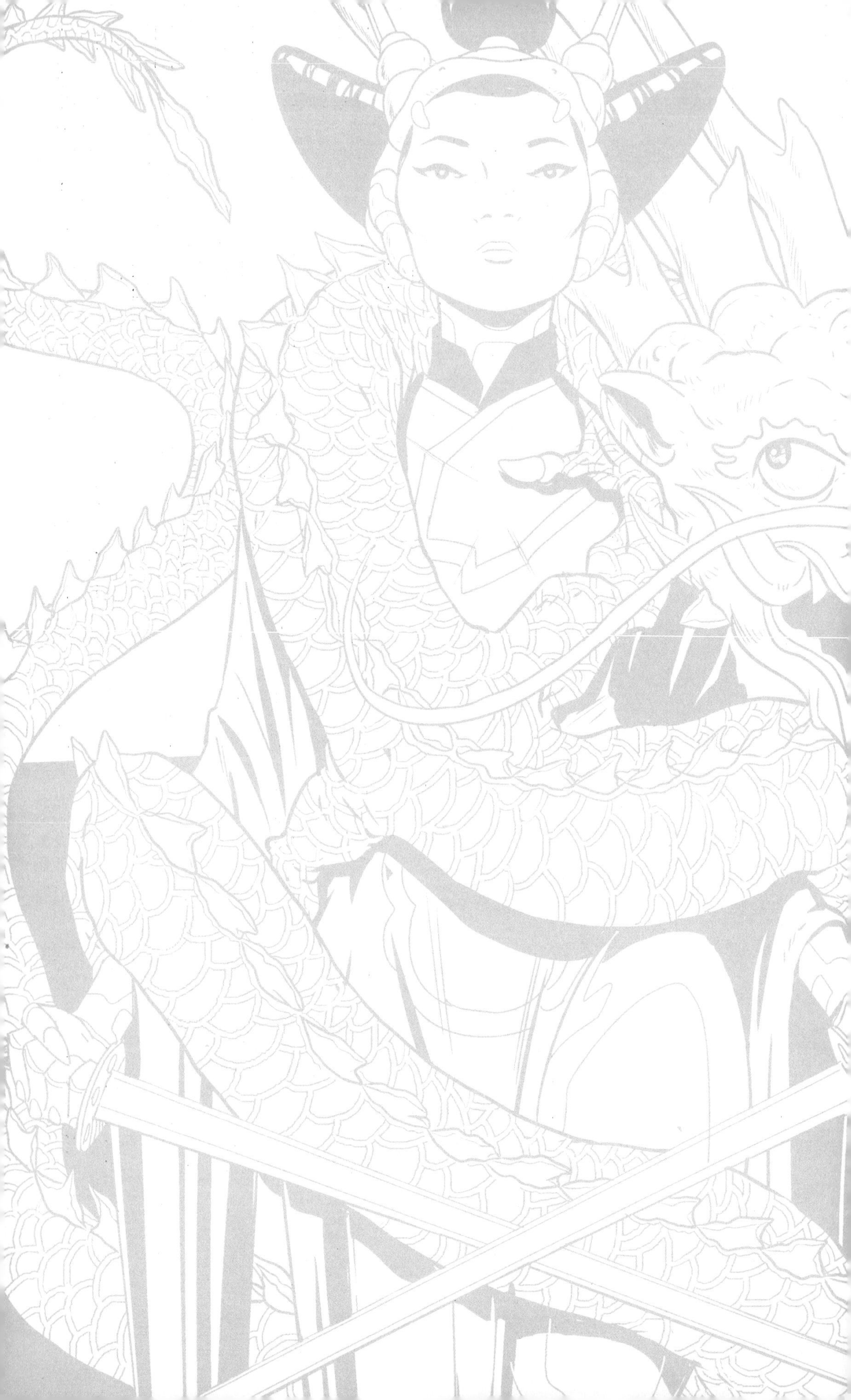

03

 THREE: THE
HOUSE OF **MAO**

IF YOU **CANNOT TRUST** YOUR EYES AS YOU LOOK AT **THE WORLD**, WHAT GOOD ARE THEY?

I CAN GIVE YOU **SOMETHING BETTER.**

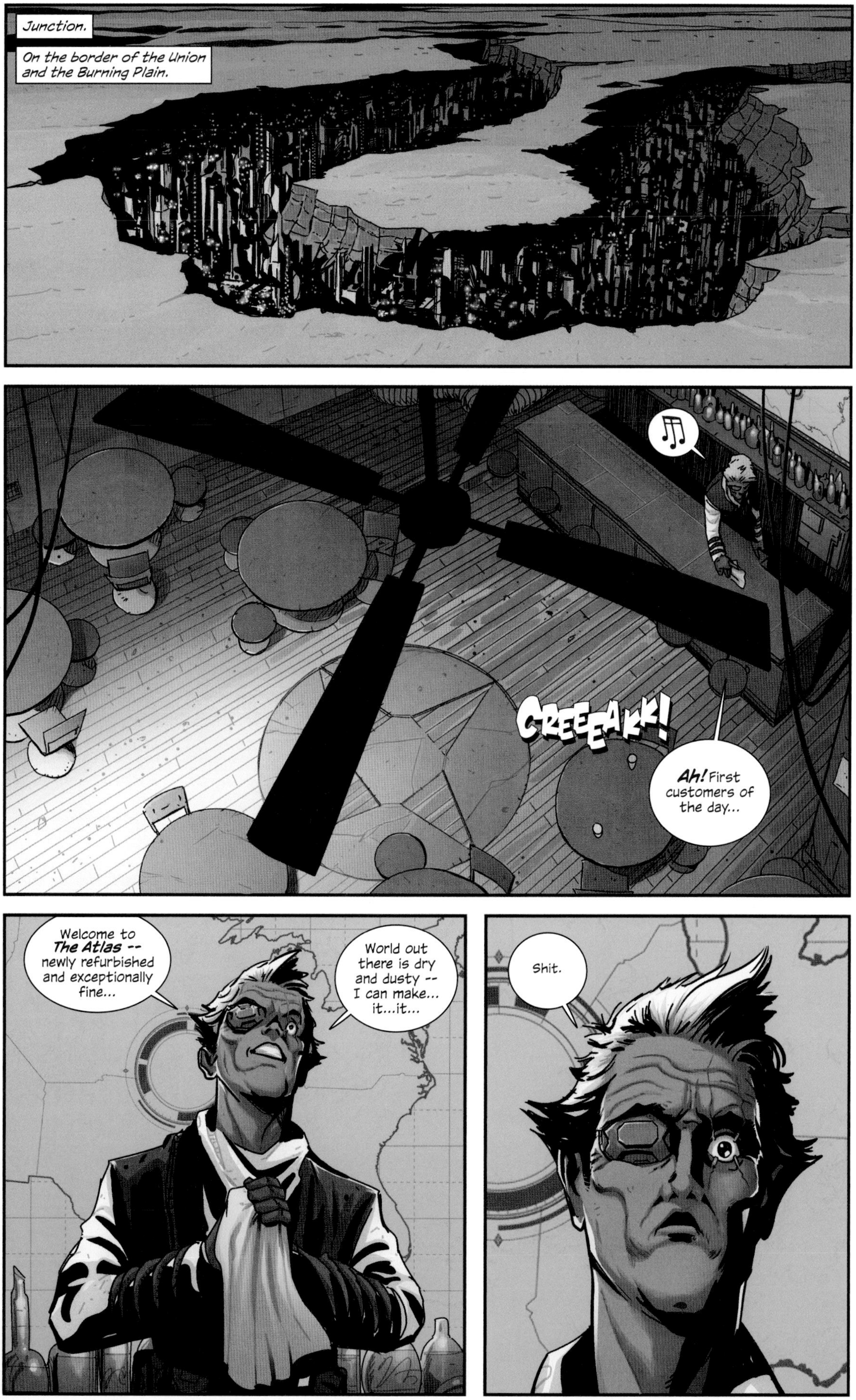
Junction.
On the border of the Union and the Burning Plain.
♬
CREEEAKK!
Ah! First customers of the day...
Welcome to The Atlas -- newly refurbished and exceptionally fine...
World out there is dry and dusty -- I can make... it...it...
Shit.

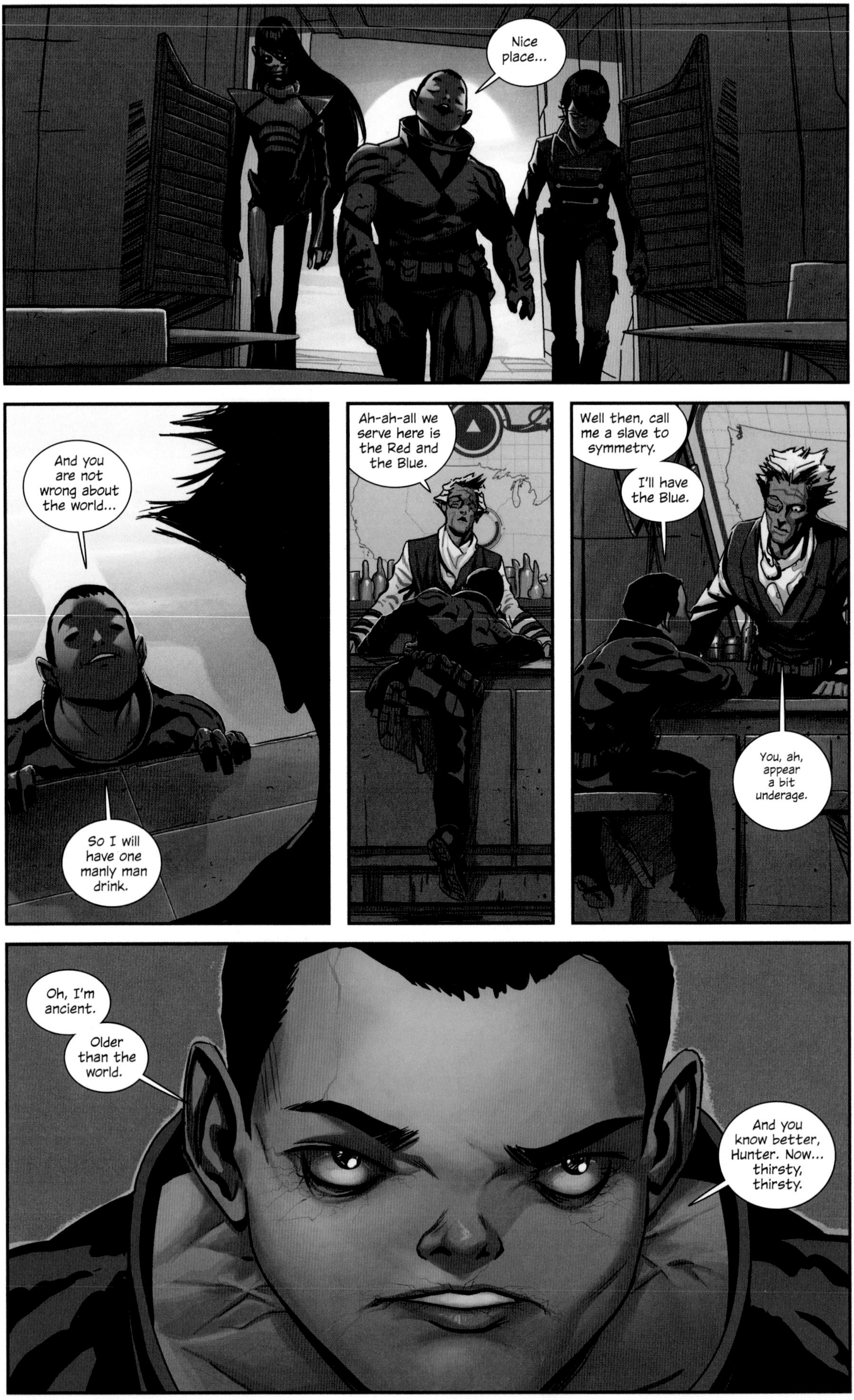
Nice place...
And you are not wrong about the world...
So I will have one manly man drink.
Ah-ah-all we serve here is the Red and the Blue.
Well then, call me a slave to symmetry.
I'll have the Blue.
You, ah, appear a bit underage.
Oh, I'm ancient.
Older than the world.
And you know better, Hunter. Now... thirsty, thirsty.

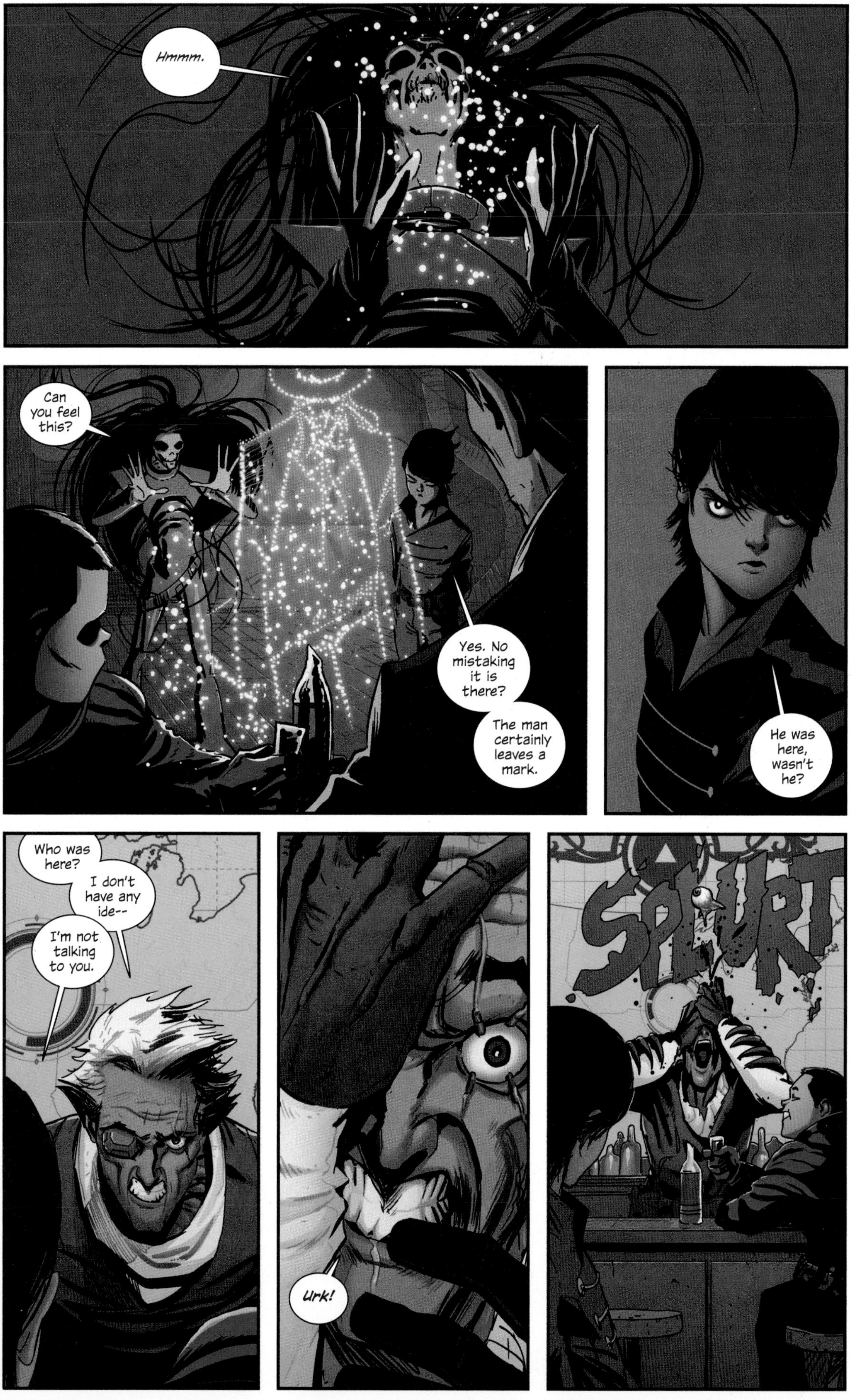
Hmmm.
Can you feel this?
Yes. No mistaking it is there?
The man certainly leaves a mark.
He was here, wasn't he?
Who was here?
I don't have any ide--
I'm not talking to you.
Urk!
SPLURT

Well?

Yesss. Yesss. Much to fear. Mister Bonesss wasss rattlin' here.

And he wasn't alone. He had a witch from the Nation with him. No, wait...more than one...

There were two witches.

Maybe that's how he lived.

Right now, I don't care about what company he was keeping...

What did he want?

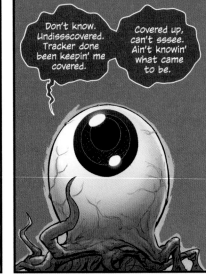

Don't know. Undissscovered. Tracker done been keepin' me covered.

Covered up, can't sssee. Ain't knowin' what came to be.

Gotcha!

So...

Do we need to start cutting off body parts, or are you going to tell us what you gave him?

There's nothing wrong with trying to hold out a bit.

Maybe show us how tough you are?

Honestly, we could use the practice.

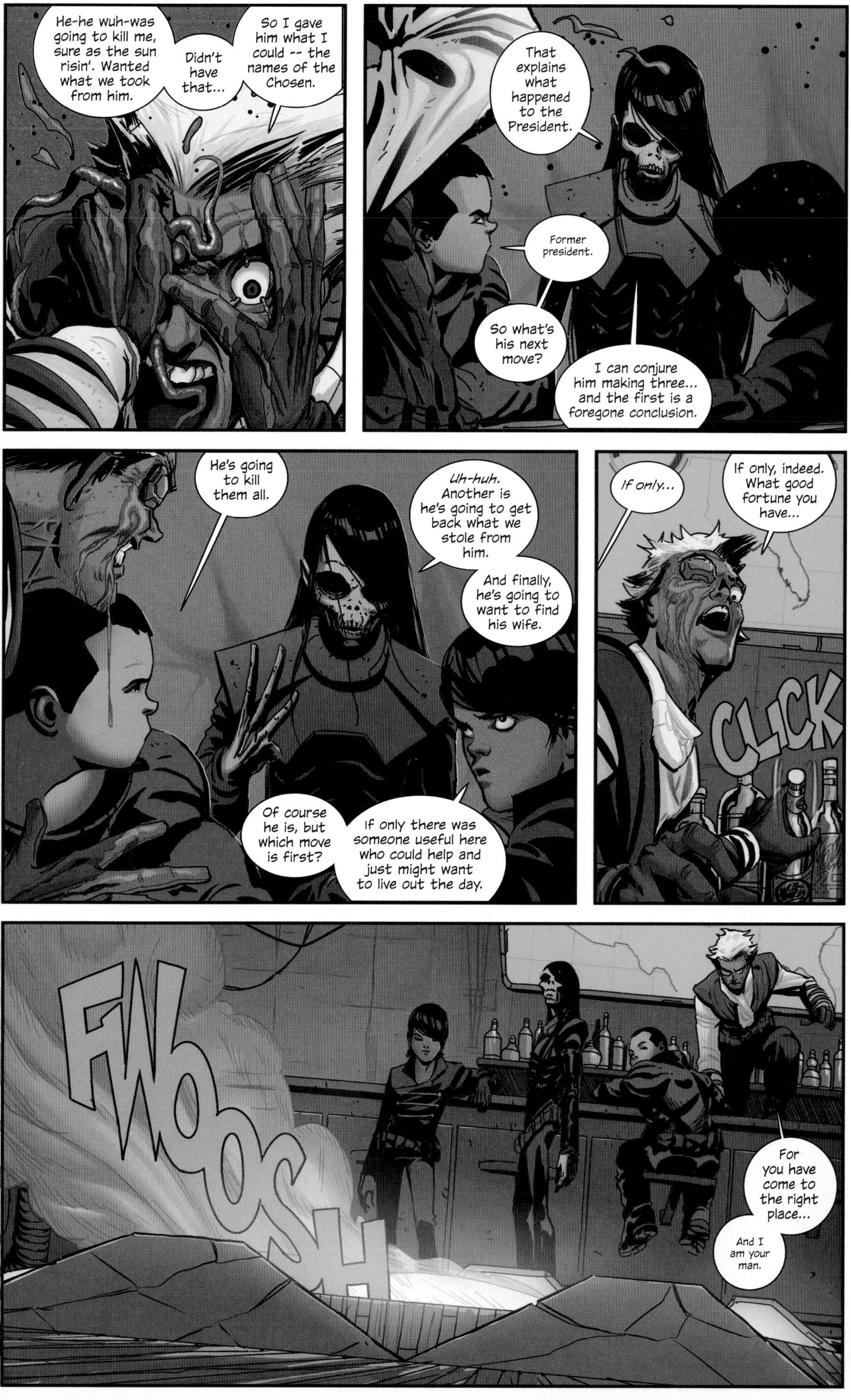
He-he wuh-was going to kill me, sure as the sun risin'. Wanted what we took from him.
Didn't have that...
So I gave him what I could -- the names of the Chosen.
That explains what happened to the President.
Former president.
So what's his next move?
I can conjure him making three... and the first is a foregone conclusion.
He's going to kill them all.
Uh-huh. Another is he's going to get back what we stole from him.
And finally, he's going to want to find his wife.
Of course he is, but which move is first?
If only there was someone useful here who could help and just might want to live out the day.
If only...
If only, indeed. What good fortune you have...
CLICK
FWOOSH!
For you have come to the right place...
And I am your man.

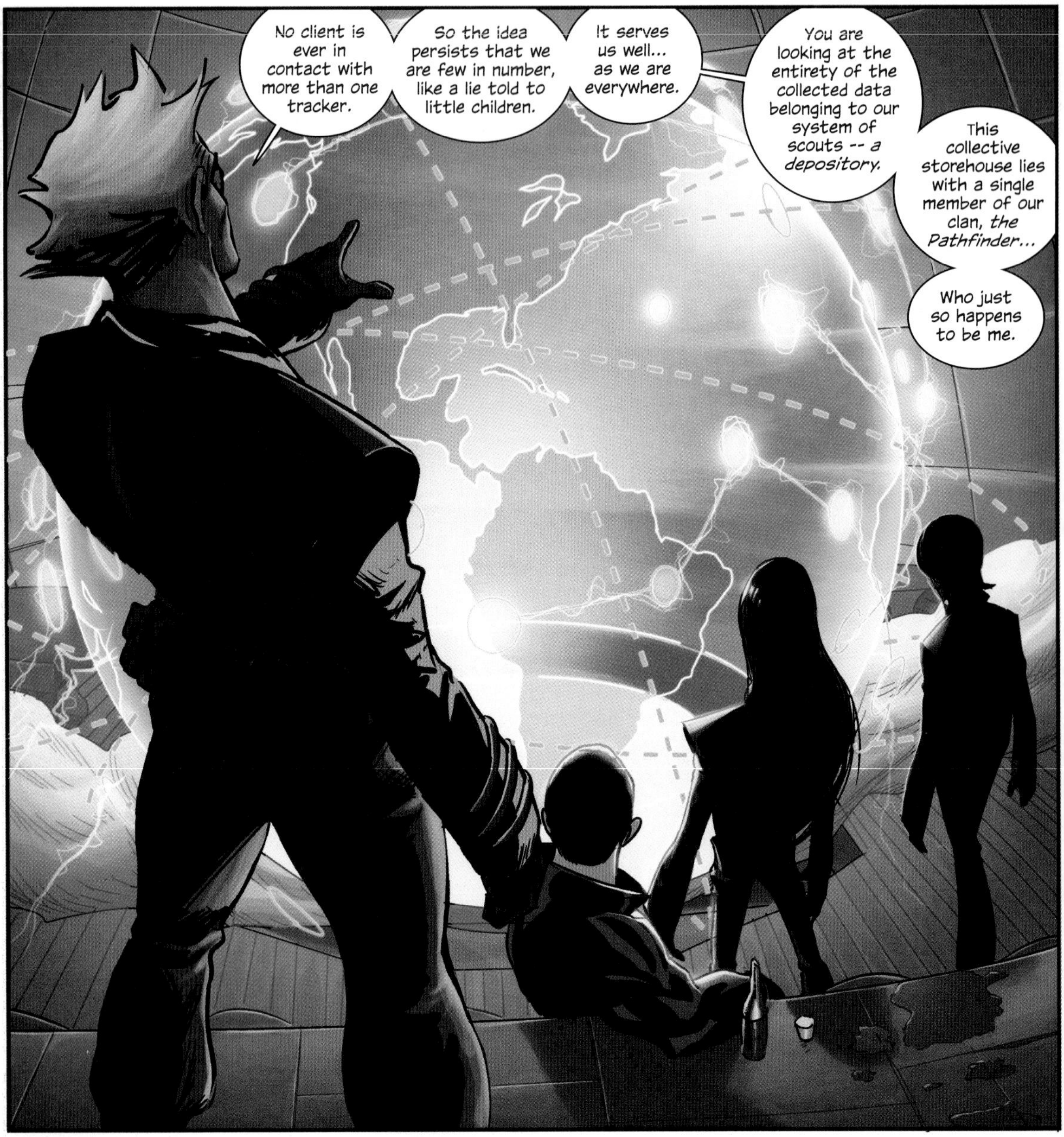
No client is ever in contact with more than one tracker.
So the idea persists that we are few in number, like a lie told to little children.
It serves us well... as we are everywhere.
You are looking at the entirety of the collected data belonging to our system of scouts -- a *depository.*
This collective storehouse lies with a single member of our clan, *the Pathfinder...*
Who just so happens to be me.

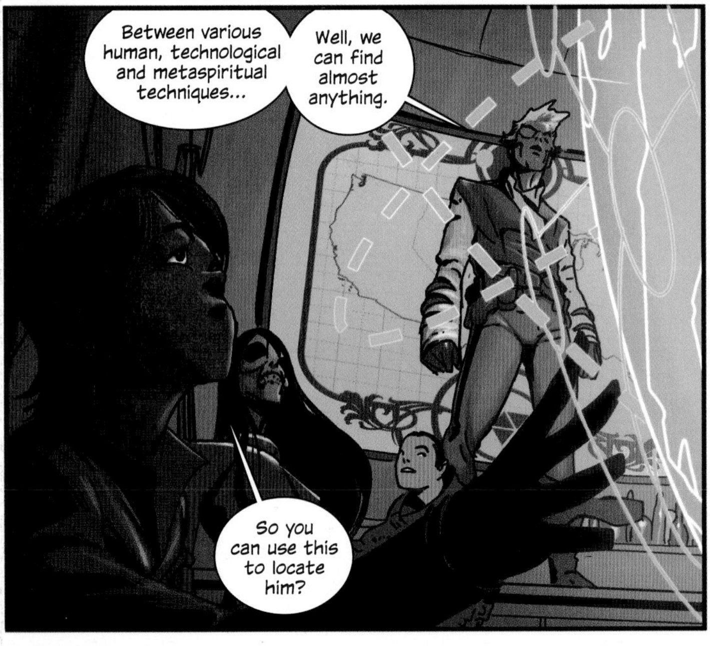
Between various human, technological and metaspiritual techniques...
Well, we can find almost anything.
So you can use this to locate him?

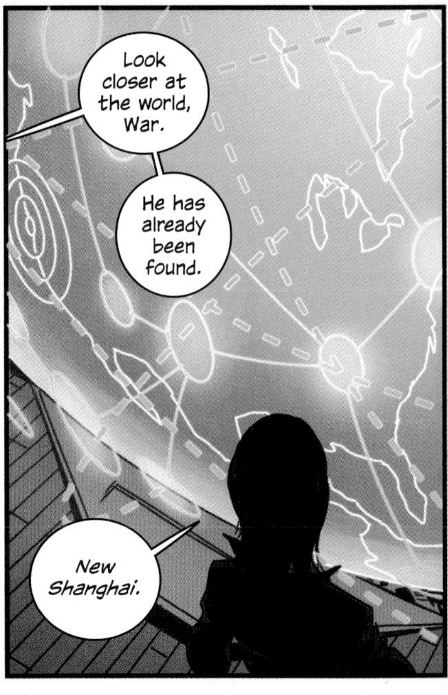
Look closer at the world, War.
He has already been found.
New Shanghai.

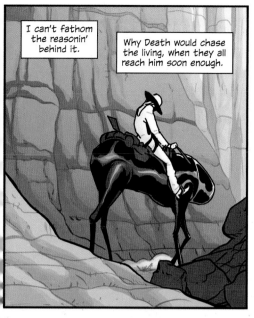

I can't fathom the reasonin' behind it.

Why Death would chase the living, when they all reach him soon enough.

...Yes, there's prophecy, but he ain't no agent for others.

Makes you wonder what he's all about though, doesn't it?

No. I don't wonder.

I know.

It's love.

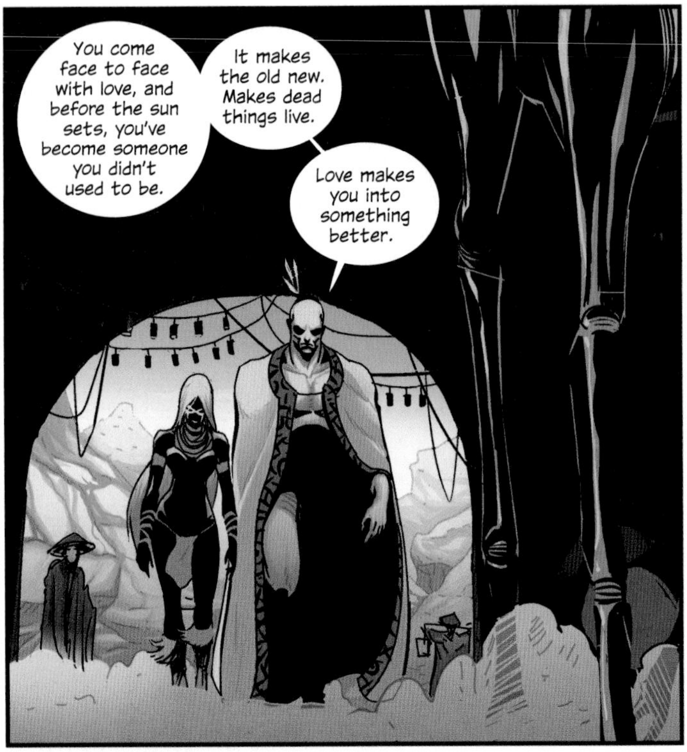
You come face to face with love, and before the sun sets, you've become someone you didn't used to be.
It makes the old new. Makes dead things live.
Love makes you into something better.

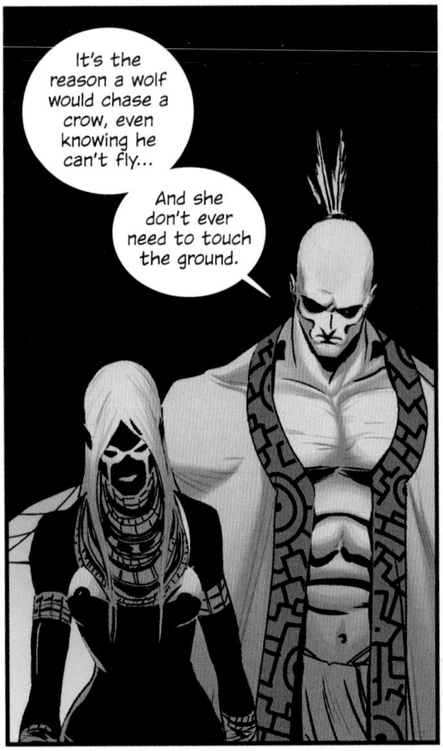
It's the reason a wolf would chase a crow, even knowing he can't fly...
And she don't ever need to touch the ground.

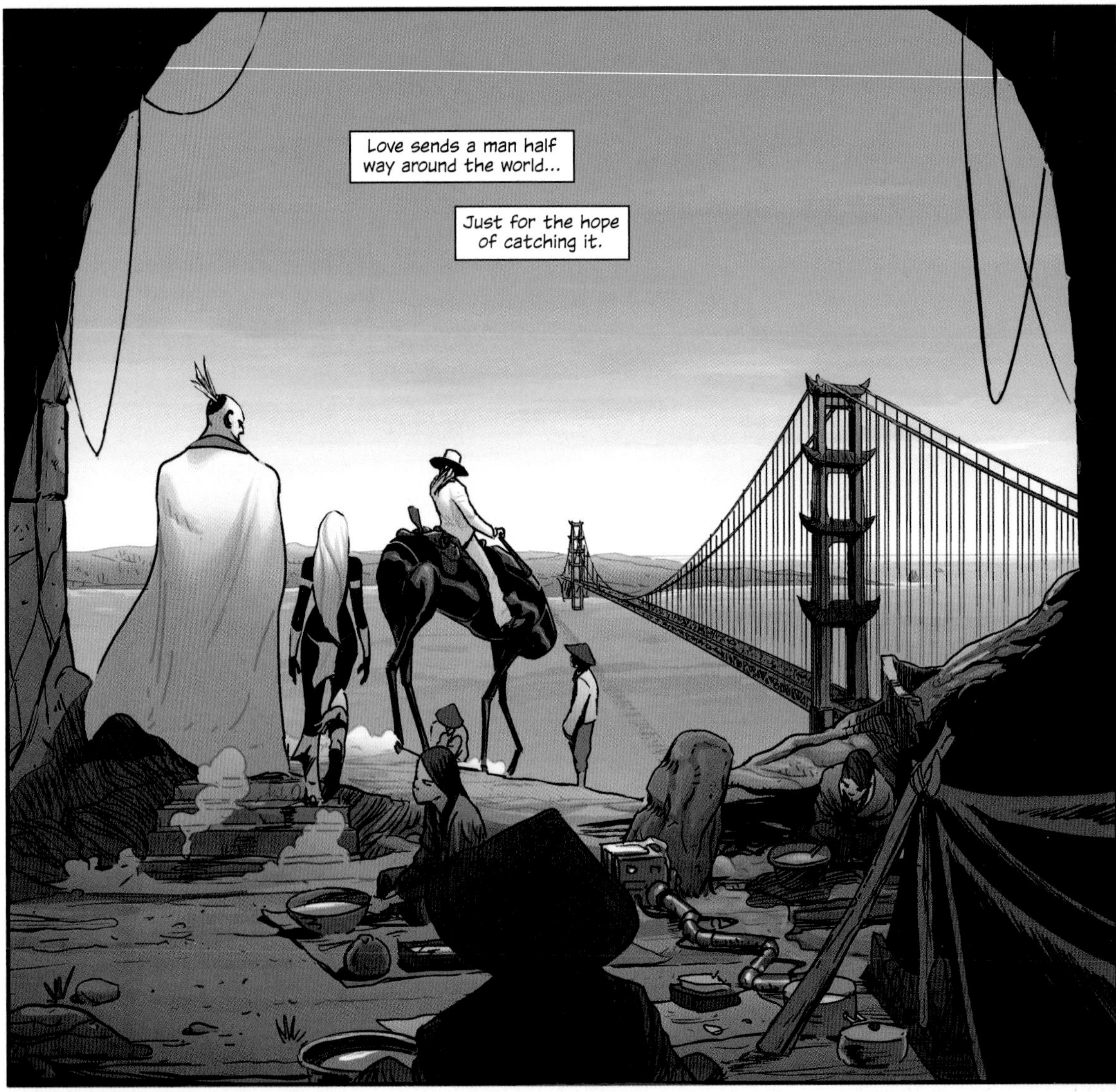
Love sends a man half way around the world...
Just for the hope of catching it.

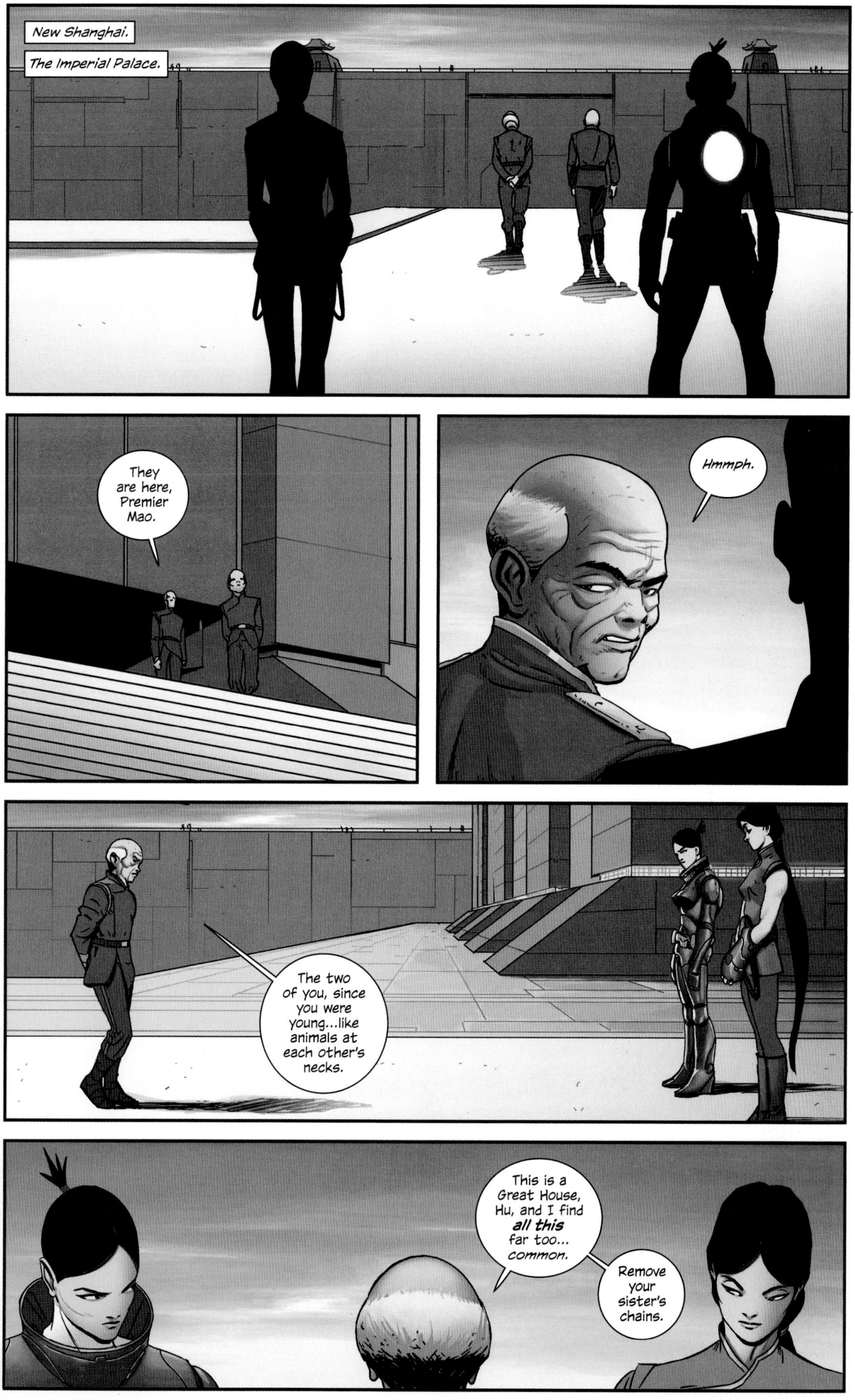
New Shanghai.
The Imperial Palace.
They are here, Premier Mao.
Hmmph.
The two of you, since you were young...like animals at each other's necks.
This is a Great House, Hu, and I find *all this* far too... *common.*
Remove your sister's chains.

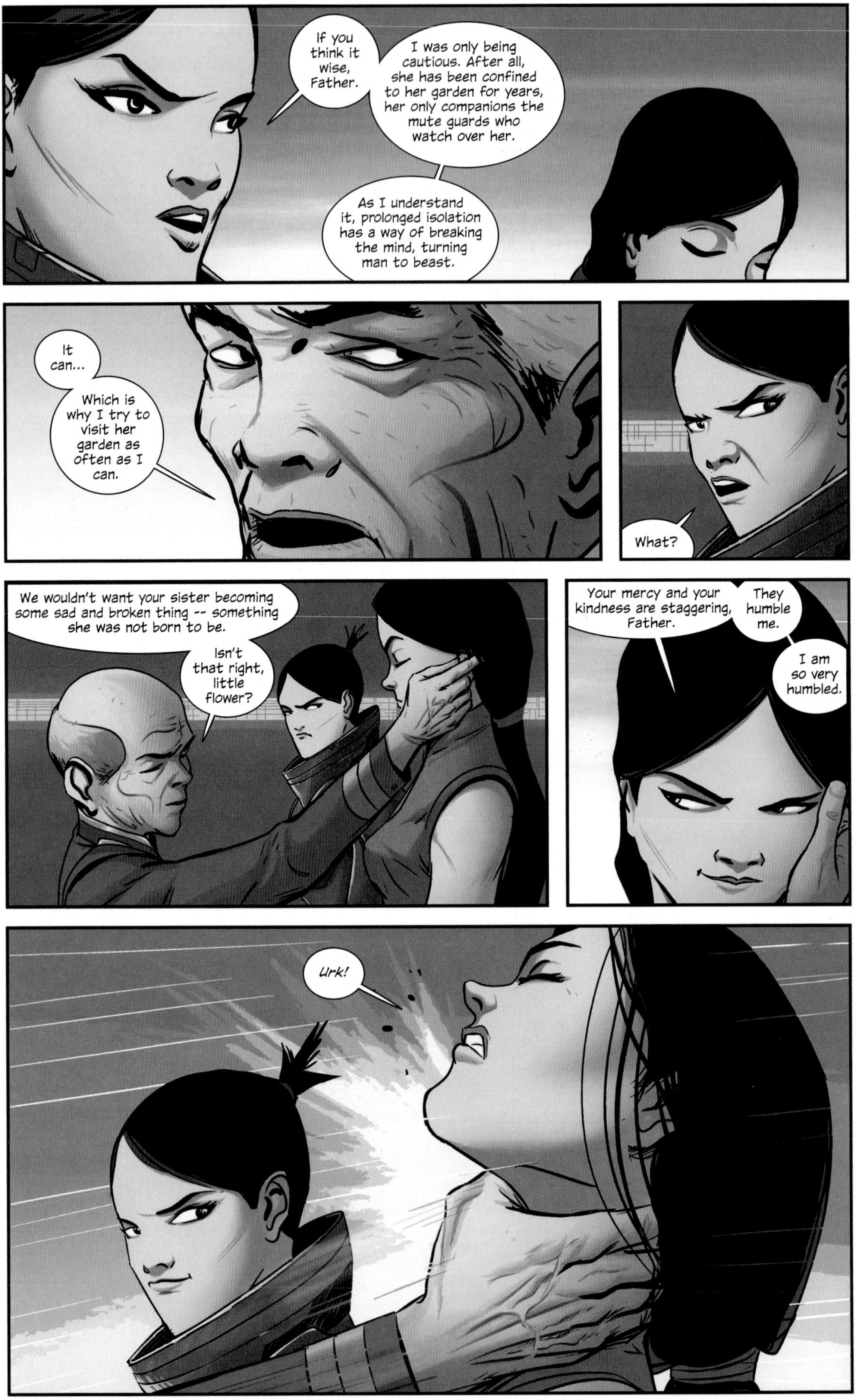
If you think it wise, Father.
I was only being cautious. After all, she has been confined to her garden for years, her only companions the mute guards who watch over her.
As I understand it, prolonged isolation has a way of breaking the mind, turning man to beast.
It can...
Which is why I try to visit her garden as often as I can.
What?
We wouldn't want your sister becoming some sad and broken thing -- something she was not born to be.
Isn't that right, little flower?
Your mercy and your kindness are staggering, Father.
They humble me.
I am so very humbled.
Urk!

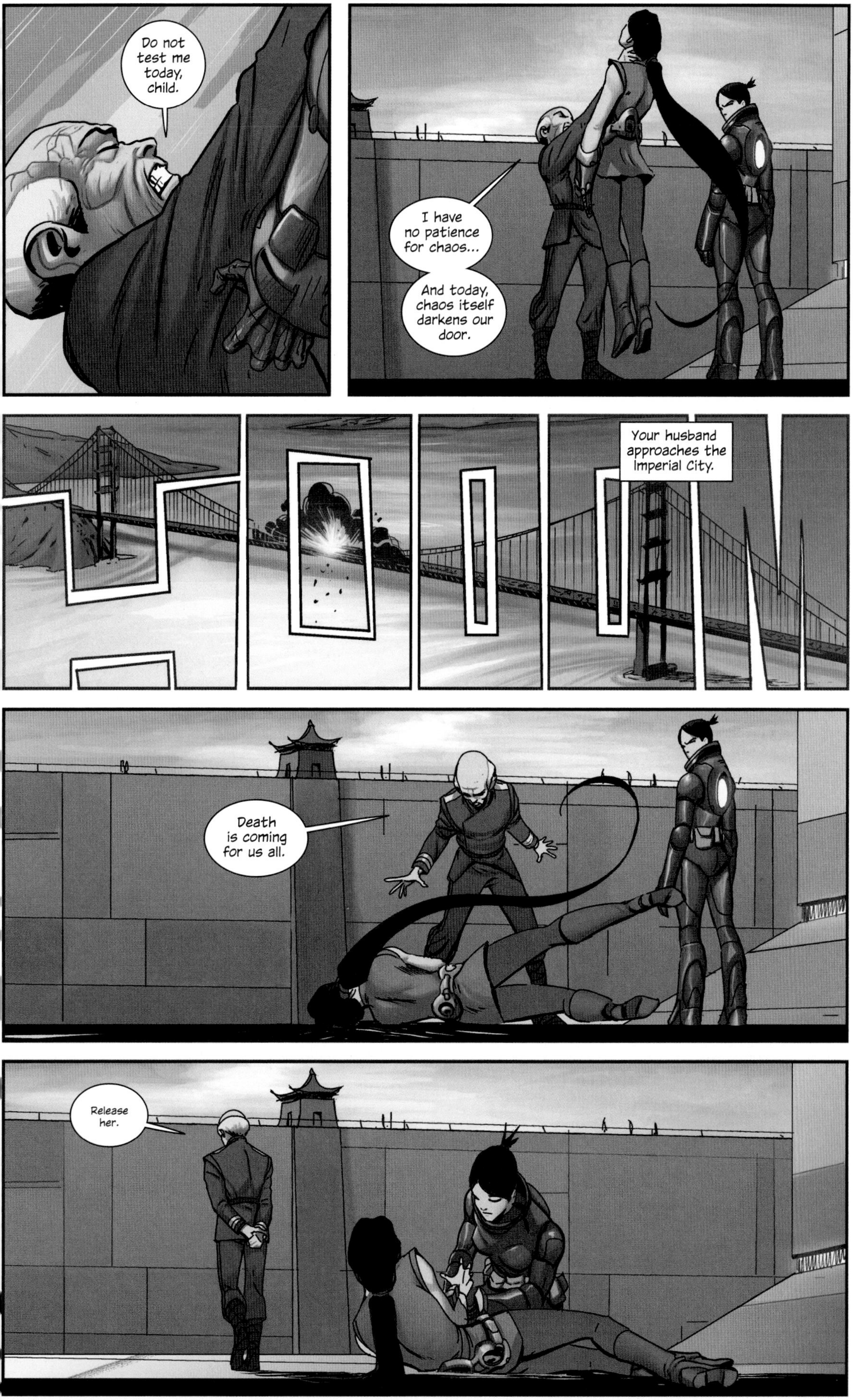
Do not test me today, child.
I have no patience for chaos...
And today, chaos itself darkens our door.
Your husband approaches the Imperial City.
Death is coming for us all.
Release her.

There is a natural order to this world... one that has been upended. A direct result of both your actions.

You with your *allegiances*...

And *you* with your *goddamned heart.*

Unchecked, this would have claimed at least one of you, possibly both. I found that unacceptable...

So I made an agreement with Hu's apocalyptists, the Chosen. It would be as if you did not exist...that no one could find you, not even Death himself.

It kept you alive, Xiaolian...and it cost me dearly.

Then we have all paid, haven't we?

You do not understand, sister.

There is no deal if your husband finds you alive. Father's sacrifice -- even your sacrifice -- will be rendered as nothing.

We Chosen are united on this.

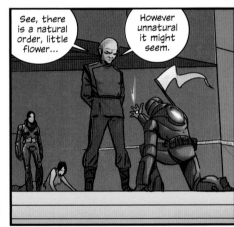

See, there is a natural order, little flower...

However unnatural it might seem.

So he has reached the edge of the city.

Yes. The forward riders have fallen...

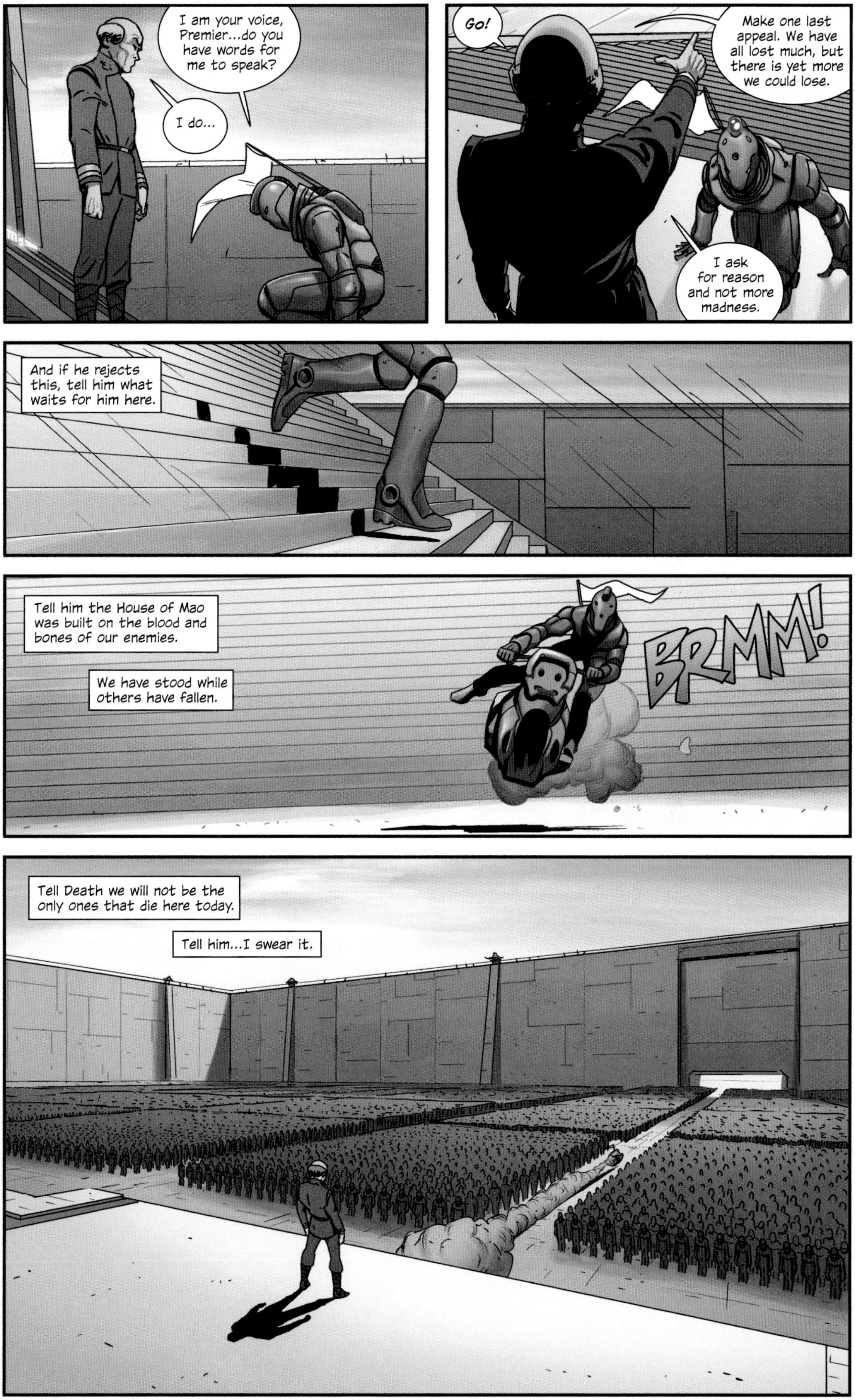
I am your voice, Premier...do you have words for me to speak?
I do...
Go!
Make one last appeal. We have all lost much, but there is yet more we could lose.
I ask for reason and not more madness.
And if he rejects this, tell him what waits for him here.
Tell him the House of Mao was built on the blood and bones of our enemies.
We have stood while others have fallen.
BRMM!
Tell Death we will not be the only ones that die here today.
Tell him...I swear it.

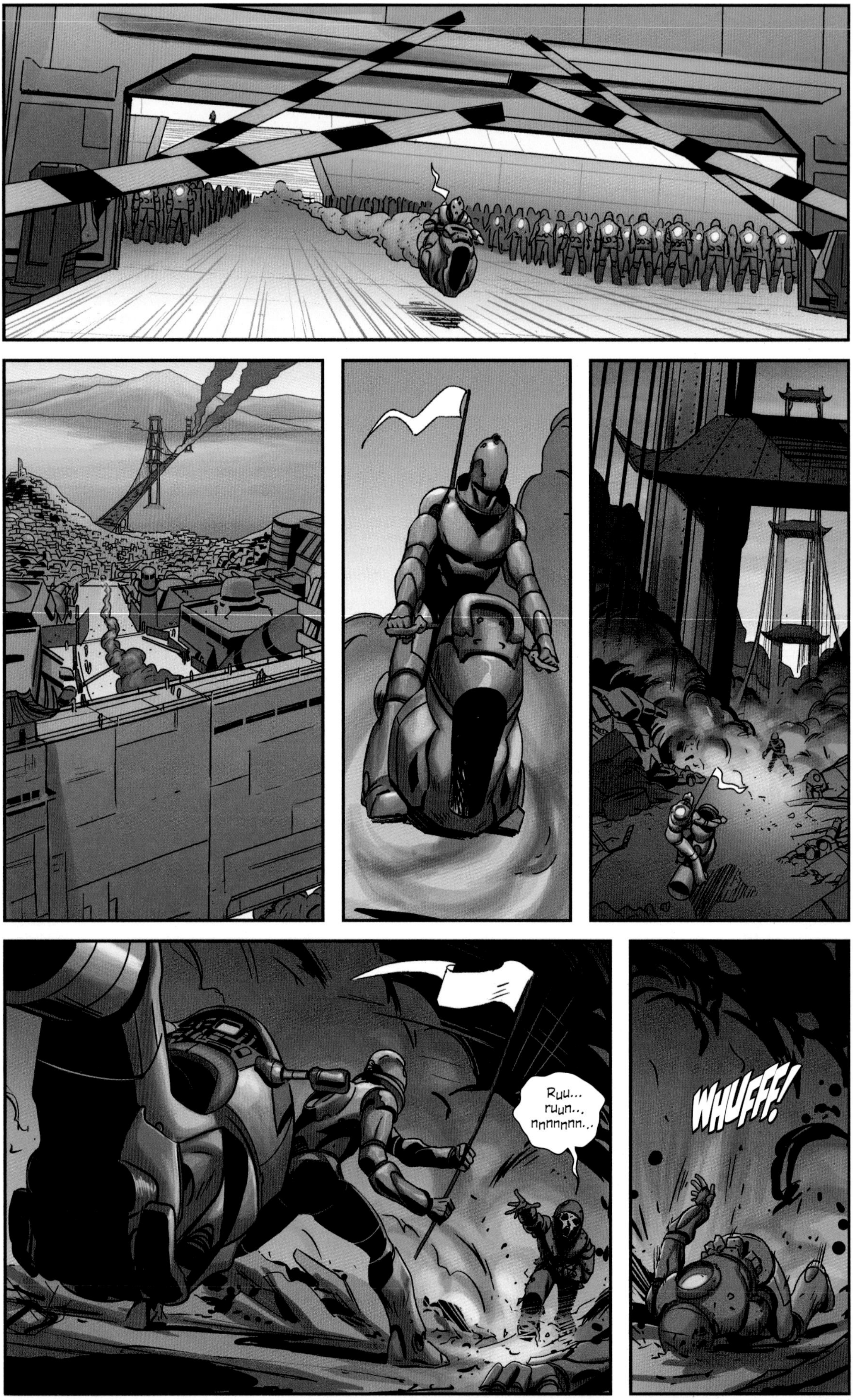
Ruu...
ruun...
nnnnnnn...
WHUFFF!

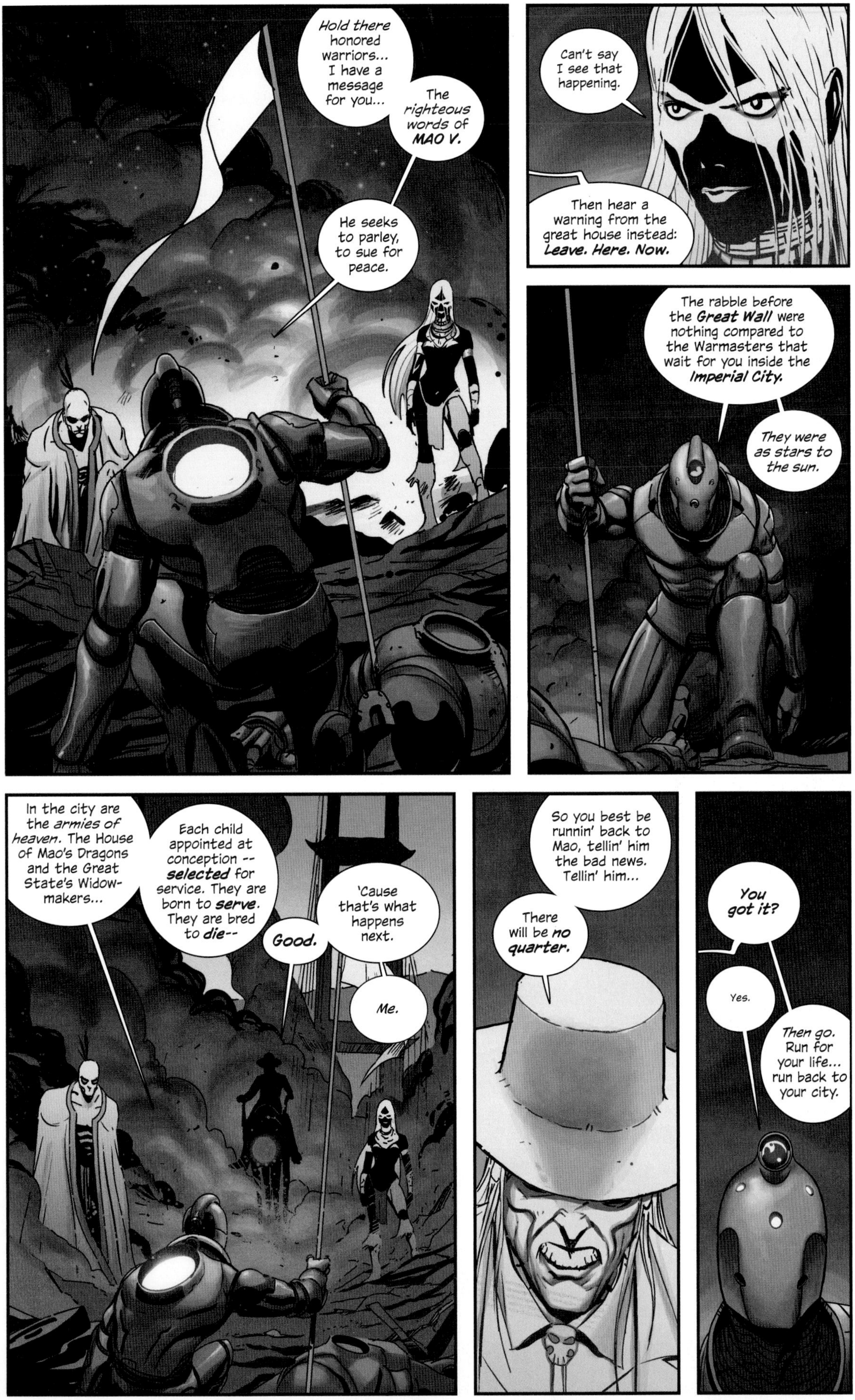
Hold there honored warriors... I have a message for you...
The righteous words of MAO V.
He seeks to parley, to sue for peace.
Can't say I see that happening.
Then hear a warning from the great house instead: Leave. Here. Now.
The rabble before the Great Wall were nothing compared to the Warmasters that wait for you inside the Imperial City.
They were as stars to the sun.
In the city are the armies of heaven. The House of Mao's Dragons and the Great State's Widow-makers...
Each child appointed at conception -- selected for service. They are born to serve. They are bred to die--
Good.
'Cause that's what happens next.
Me.
So you best be runnin' back to Mao, tellin' him the bad news. Tellin' him...
There will be no quarter.
You got it?
Yes.
Then go. Run for your life... run back to your city.

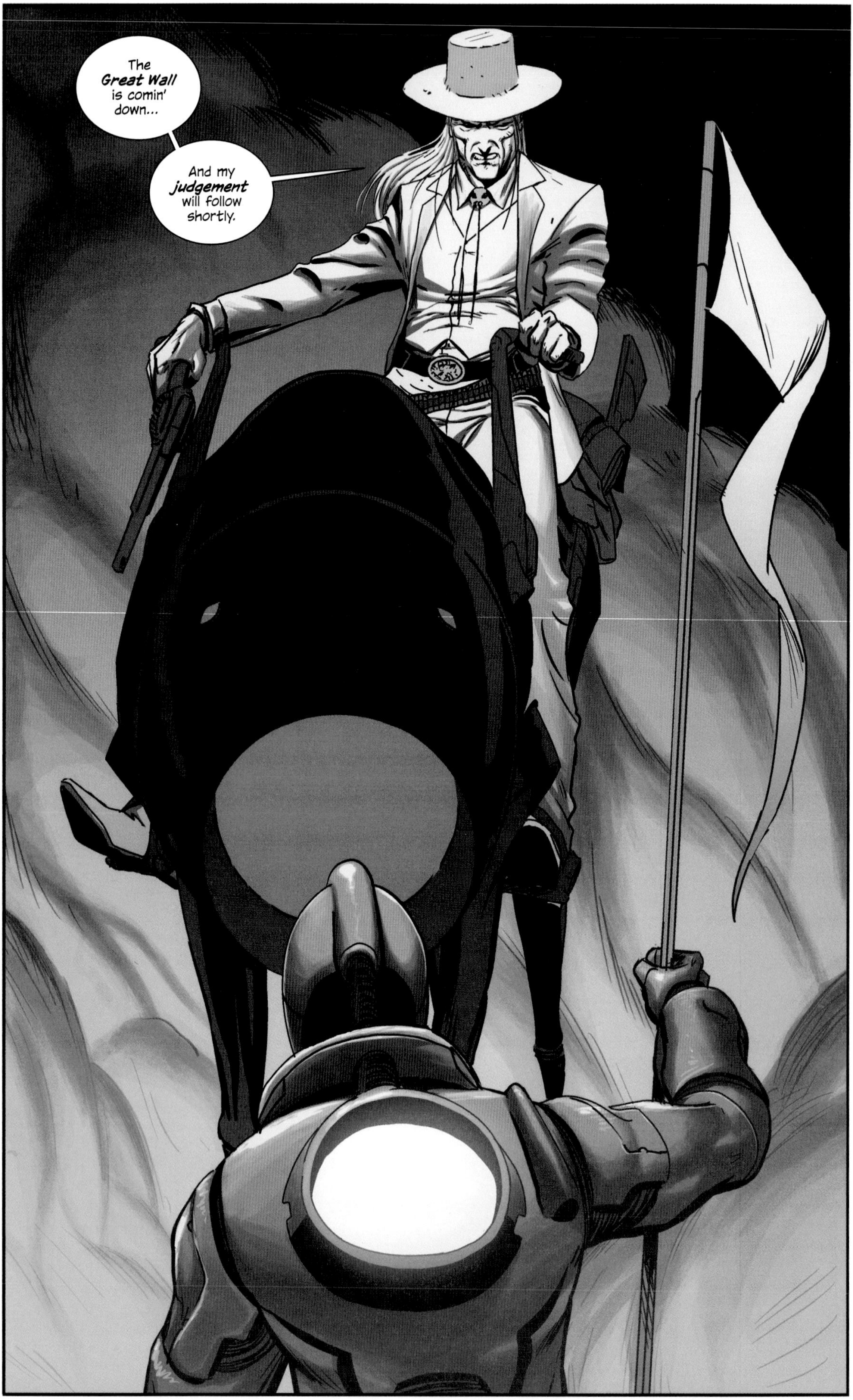
The **Great Wall** is comin' down...
And my ***judgement*** will follow shortly.

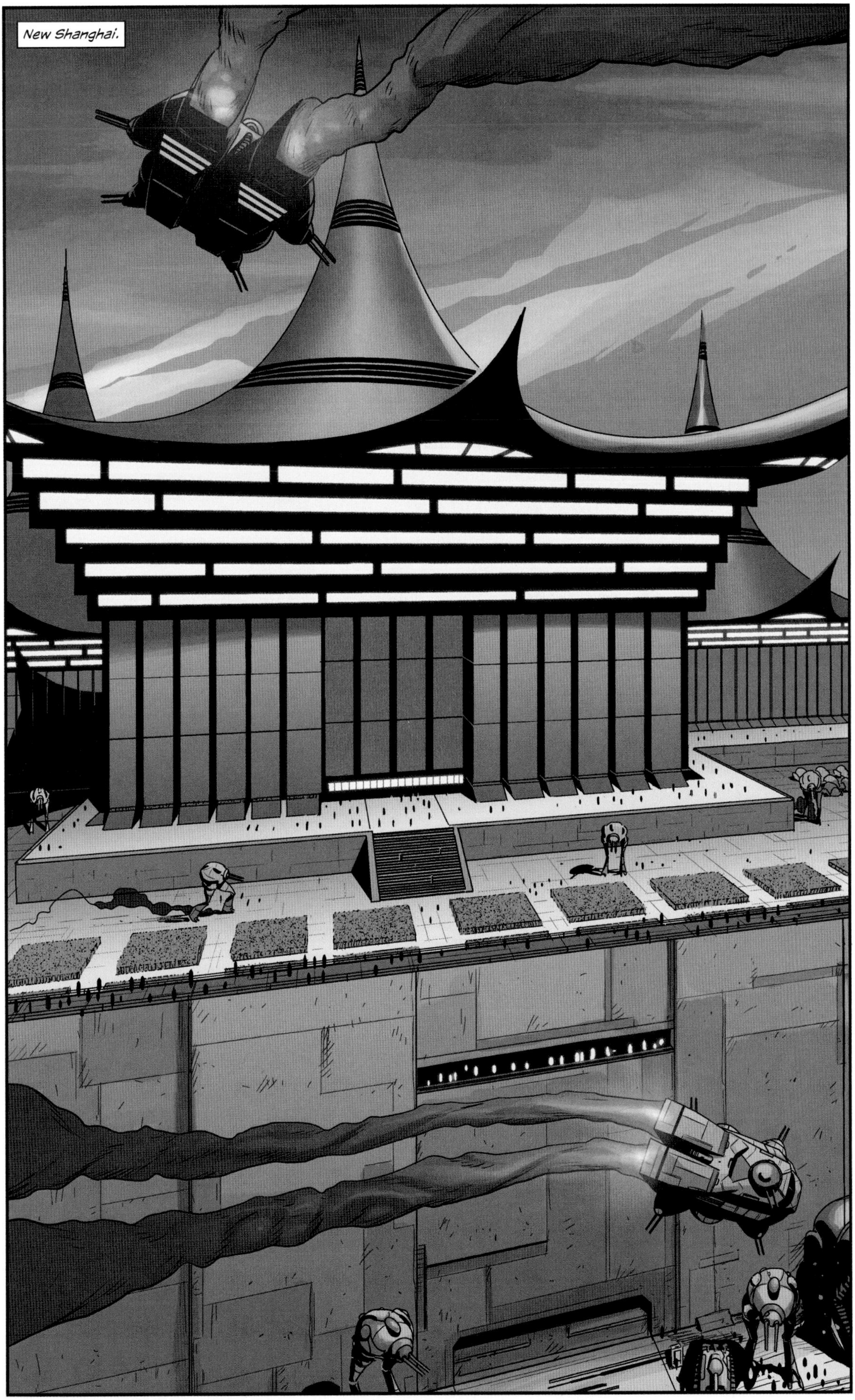
New Shanghai.

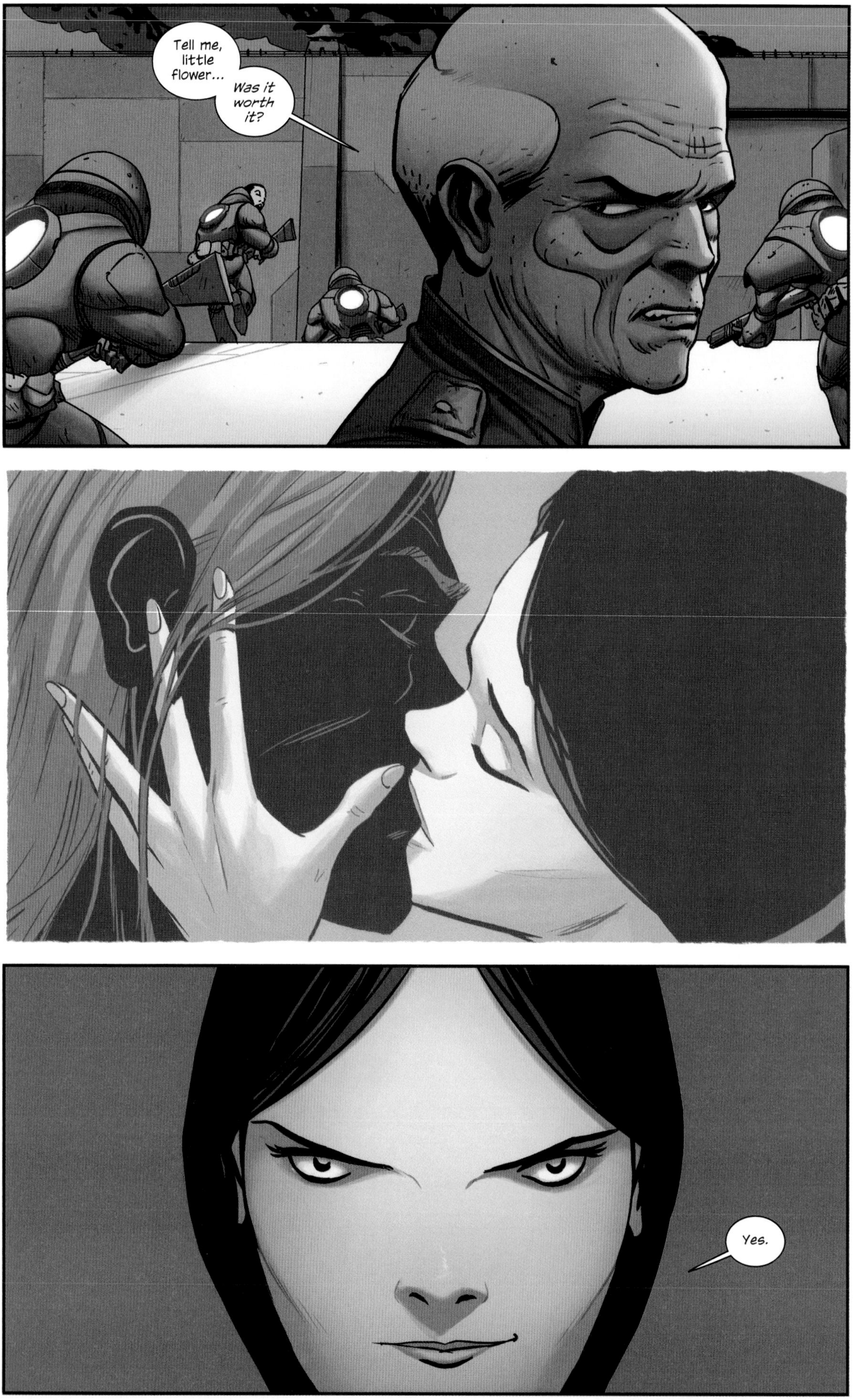
Tell me, little flower...
Was it worth it?
Yes.

WHEN I WAS A CHILD, YOU
TAUGHT ME **REGRET** WAS FOR
THE WEAK.

HOW CAN YOU EXPECT ME TO
FEEL **SUCH A THING** NOW?

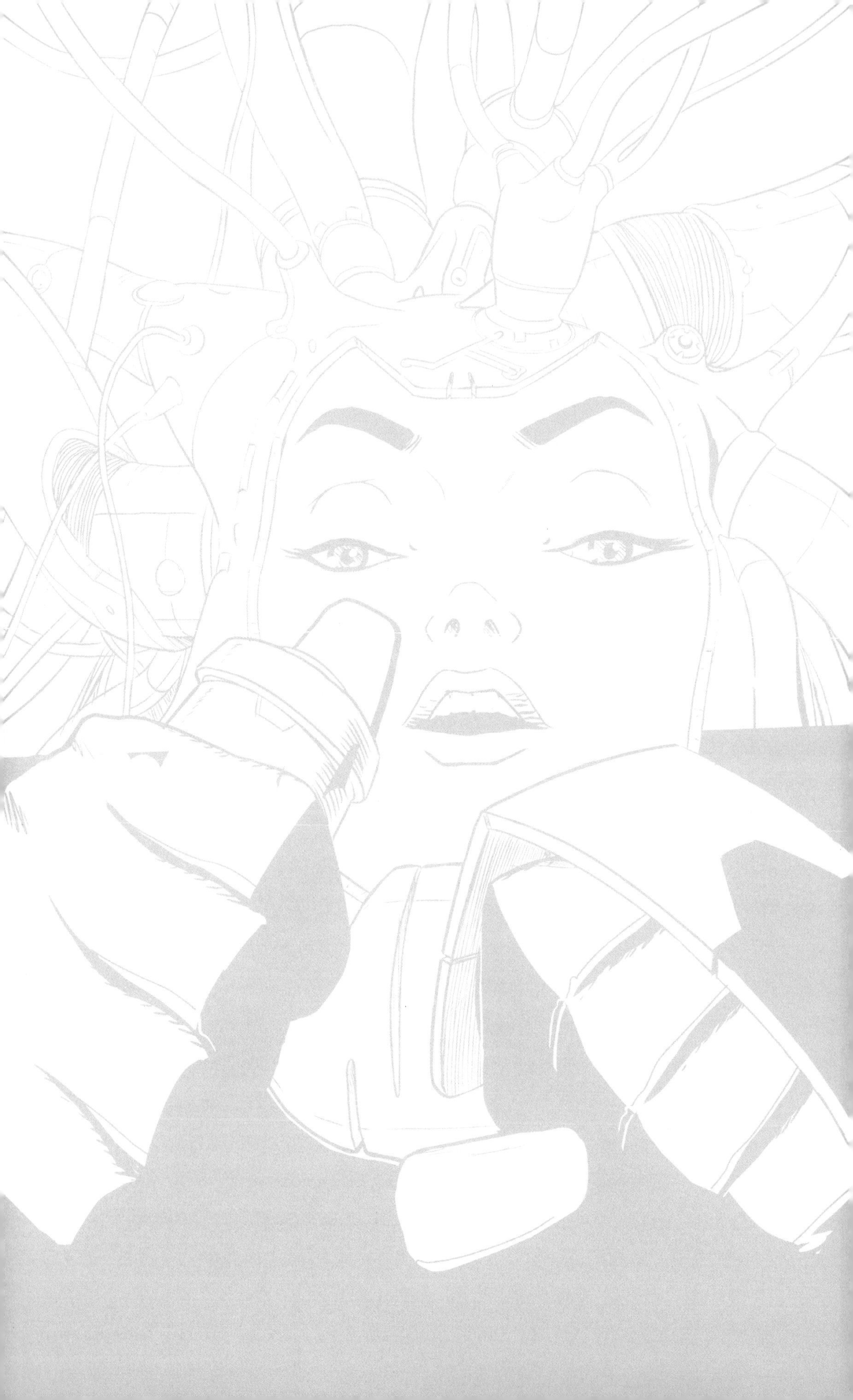

04

FOUR: LAST DEALS
OF **DEAD MEN**

KEEP YOUR GREAT SOCIETY.

TAKE IT WITH YOU TO THE
GRAVE.

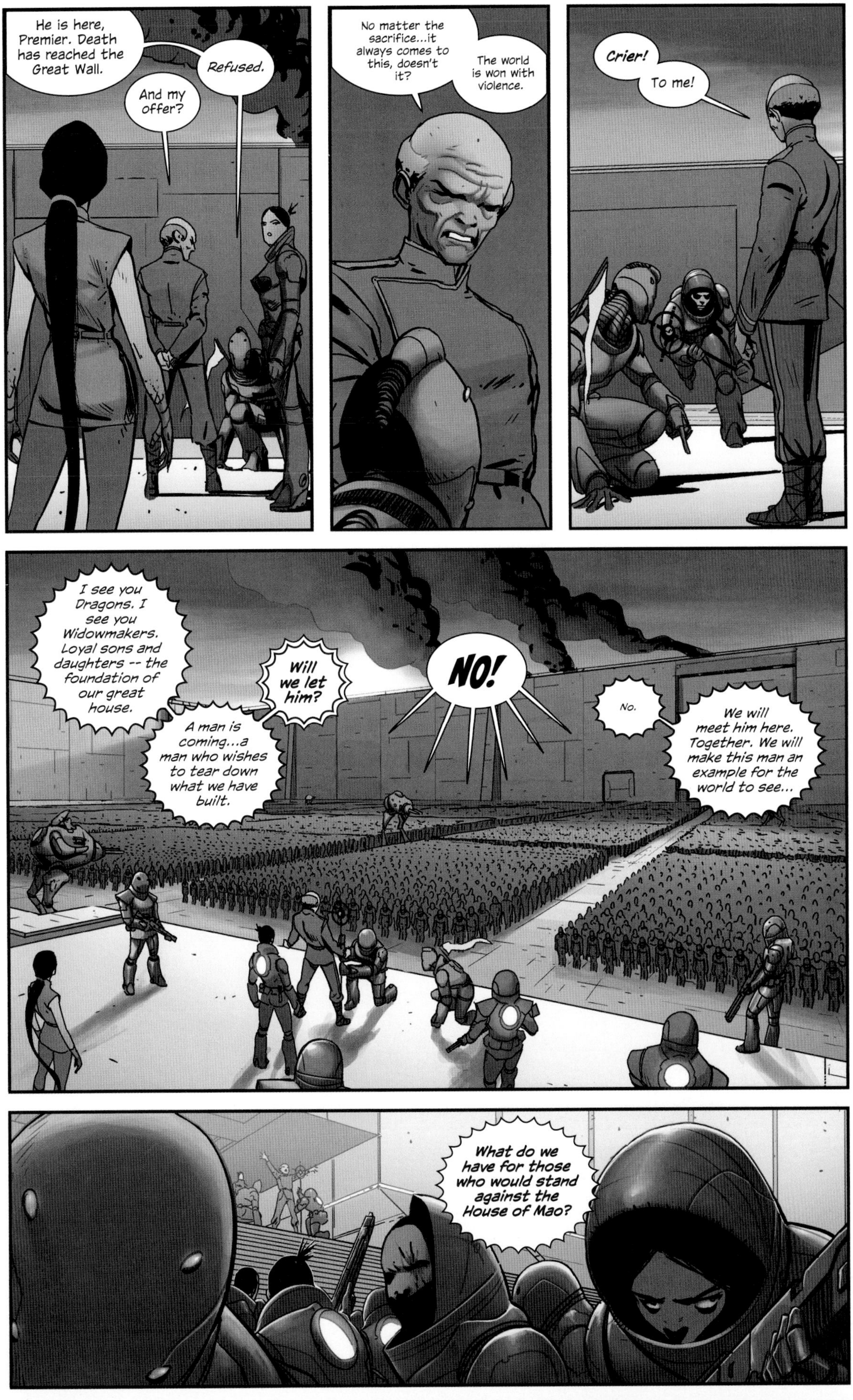
He is here, Premier. Death has reached the Great Wall.
Refused.
And my offer?
No matter the sacrifice...it always comes to this, doesn't it?
The world is won with violence.
Crier!
To me!
I see you Dragons. I see you Widowmakers. Loyal sons and daughters -- the foundation of our great house.
A man is coming...a man who wishes to tear down what we have built.
Will we let him?
NO!
No.
We will meet him here. Together. We will make this man an example for the world to see...
What do we have for those who would stand against the House of Mao?

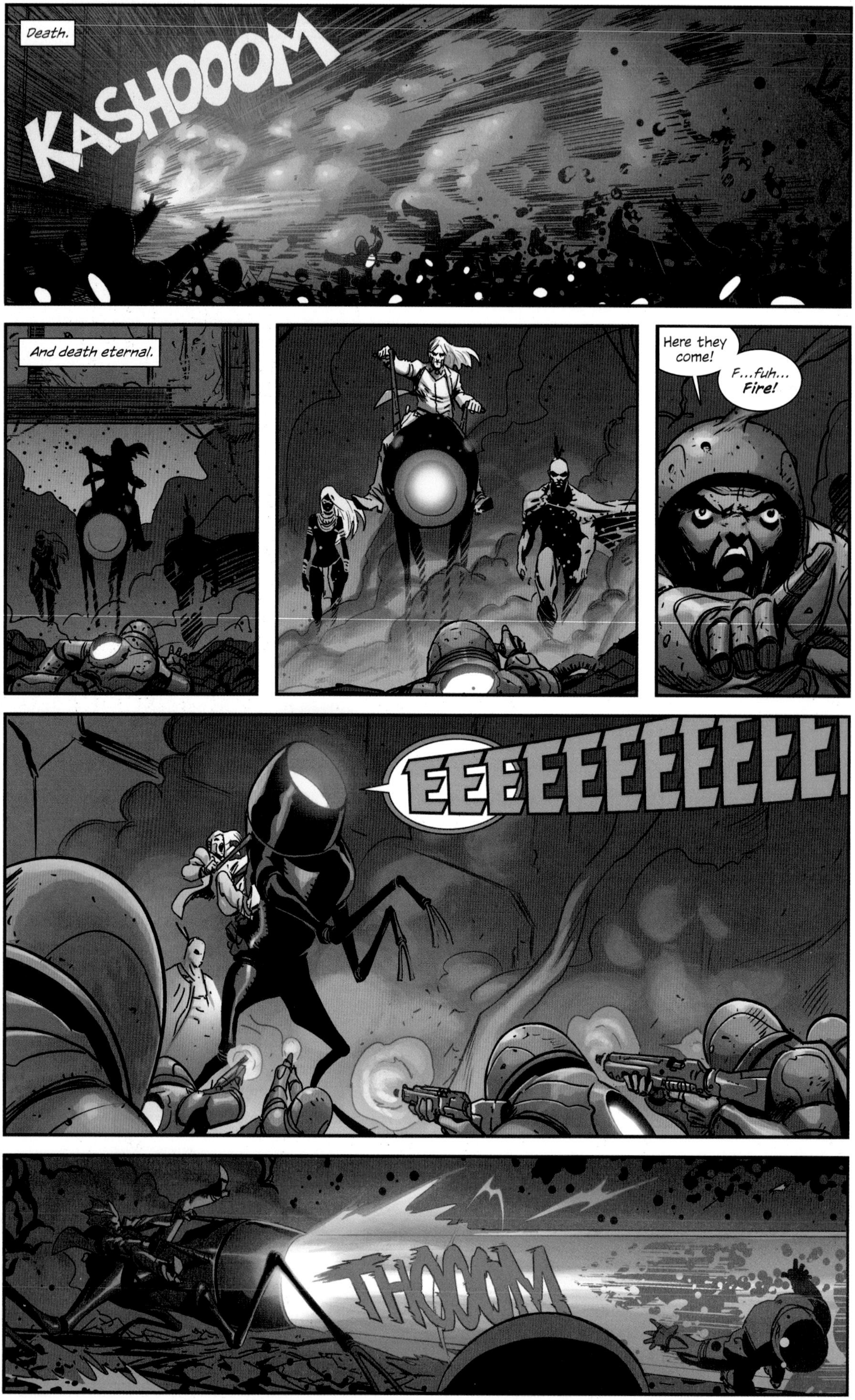
Death.
KASHOOOM
And death eternal.
Here they come!
F...fuh... Fire!
EEEEEEEEEEEEE
THOOOM

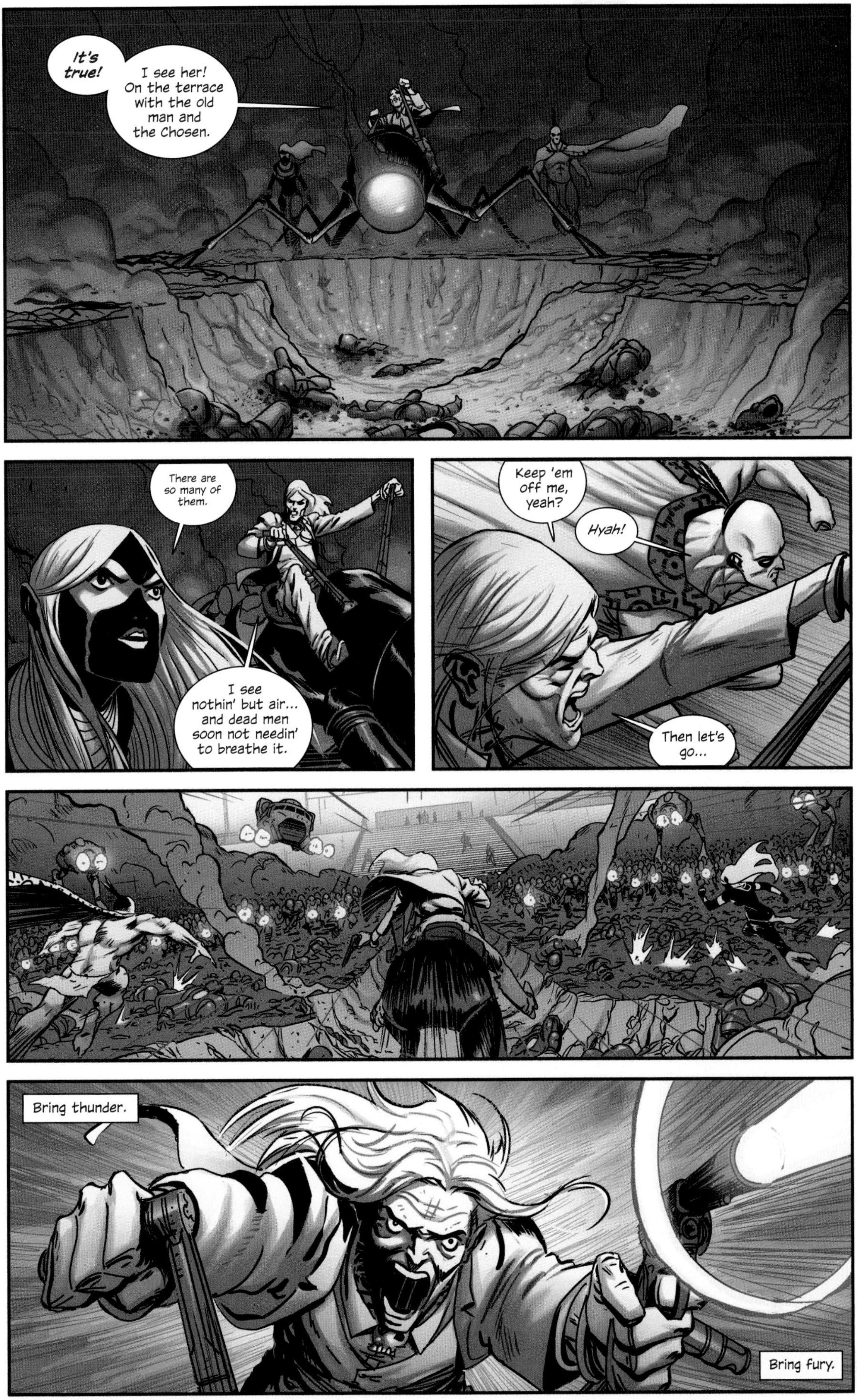
It's true!
I see her! On the terrace with the old man and the Chosen.
There are so many of them.
I see nothin' but air... and dead men soon not needin' to breathe it.
Keep 'em off me, yeah?
Hyah!
Then let's go...
Bring thunder.
Bring fury.

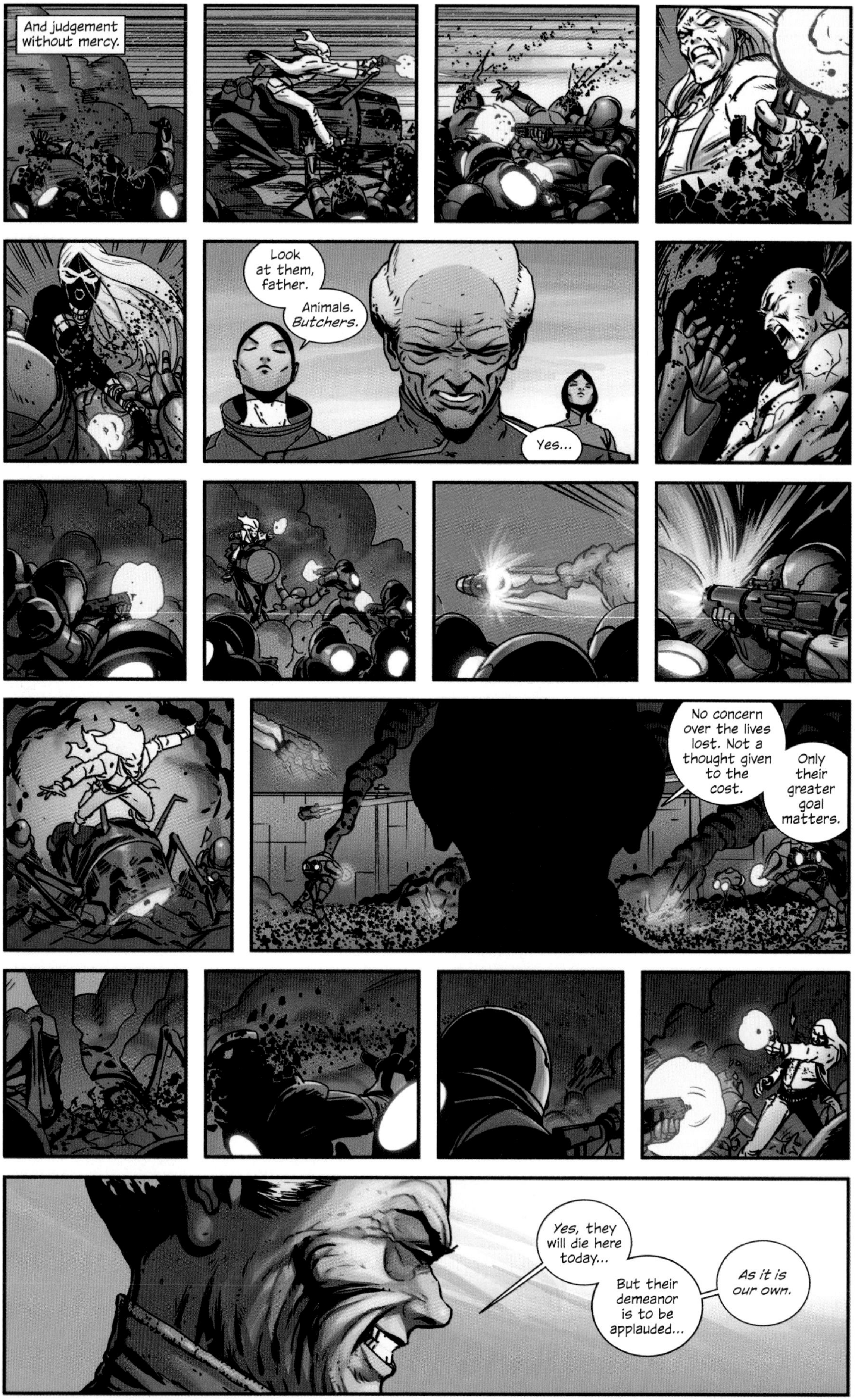

And judgement without mercy.
Look at them, father.
Animals. *Butchers.*
Yes...
No concern over the lives lost. Not a thought given to the cost.
Only their greater goal matters.
Yes, they will die here today...
But their demeanor is to be applauded...
As it is our own.

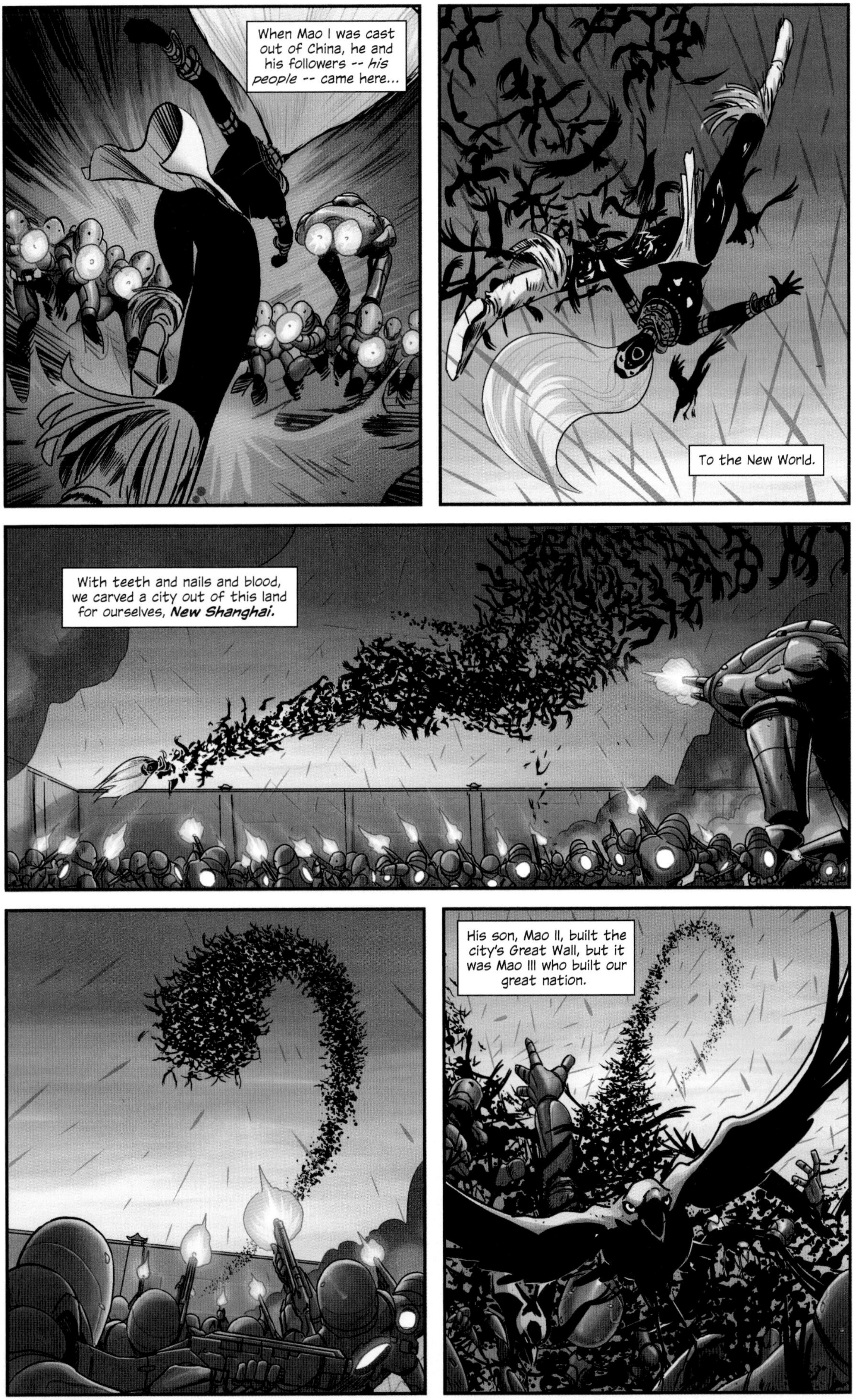
When Mao I was cast out of China, he and his followers -- *his people* -- came here...
To the New World.
With teeth and nails and blood, we carved a city out of this land for ourselves, ***New Shanghai.***
His son, Mao II, built the city's Great Wall, but it was Mao III who built our great nation.

Civil Wars had left the land weak and full of opportunity, so he created the Armies of Heaven -- our Dragons, our Widowmakers -- and then he released them onto an unsuspecting world.

Within a generation we had taken one-third of this land.

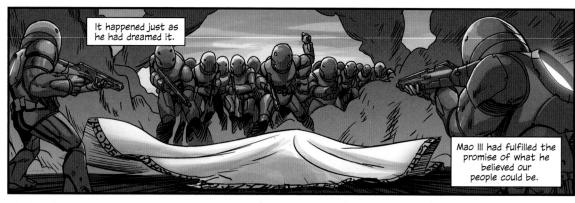

It happened just as he had dreamed it.

Mao III had fulfilled the promise of what he believed our people could be.

Twenty million loyal soldiers died to realize his vision.

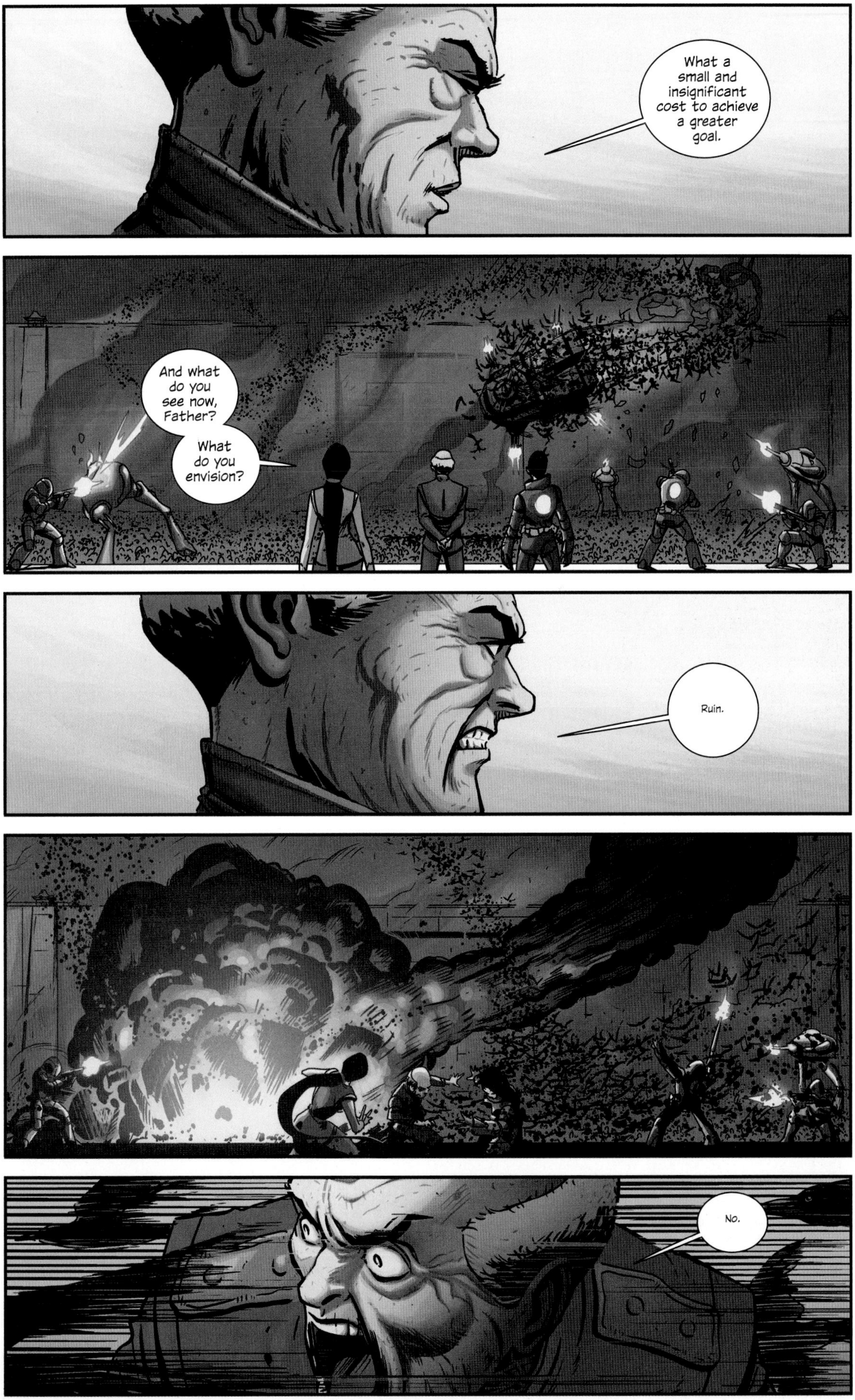
What a small and insignificant cost to achieve a greater goal.
And what do you see now, Father?
What do you envision?
Ruin.
No.

NO!

There's a thing, Father, where men who have thought they were giants their entire lives actually see one for the first time.

It sparks a reaction.

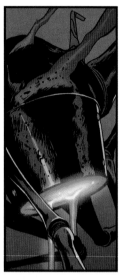

It shows them their true worth.

BLAM

It shows them their place.

BLAM BLAM   BLAM   BLAM
BLAM
BLAM

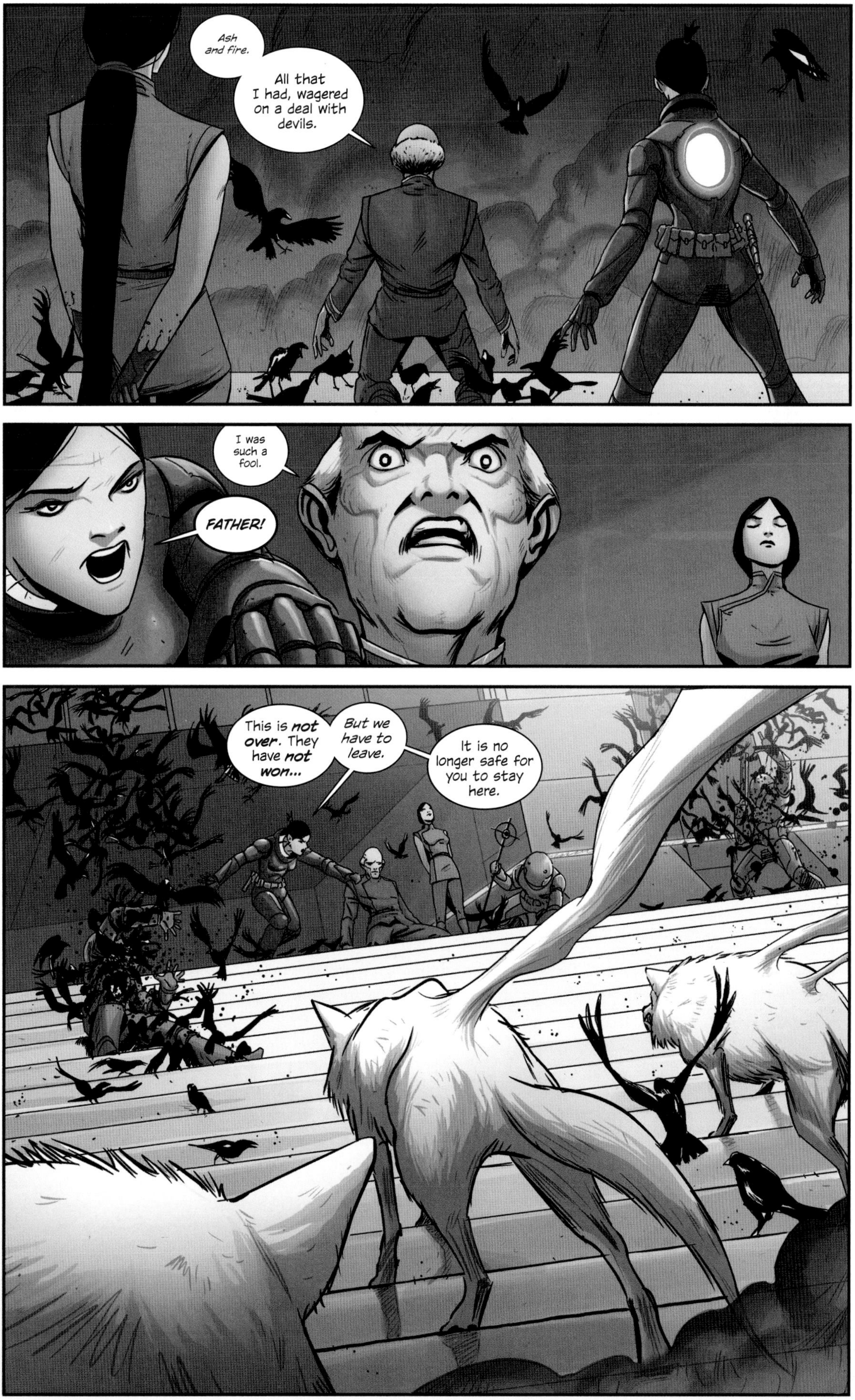

Ash and fire.
All that I had, wagered on a deal with devils.
I was such a fool.
FATHER!
This is **not over**. They have **not won**...
But we have to leave.
It is no longer safe for you to stay here.

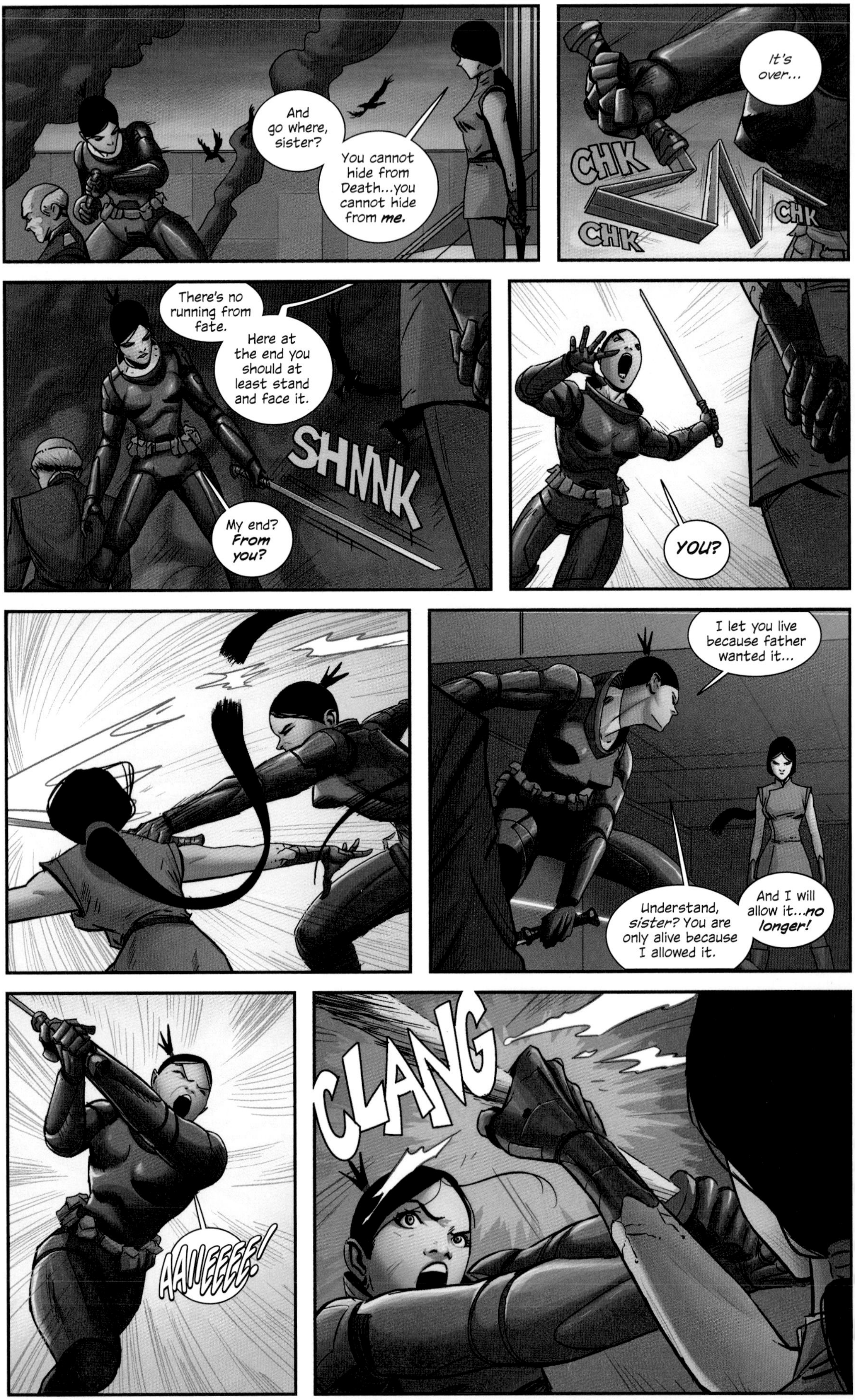
And go where, sister?
You cannot hide from Death...you cannot hide from *me.*
It's over...
CHK
CHK
CHK
There's no running from fate.
Here at the end you should at least stand and face it.
SHNNK
My end? *From you?*
YOU?
I let you live because father wanted it...
Understand, *sister?* You are only alive because I allowed it.
And I will allow it...*no longer!*
AAIIEEEE!
CLANG

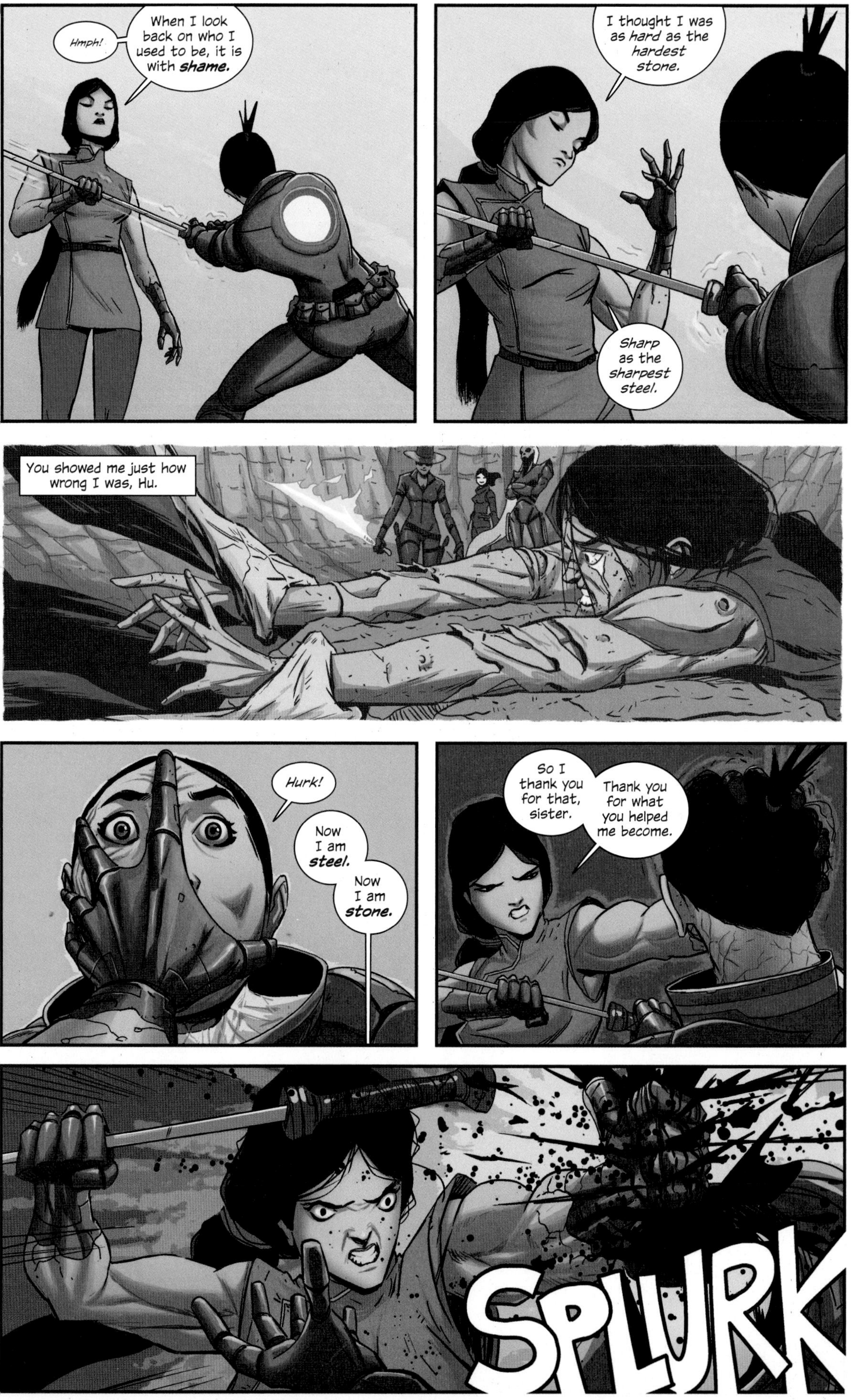

Hmph!
When I look back on who I used to be, it is with **shame.**
I thought I was as *hard* as the *hardest* stone.
Sharp as the *sharpest* *steel.*
You showed me just how wrong I was, Hu.
Hurk!
Now I am **steel.**
Now I am **stone.**
So I thank you for that, sister.
Thank you for what you helped me become.
SPLURK

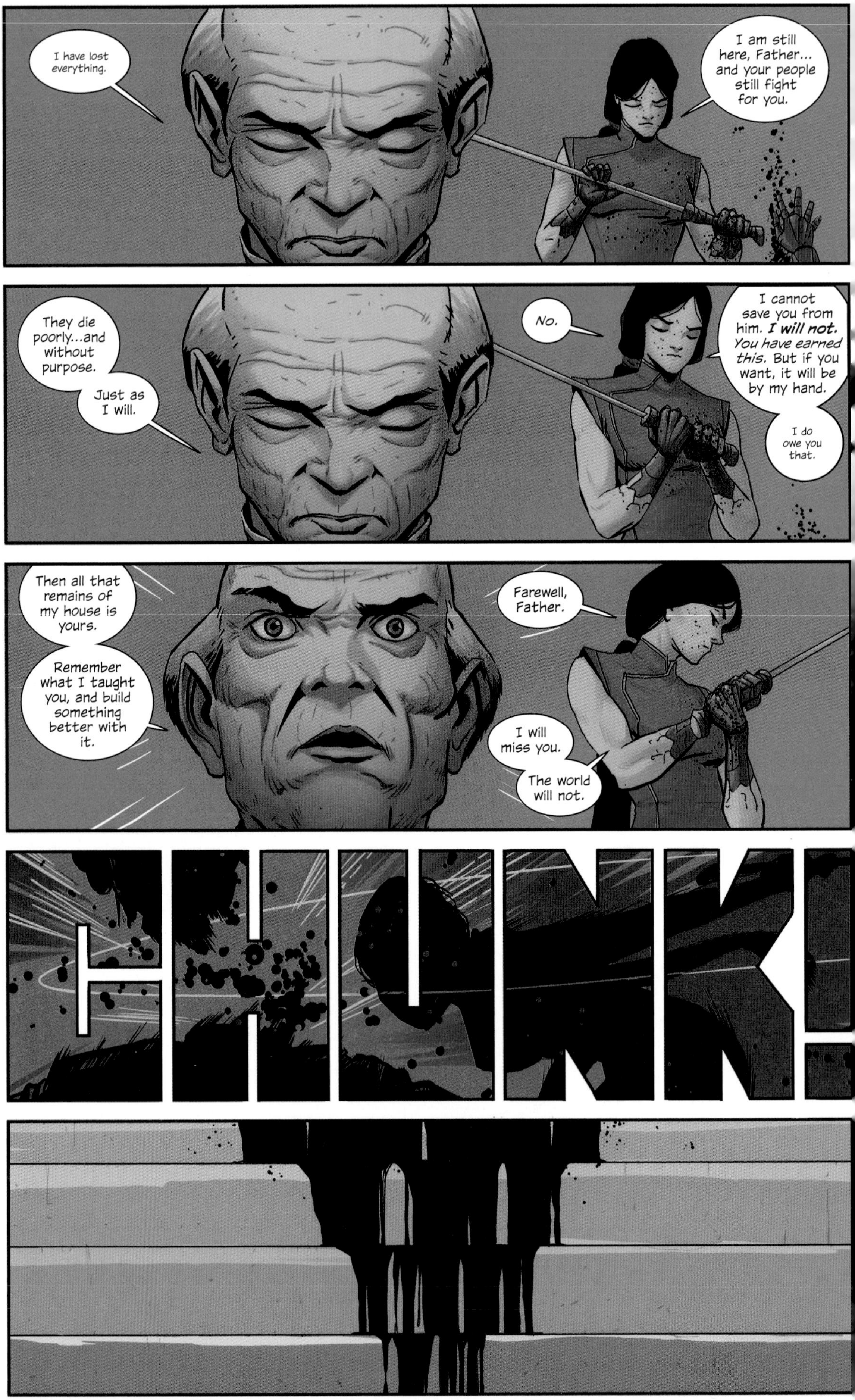
I have lost everything.
I am still here, Father... and your people still fight for you.
They die poorly...and without purpose.
Just as I will.
No.
I cannot save you from him. ***I will not.*** *You have earned this.* But if you want, it will be by my hand.
I do owe you that.
Then all that remains of my house is yours.
Remember what I taught you, and build something better with it.
Farewell, Father.
I will miss you.
The world will not.
CHUNK!

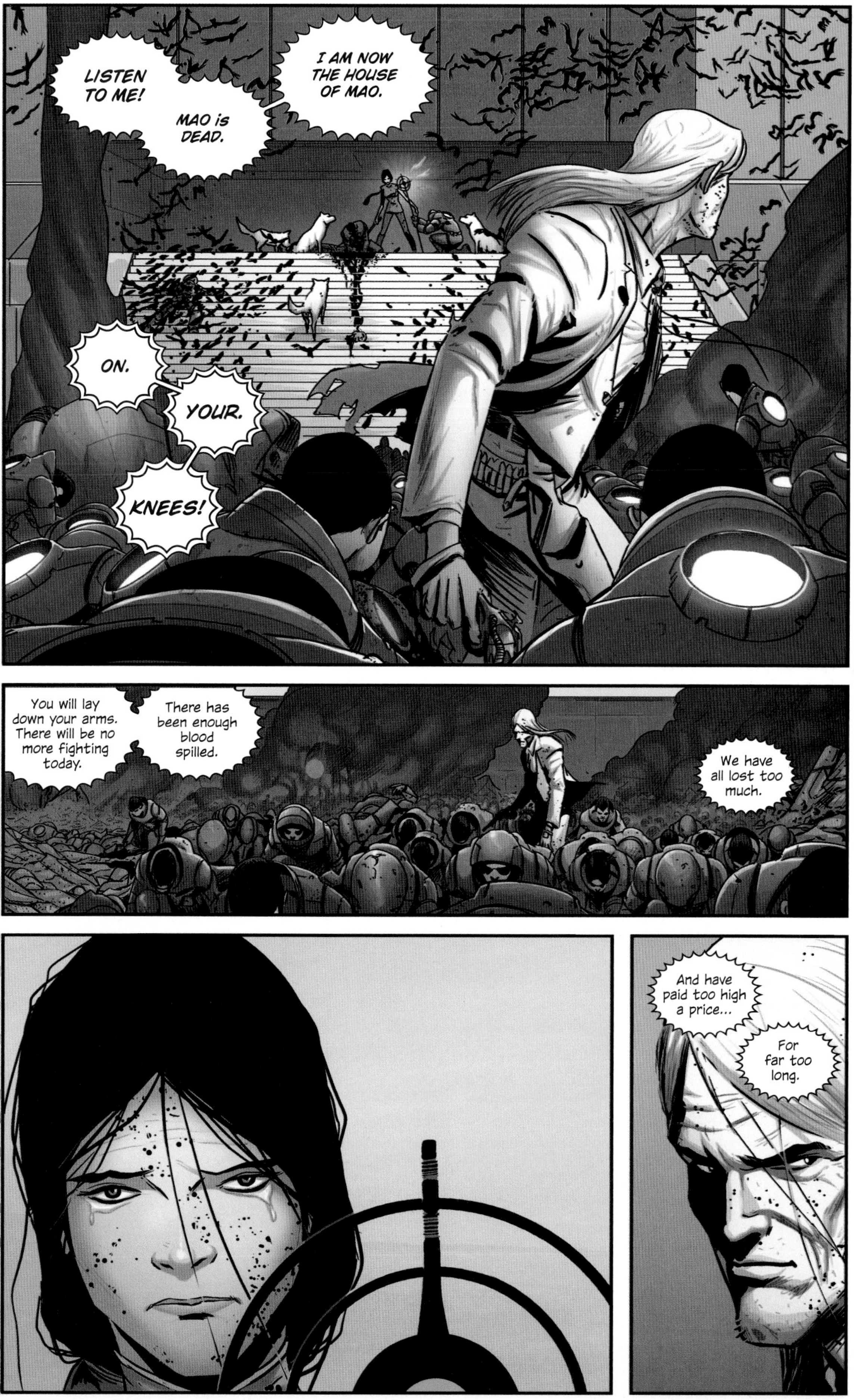
LISTEN TO ME!
MAO is DEAD.
I AM NOW THE HOUSE OF MAO.
ON.
YOUR.
KNEES!
You will lay down your arms. There will be no more fighting today.
There has been enough blood spilled.
We have all lost too much.
And have paid too high a price...
For far too long.

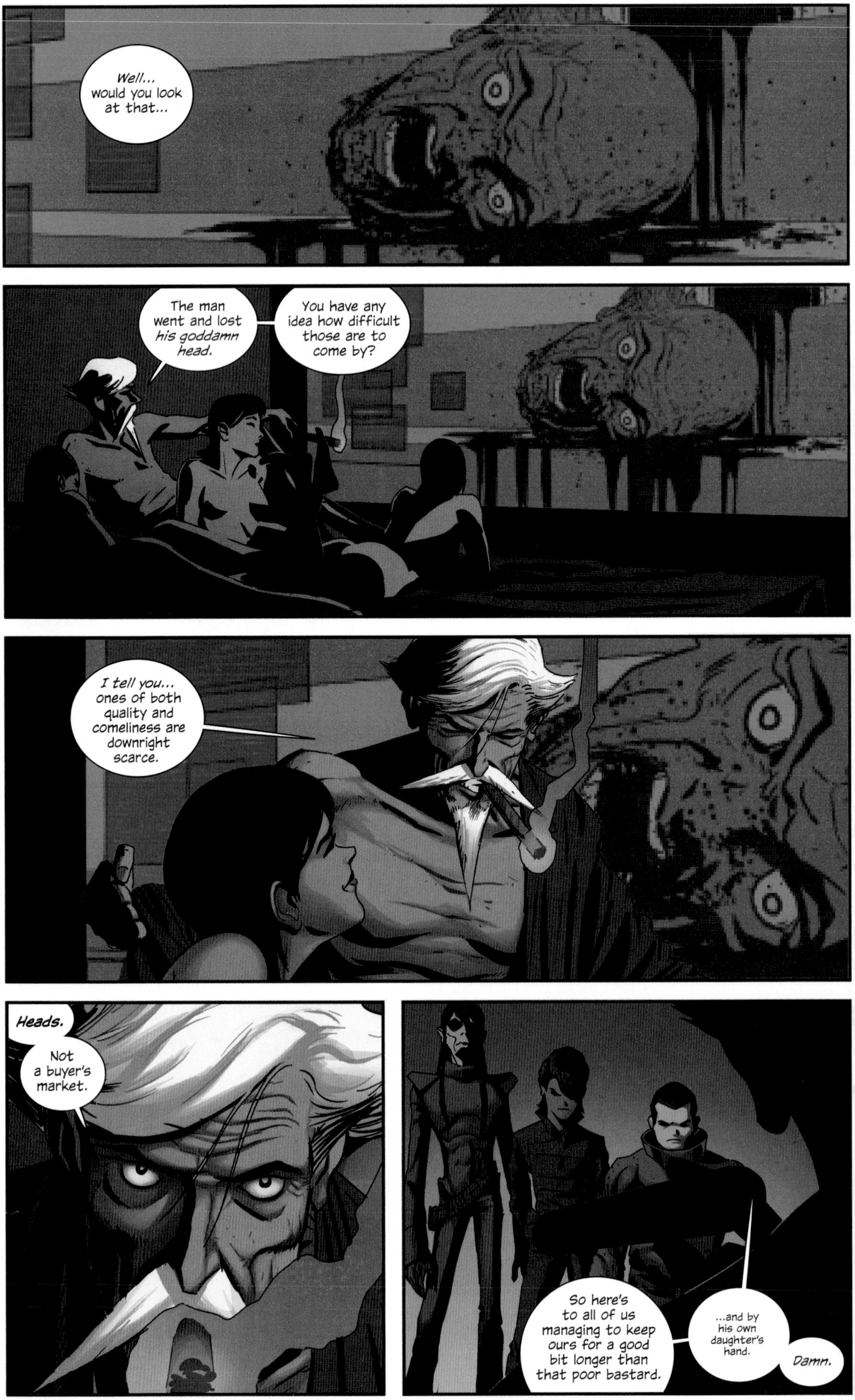
Well... would you look at that...
The man went and lost his goddamn head.
You have any idea how difficult those are to come by?
I tell you... ones of both quality and comeliness are downright scarce.
Heads.
Not a buyer's market.
So here's to all of us managing to keep ours for a good bit longer than that poor bastard.
...and by his own daughter's hand.
Damn.

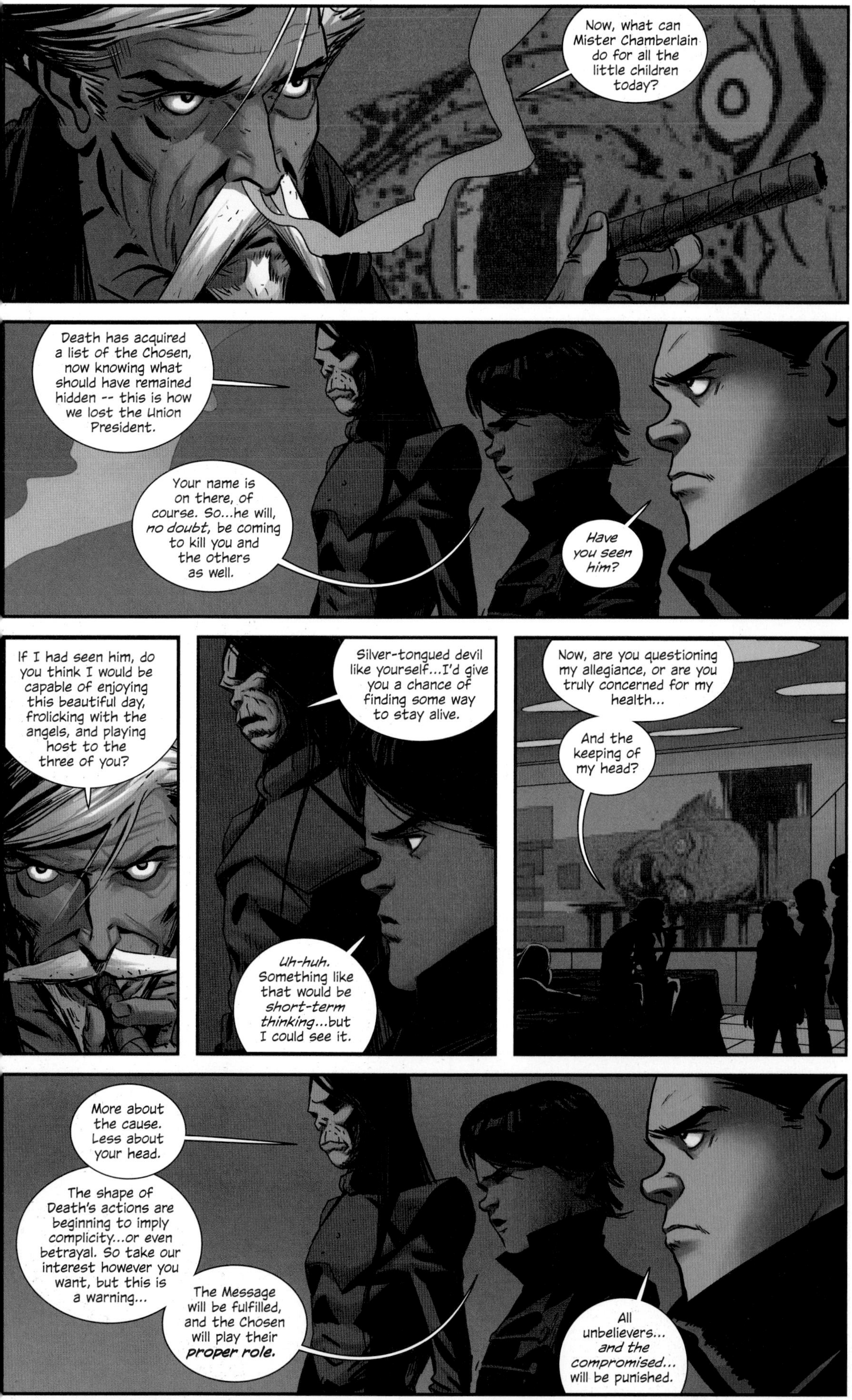

Now, what can Mister Chamberlain do for all the little children today?
Death has acquired a list of the Chosen, now knowing what should have remained hidden -- this is how we lost the Union President.
Your name is on there, of course. So...he will, *no doubt*, be coming to kill you and the others as well.
Have you seen him?
If I had seen him, do you think I would be capable of enjoying this beautiful day, frolicking with the angels, and playing host to the three of you?
Silver-tongued devil like yourself...I'd give you a chance of finding some way to stay alive.
Uh-huh. Something like that would be *short-term thinking*...but I could see it.
Now, are you questioning my allegiance, or are you truly concerned for my health...
And the keeping of my head?
More about the cause. Less about your head.
The shape of Death's actions are beginning to imply complicity...or even betrayal. So take our interest however you want, but this is a warning...
The Message will be fulfilled, and the Chosen will play their ***proper role.***
All unbelievers... *and the compromised...* will be punished.

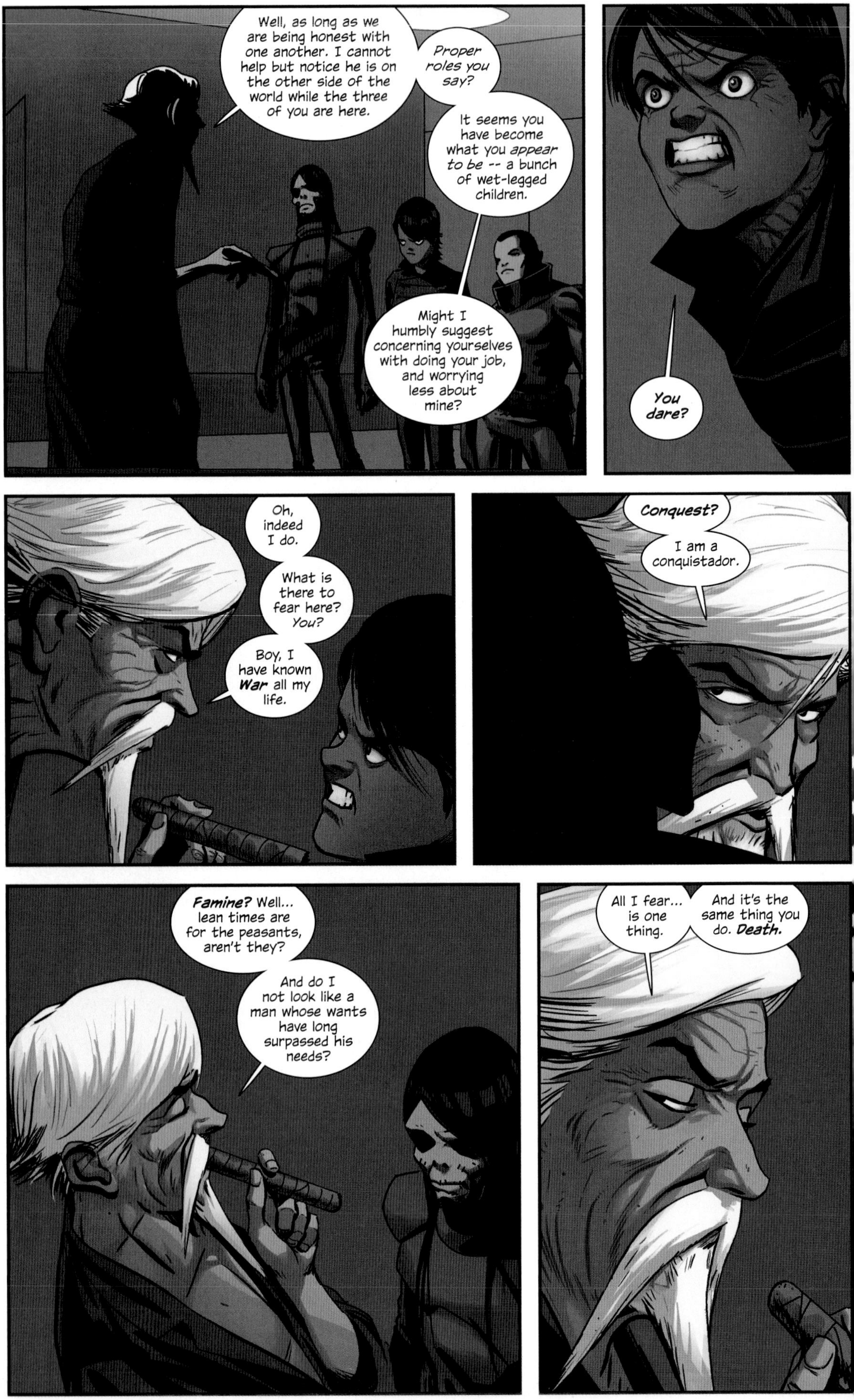
Well, as long as we are being honest with one another. I cannot help but notice he is on the other side of the world while the three of you are here.
Proper roles you say?
It seems you have become what you *appear to be* -- a bunch of wet-legged children.
Might I humbly suggest concerning yourselves with doing your job, and worrying less about mine?
You dare?
Oh, indeed I do.
What is there to fear here? *You?*
Boy, I have known ***War*** all my life.
Conquest?
I am a conquistador.
Famine? Well... lean times are for the peasants, aren't they?
And do I not look like a man whose wants have long surpassed his needs?
All I fear... is one thing.
And it's the same thing you do. ***Death.***

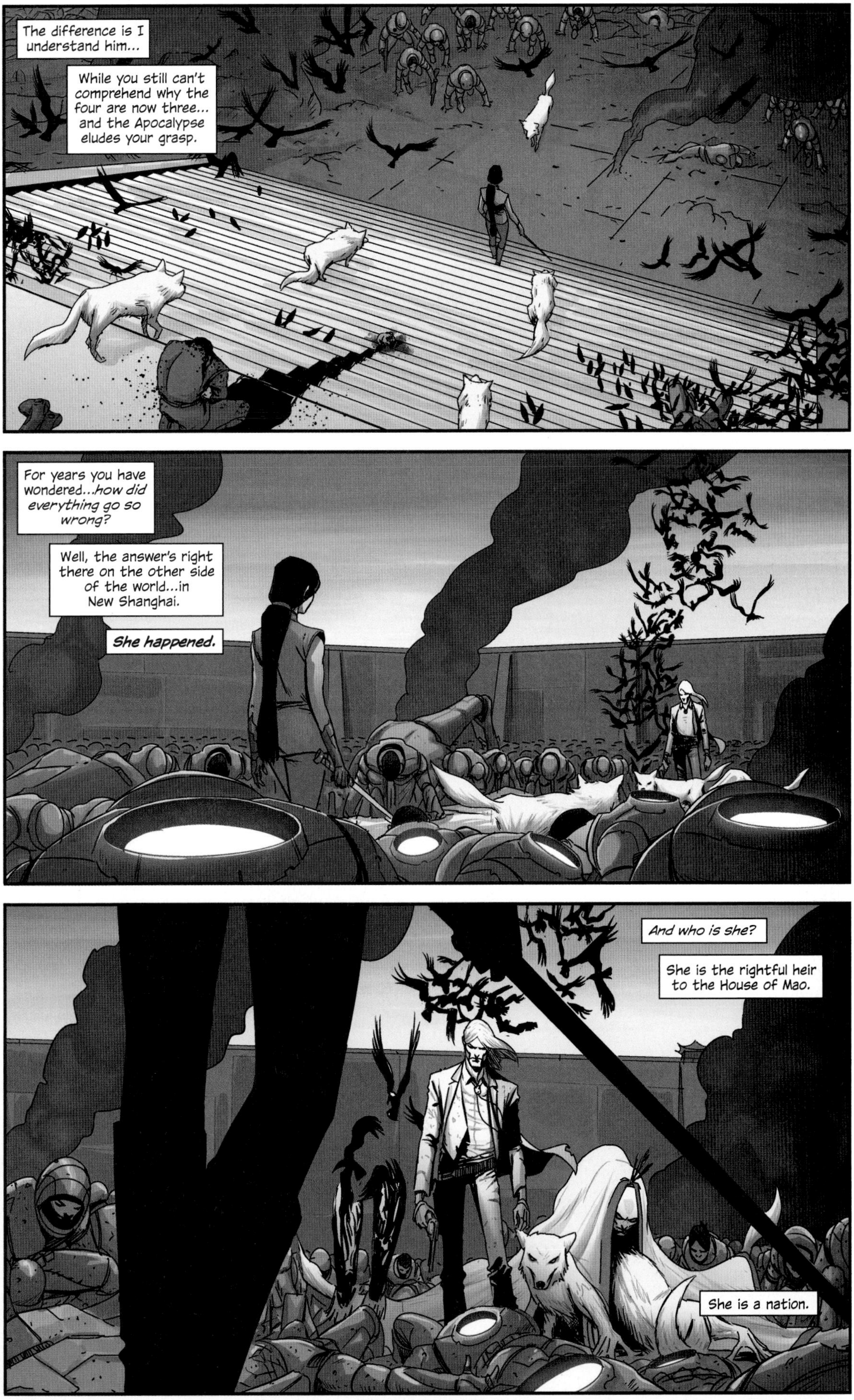

The difference is I understand him...
While you still can't comprehend why the four are now three... and the Apocalypse eludes your grasp.
For years you have wondered...*how did everything go so wrong?*
Well, the answer's right there on the other side of the world...in New Shanghai.
She happened.
And who is she?
She is the rightful heir to the House of Mao.
She is a nation.

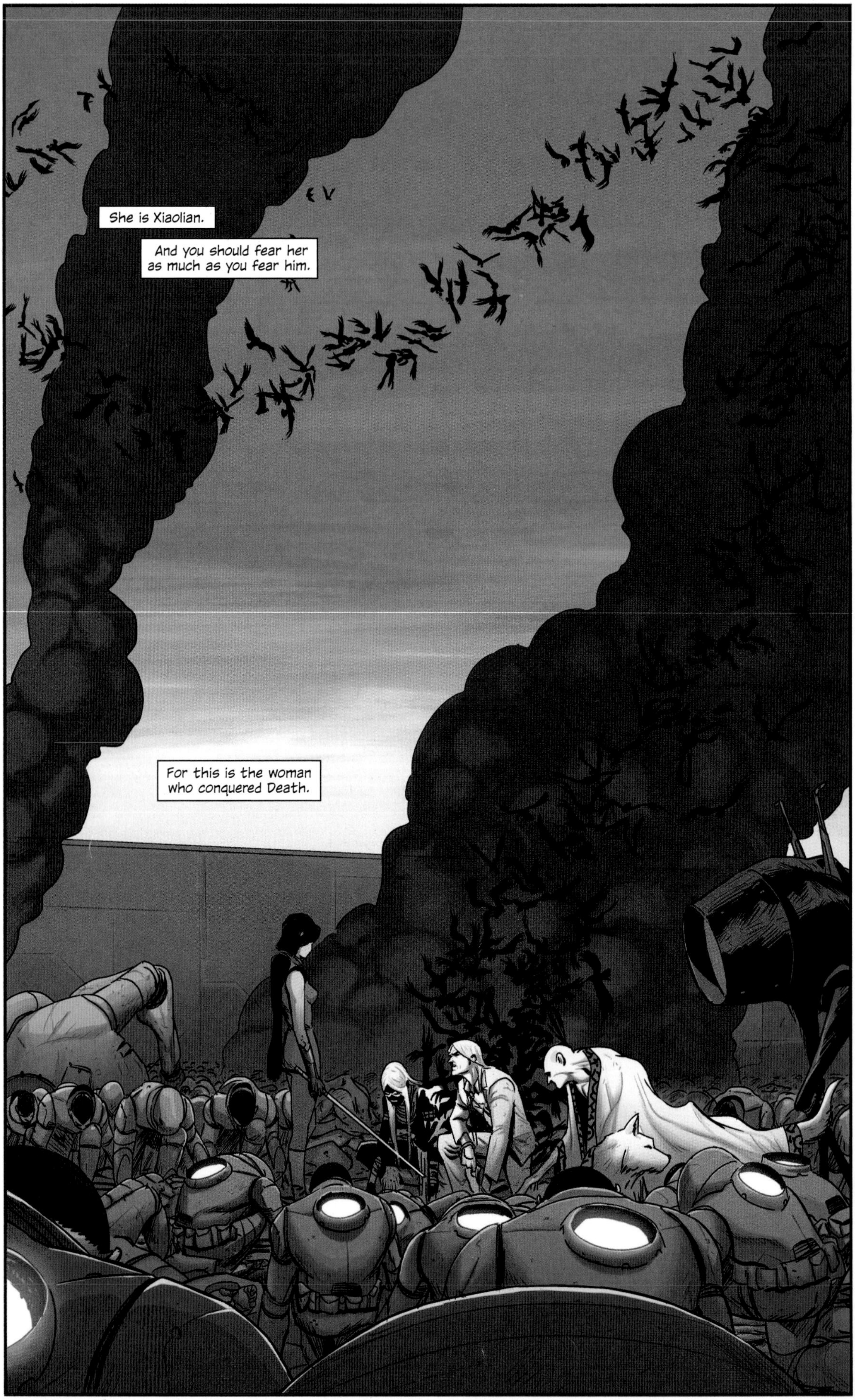
She is Xiaolian.
And you should fear her as much as you fear him.
For this is the woman who conquered Death.

HAVE YOU HEARD **THE
MESSAGE?**

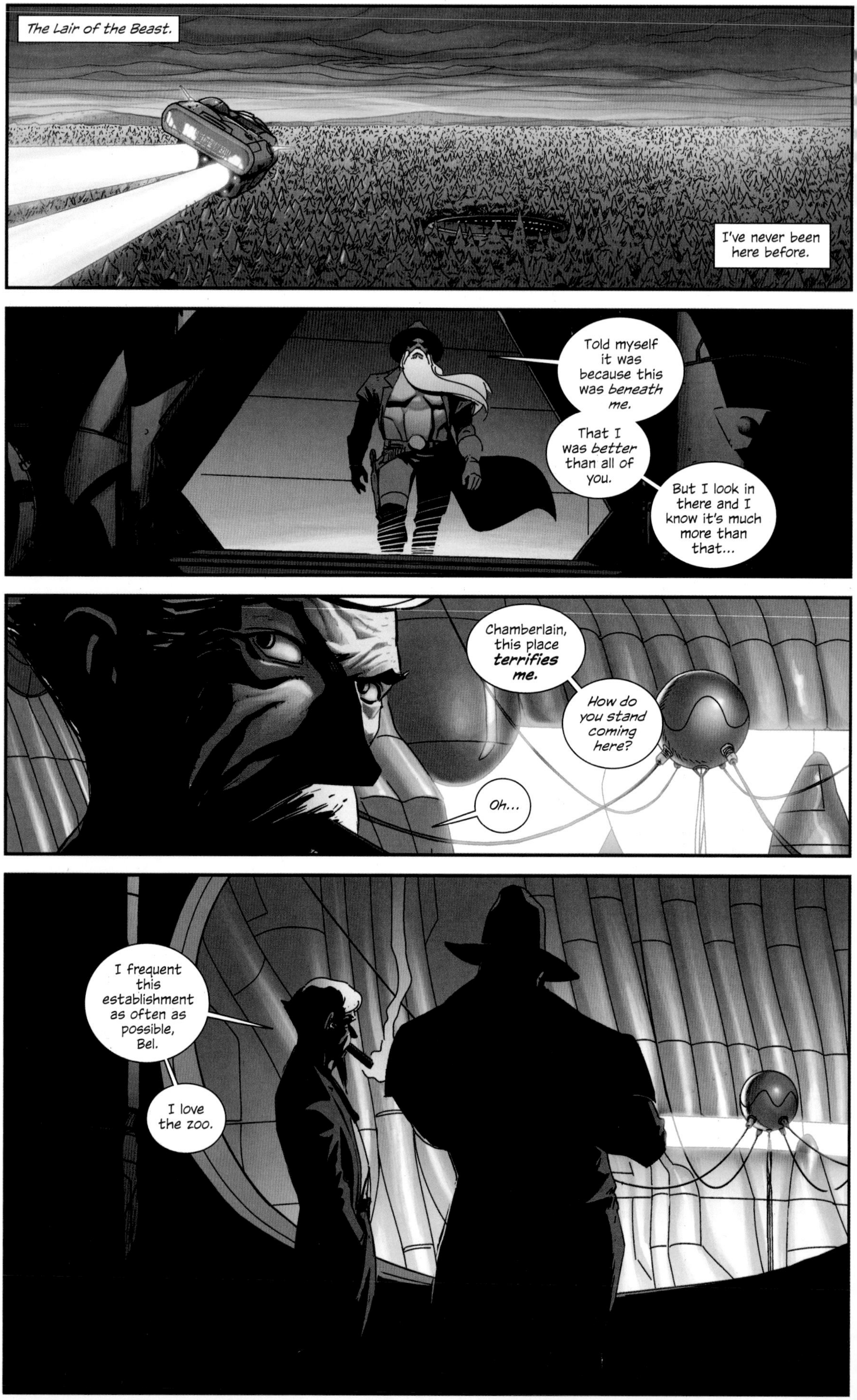

The Lair of the Beast.
I've never been here before.
Told myself it was because this was *beneath* me.
That I was *better* than all of you.
But I look in there and I know it's much more than that...
Chamberlain, this place ***terrifies me.***
How do you stand coming here?
Oh...
I frequent this establishment as often as possible, Bel.
I love the zoo.

BORN OF THE **EAST,** CHILD OF
THE **WEST,** THE ONE **TRUE**
SON OF **AMERICA.**

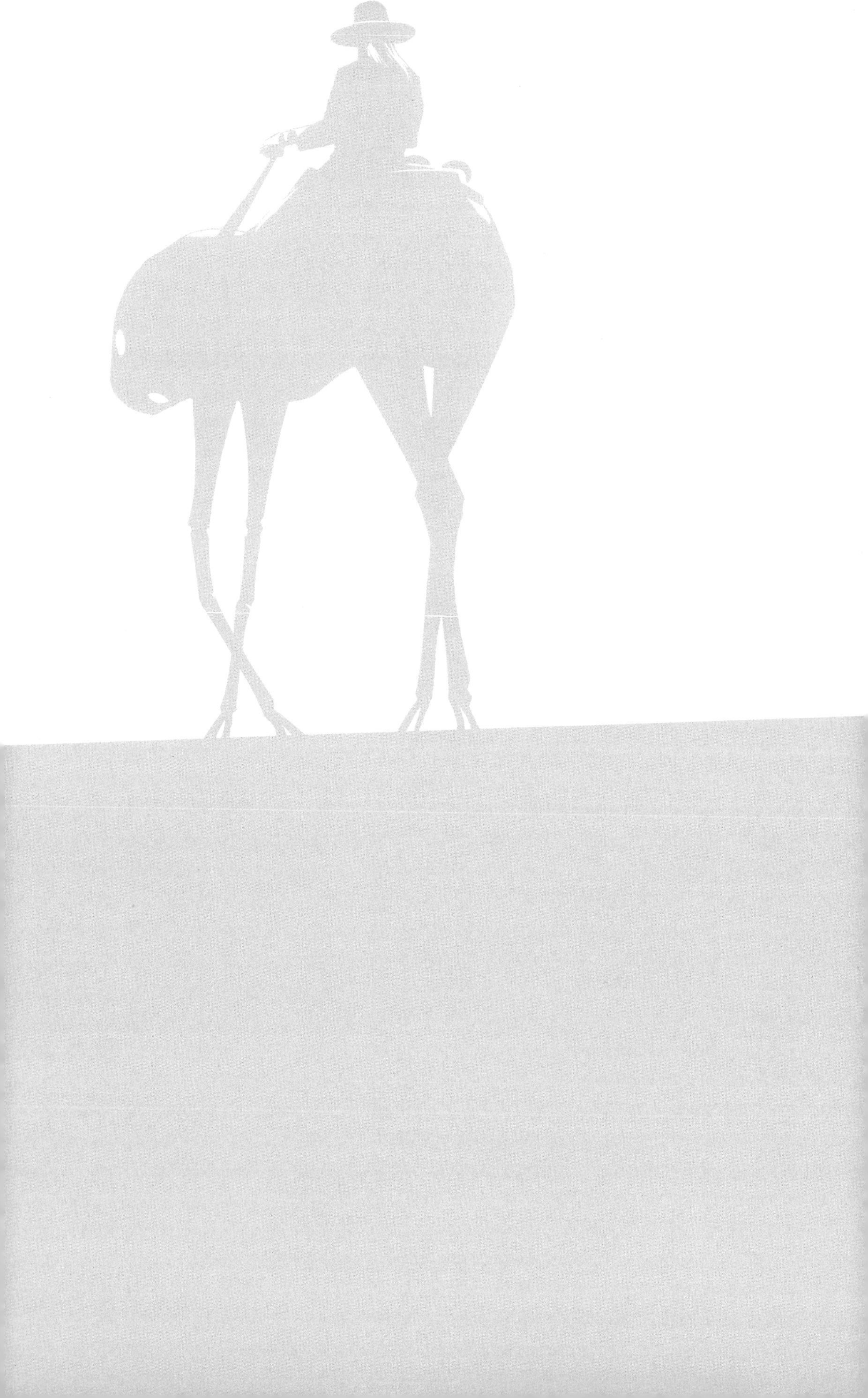

05

FIVE: THE
MESSAGE

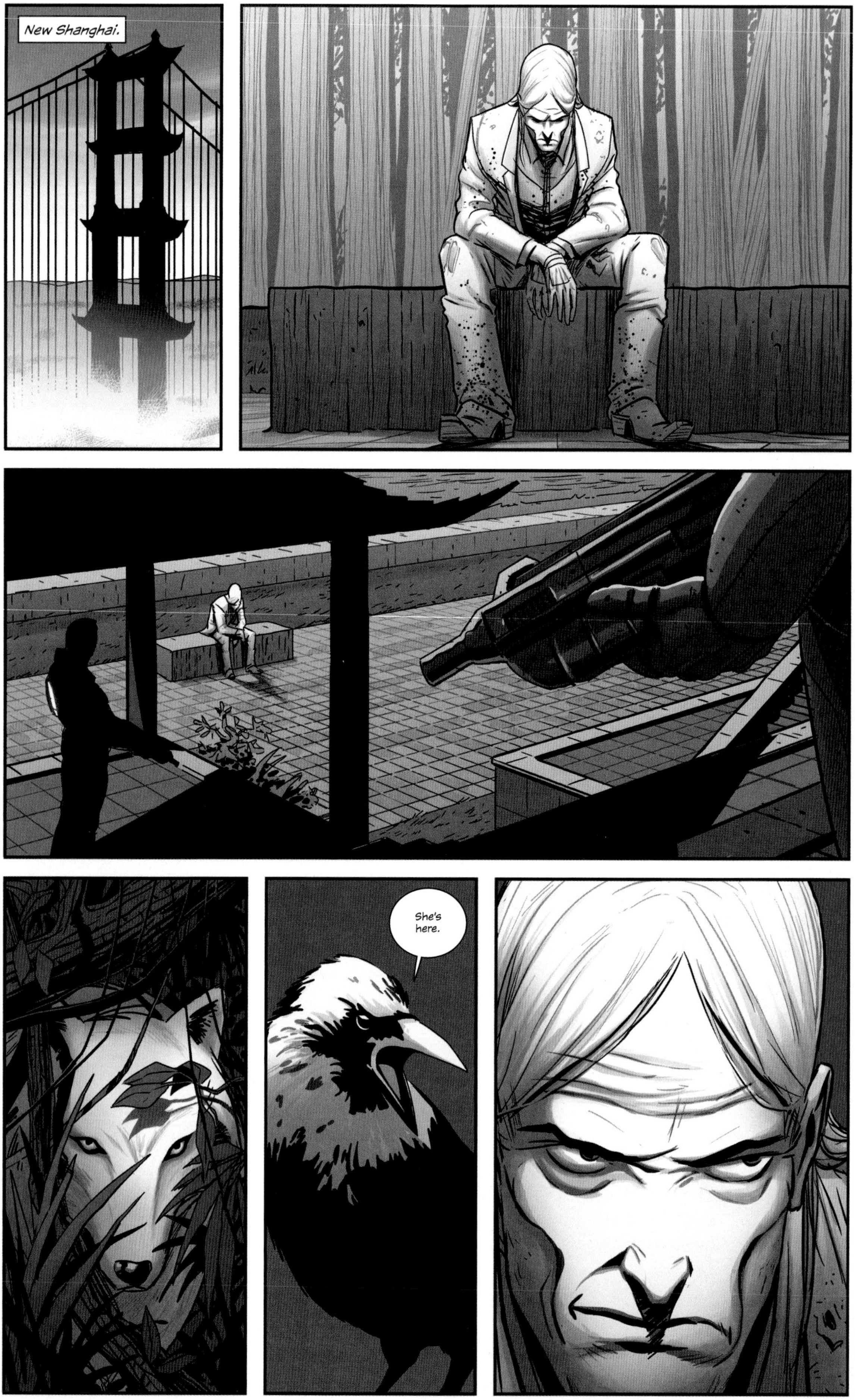
New Shanghai.
She's here.

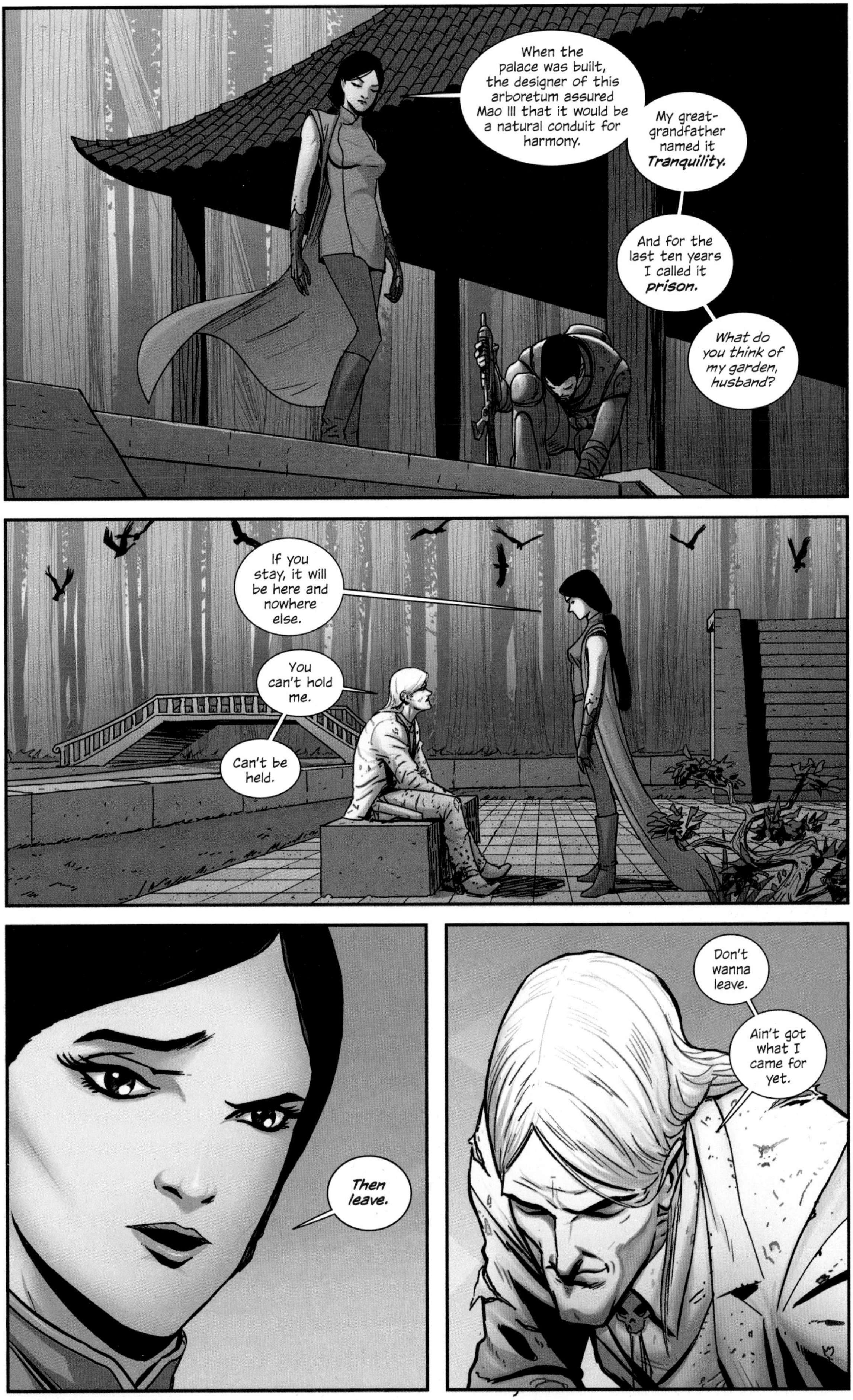
When the palace was built, the designer of this arboretum assured Mao III that it would be a natural conduit for harmony.
My great-grandfather named it *Tranquility.*
And for the last ten years I called it **prison.**
What do you think of my garden, husband?
If you stay, it will be here and nowhere else.
You can't hold me.
Can't be held.
Then leave.
Don't wanna leave.
Ain't got what I came for yet.

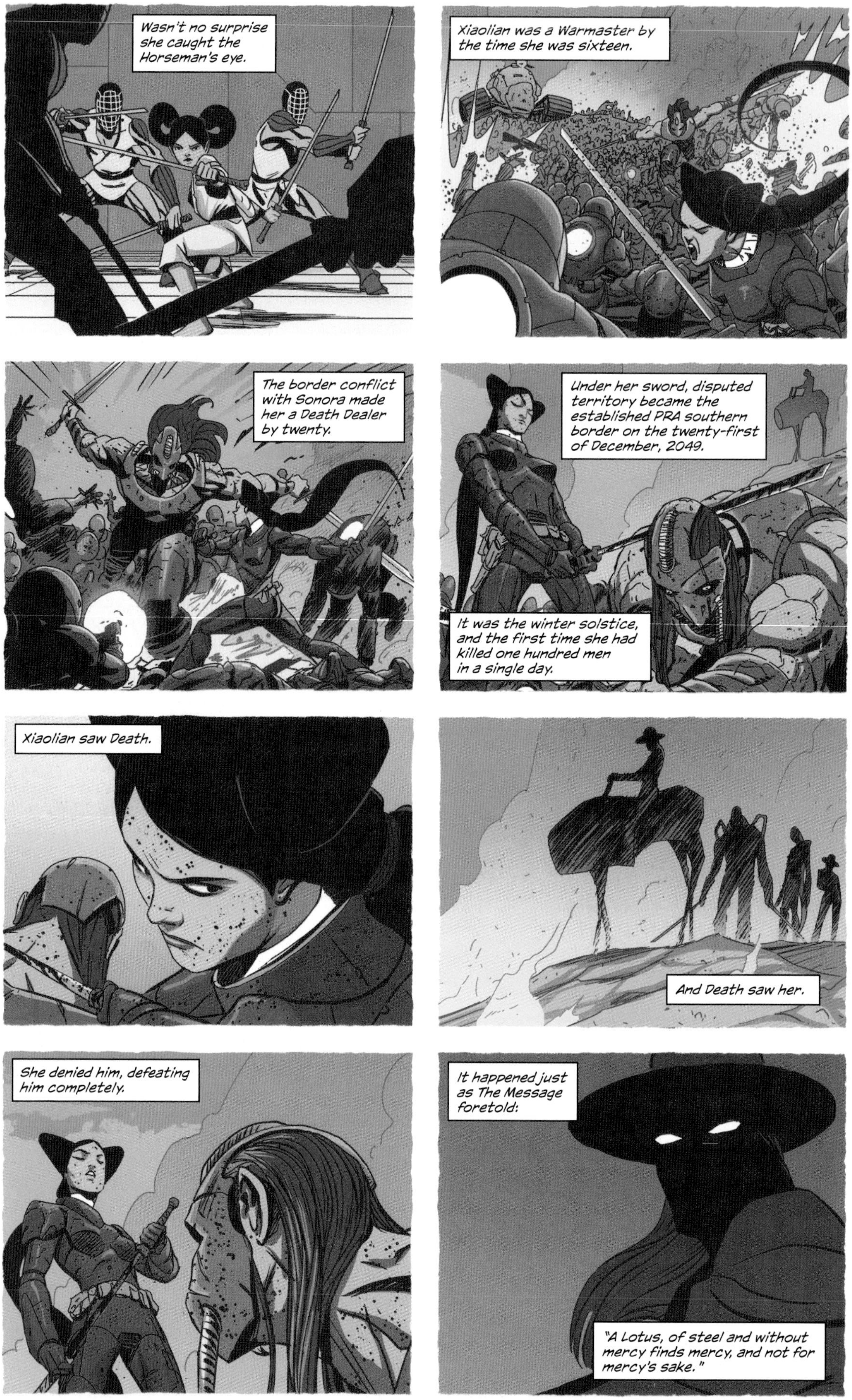
Wasn't no surprise she caught the Horseman's eye.
Xiaolian was a Warmaster by the time she was sixteen.
The border conflict with Sonora made her a Death Dealer by twenty.
Under her sword, disputed territory became the established PRA southern border on the twenty-first of December, 2049.
It was the winter solstice, and the first time she had killed one hundred men in a single day.
Xiaolian saw Death.
And Death saw her.
She denied him, defeating him completely.
It happened just as The Message foretold:
"A Lotus, of steel and without mercy finds mercy, and not for mercy's sake."

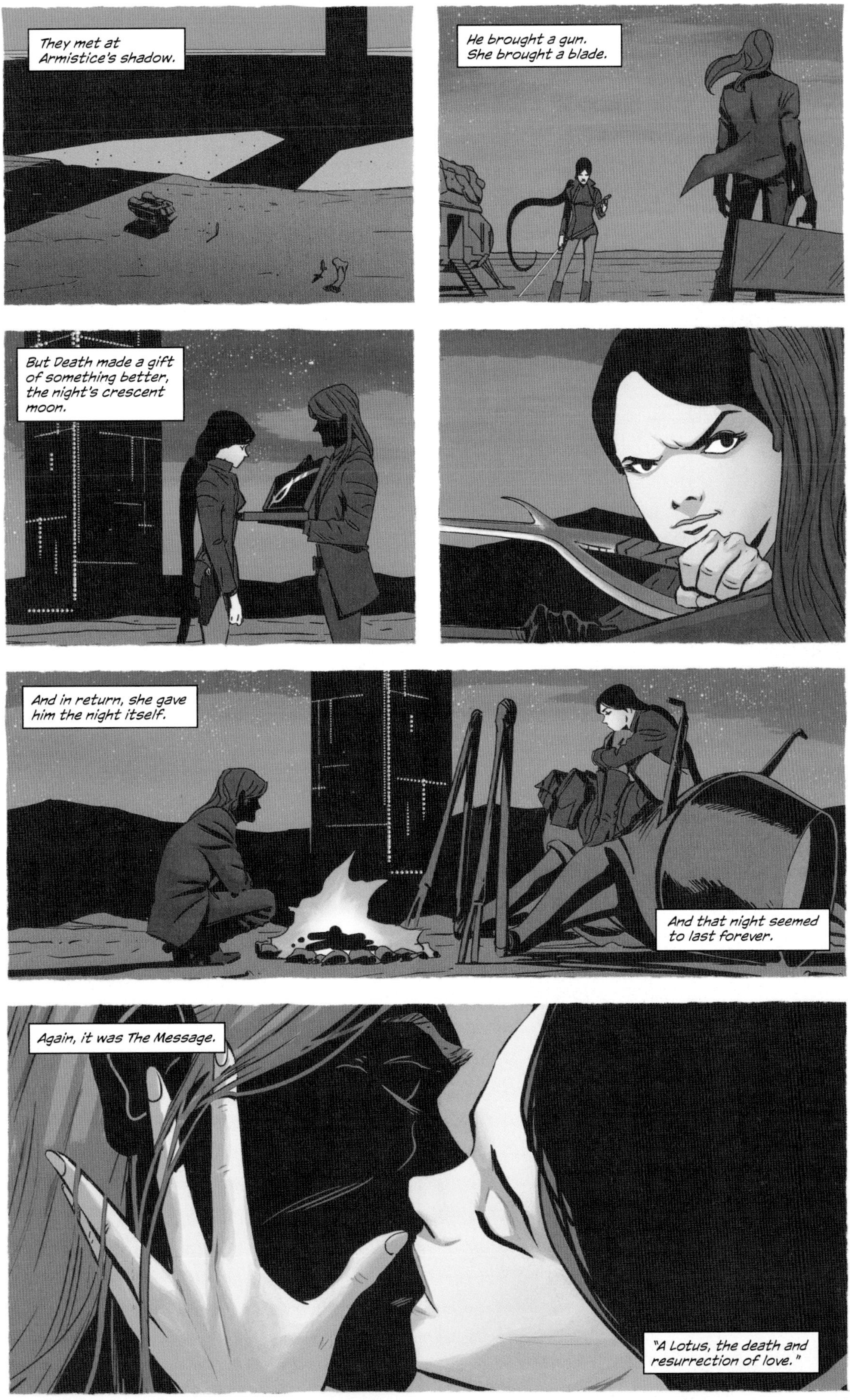
They met at
Armistice's shadow.
He brought a gun.
She brought a blade.
But Death made a gift
of something better,
the night's crescent
moon.
And in return, she gave
him the night itself.
And that night seemed
to last forever.
Again, it was The Message.
"A Lotus, the death and
resurrection of love."

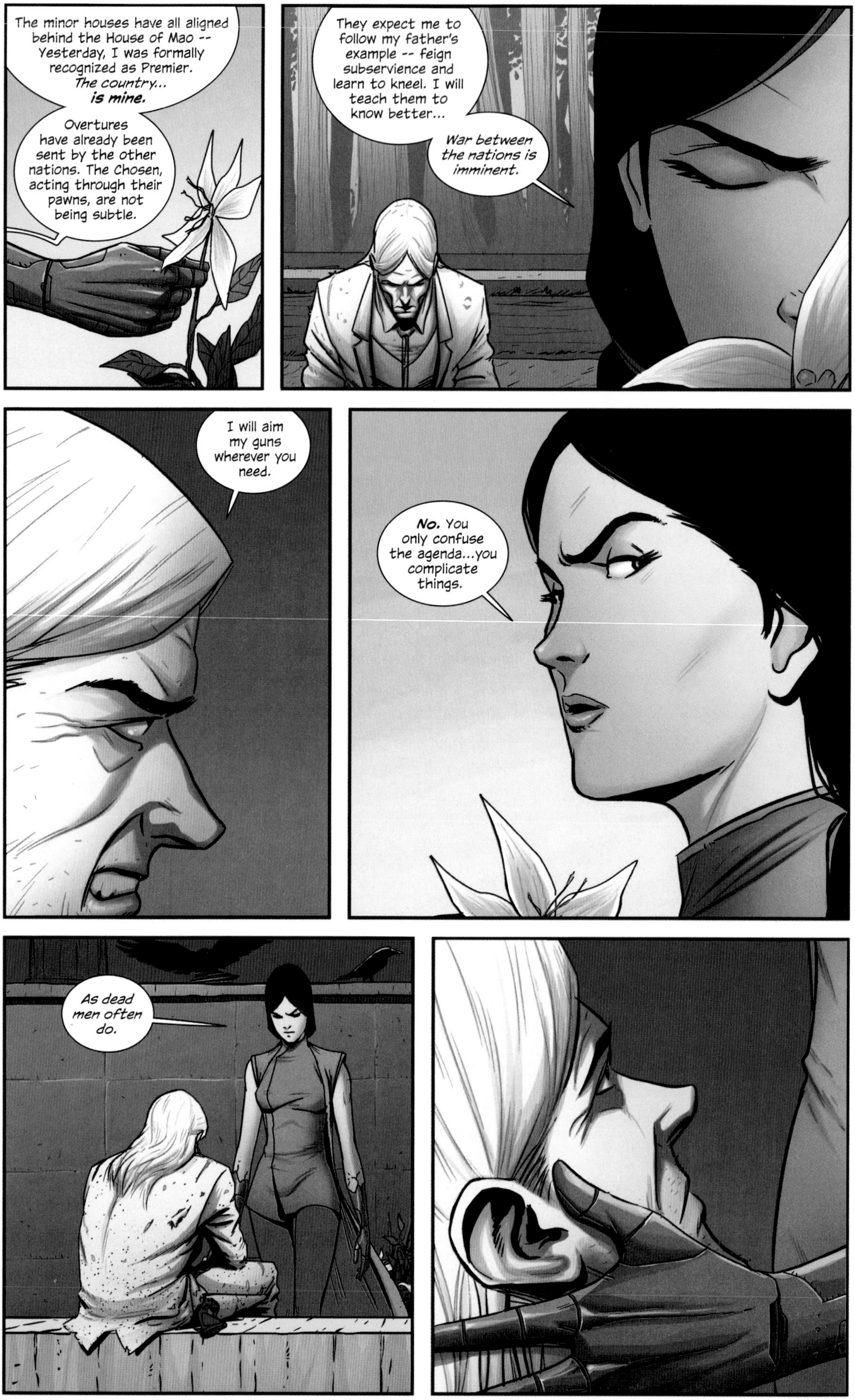
The minor houses have all aligned behind the House of Mao -- Yesterday, I was formally recognized as Premier. *The country...* ***is mine.***
Overtures have already been sent by the other nations. The Chosen, acting through their pawns, are not being subtle.
They expect me to follow my father's example -- feign subservience and learn to kneel. I will teach them to know better...
War between the nations is imminent.
I will aim my guns wherever you need.
No. You only confuse the agenda...you complicate things.
As dead men often do.

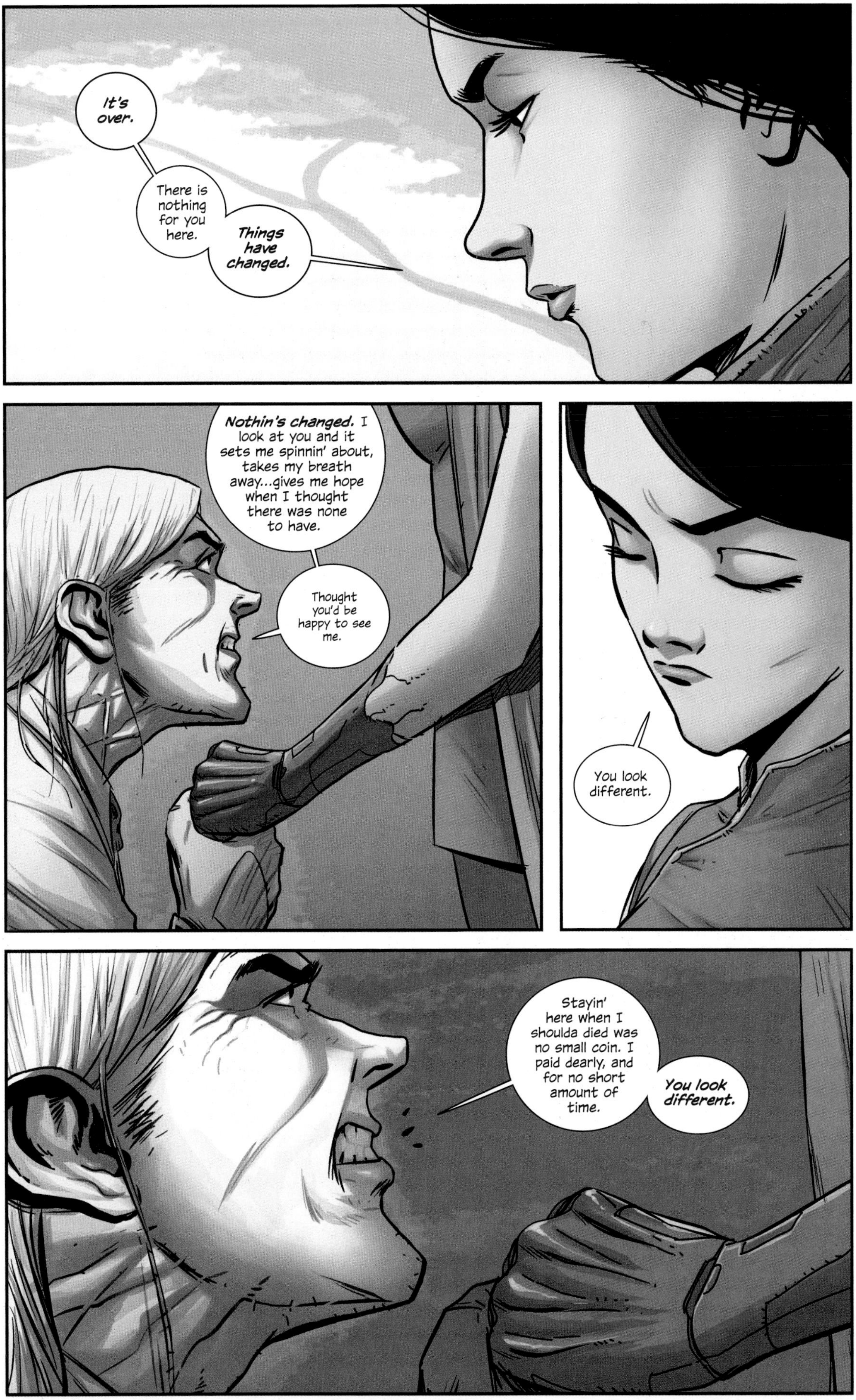

It's over.
There is nothing for you here.
Things have changed.
Nothin's changed. I look at you and it sets me spinnin' about, takes my breath away...gives me hope when I thought there was none to have.
Thought you'd be happy to see me.
You look different.
Stayin' here when I shoulda died was no small coin. I paid dearly, and for no short amount of time.
You look different.

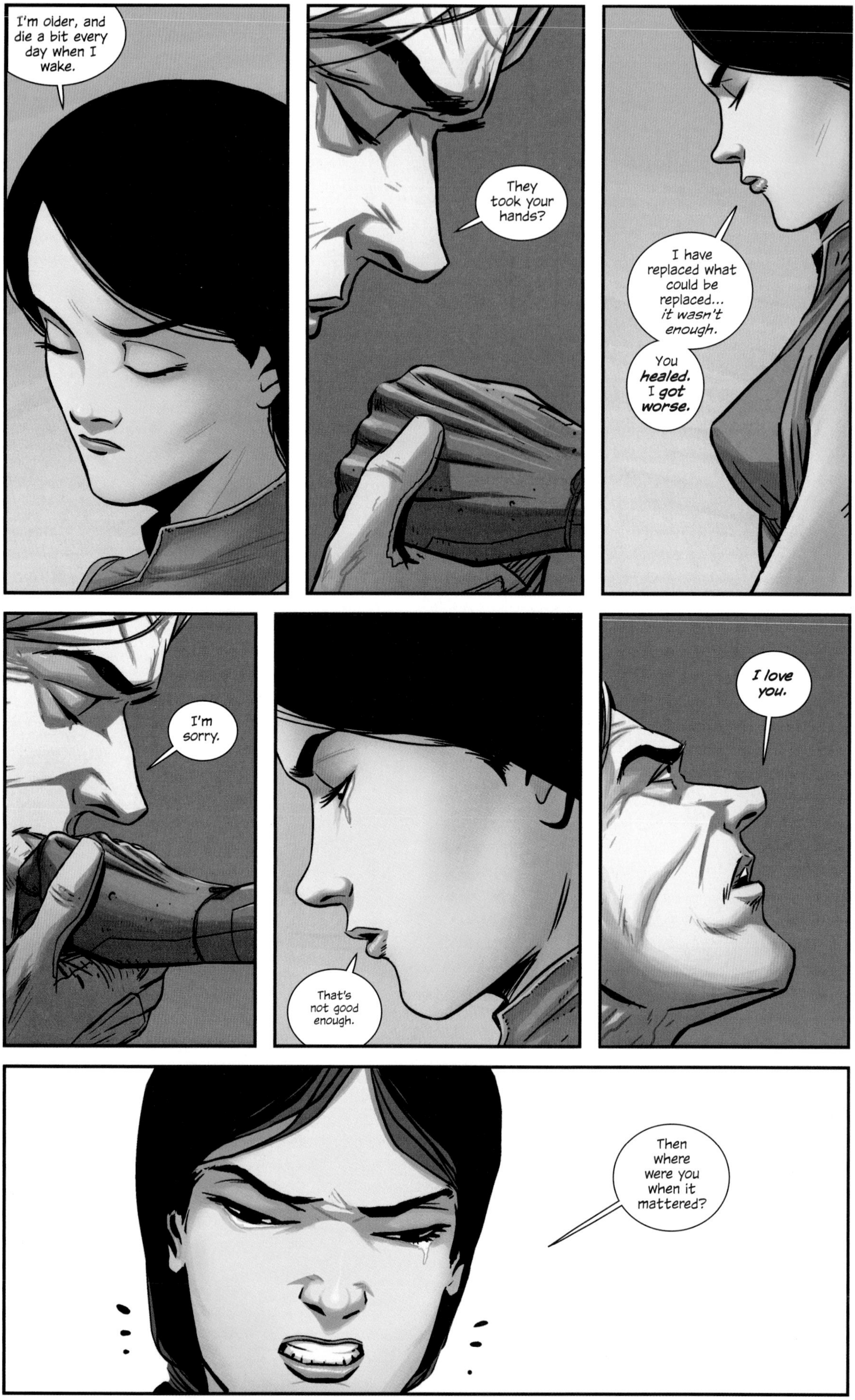
I'm older, and die a bit every day when I wake.
They took your hands?
I have replaced what could be replaced... *it wasn't enough.*
You **healed.** I **got worse.**
I'm sorry.
That's not good enough.
I love you.
Then where were you when it mattered?

They tried to leave the world behind.

Xiaolian, no longer a Death Dealer.

Death himself, no longer Death.

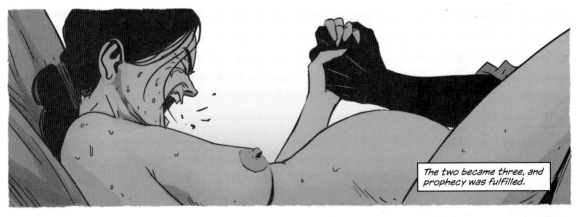

The two became three, and prophecy was fulfilled.

"Of the third, but not of the three."

"A cup, of a cup. A chalice, of a chalice."

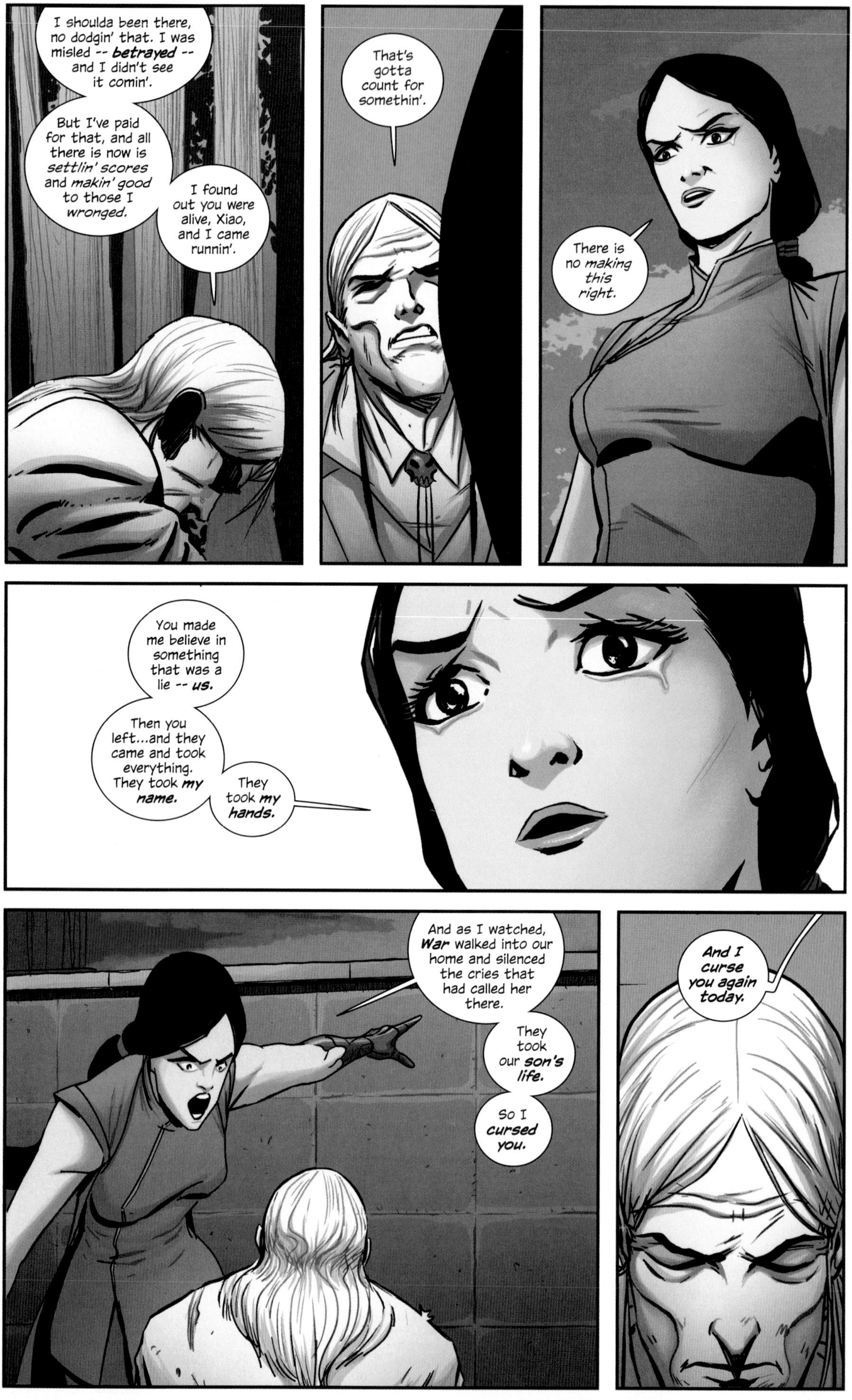
I shoulda been there, no dodgin' that. I was misled -- **betrayed** -- and I didn't see it comin'.
But I've paid for that, and all there is now is *settlin' scores* and *makin' good* to those I *wronged.*
I found out you were alive, Xiao, and I came runnin'.
That's gotta count for somethin'.
There is no *making this right.*
You made me believe in something that was a lie -- ***us.***
Then you left...and they came and took everything. They took ***my name.***
They took ***my hands.***
And as I watched, ***War*** walked into our home and silenced the cries that had called her there.
They took our ***son's life.***
So I ***cursed you.***
And I curse you again today.

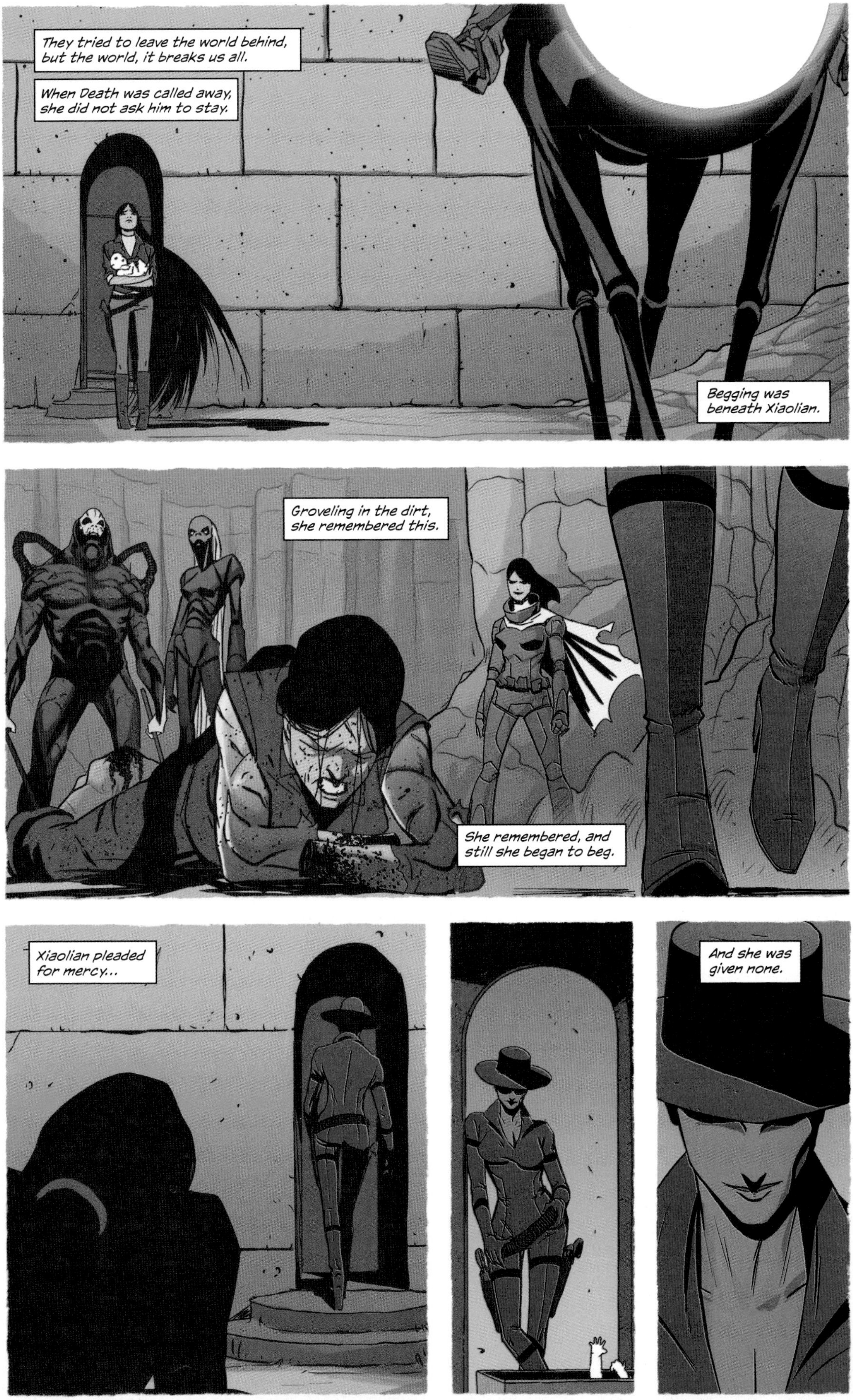
They tried to leave the world behind, but the world, it breaks us all.
When Death was called away, she did not ask him to stay.
Begging was beneath Xiaolian.
Groveling in the dirt, she remembered this.
She remembered, and still she began to beg.
Xiaolian pleaded for mercy...
And she was given none.

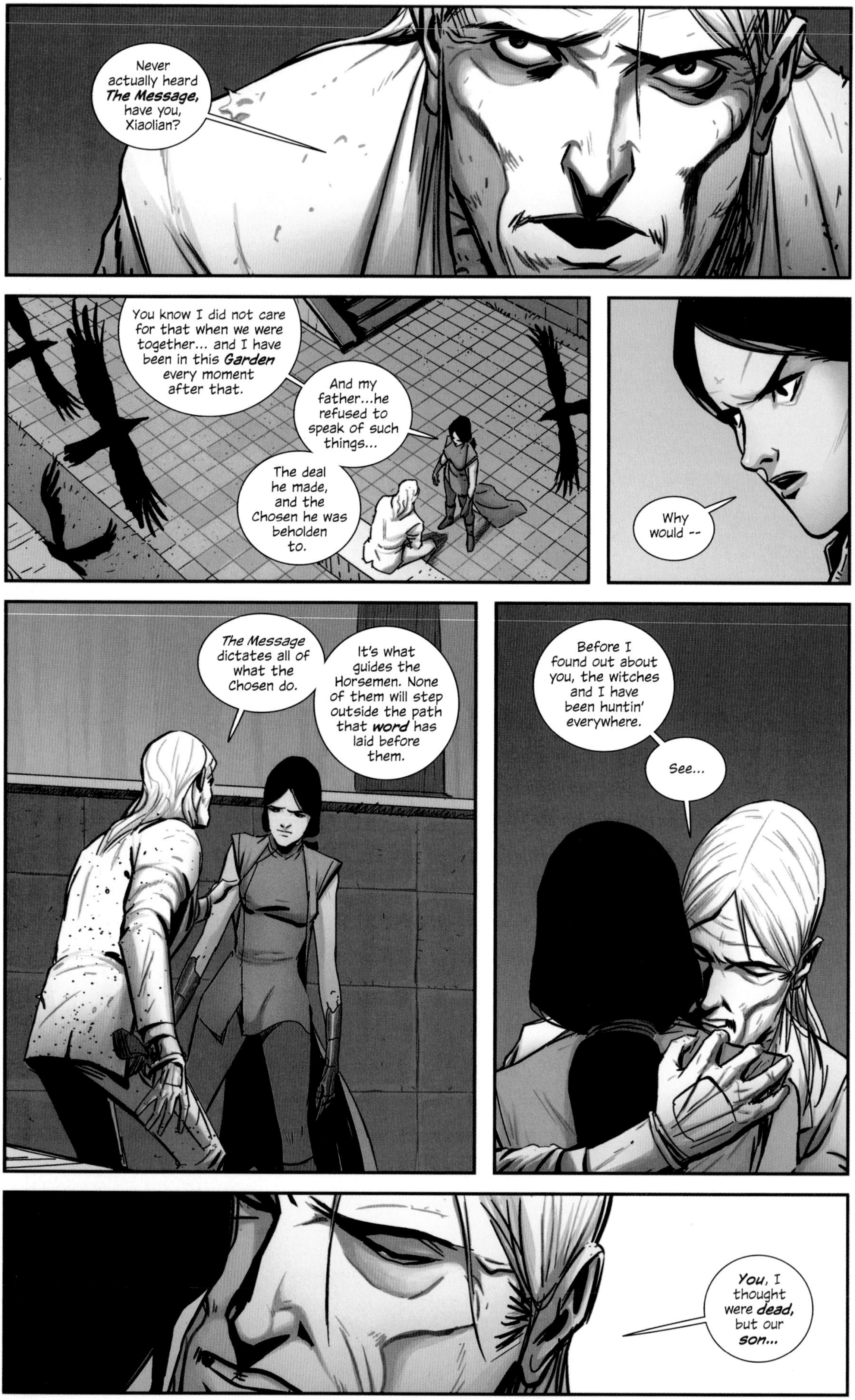

Never actually heard ***The Message,*** have you, Xiaolian?
You know I did not care for that when we were together... and I have been in this ***Garden*** every moment after that.
And my father...he refused to speak of such things...
The deal he made, and the Chosen he was beholden to.
Why would --
The Message dictates all of what the Chosen do.
It's what guides the Horsemen. None of them will step outside the path that ***word*** has laid before them.
Before I found out about you, the witches and I have been huntin' everywhere.
See...
You, I thought were ***dead,*** but our ***son...***

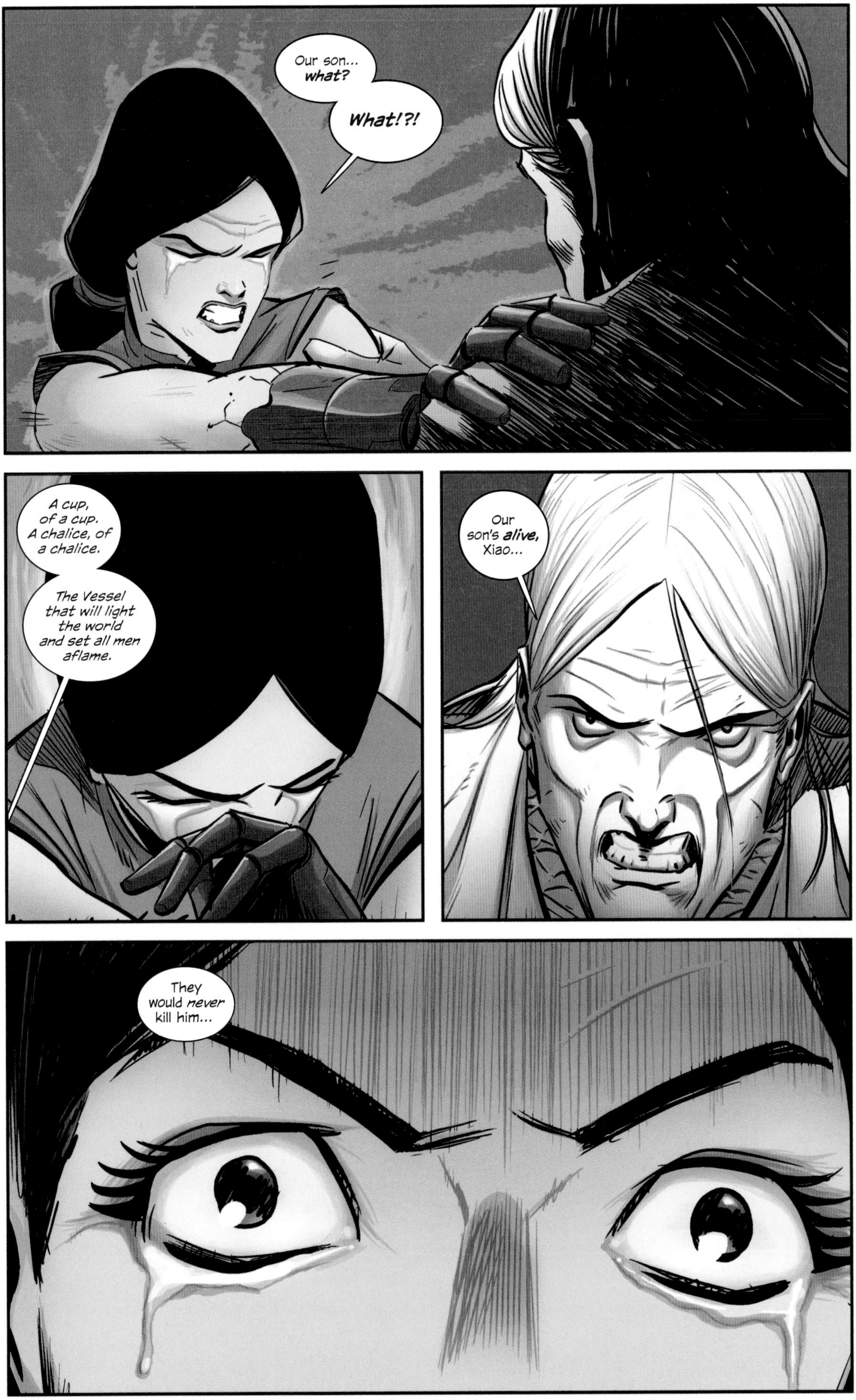
Our son... *what?*
What!?!
A cup, of a cup. A chalice, of a chalice.
The Vessel that will light the world and set all men aflame.
Our son's *alive,* Xiao...
They would *never* kill him...

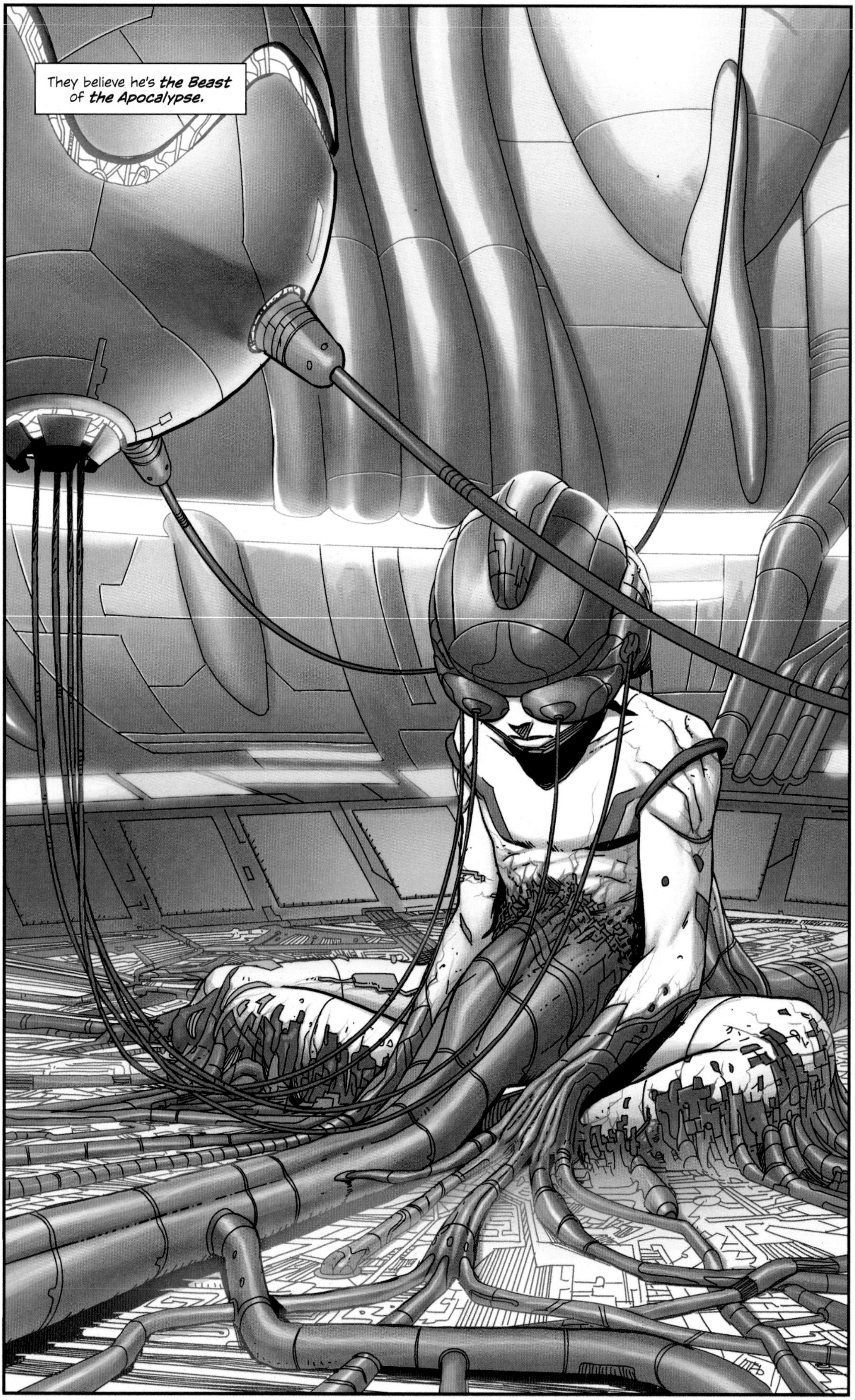
They believe he's the Beast of the Apocalypse.

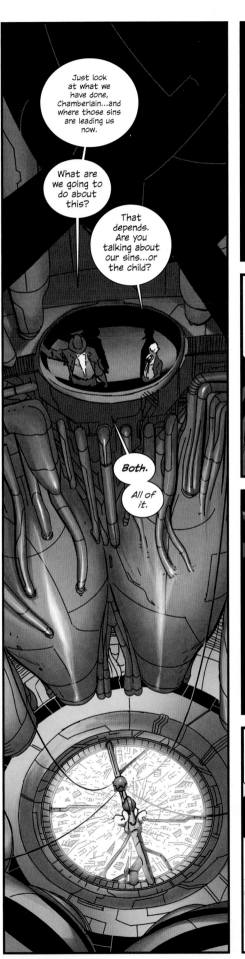

Just look at what we have done, Chamberlain...and where those sins are leading us now.

What are we going to do about this?

That depends. Are you talking about our sins...or the child?

Both.

All of it.

I wanted us to meet because the others...well, they are *true believers*.

And we are *not*? Are you questioning my faith, Mister Solomon?

You *wound* me.

I never believed any of this. I joined the Chosen because I figured selling my soul was worth protecting my nation...*saving them* from the ambitious and power mad.

But now *I* know it's real, and they're actually going to attempt to manufacture the end of the world.

It'll be some show.

That cannot be denied.

There isn't one thing amusing about this, Archibald.

Take a *closer look* at what they are creating down there.

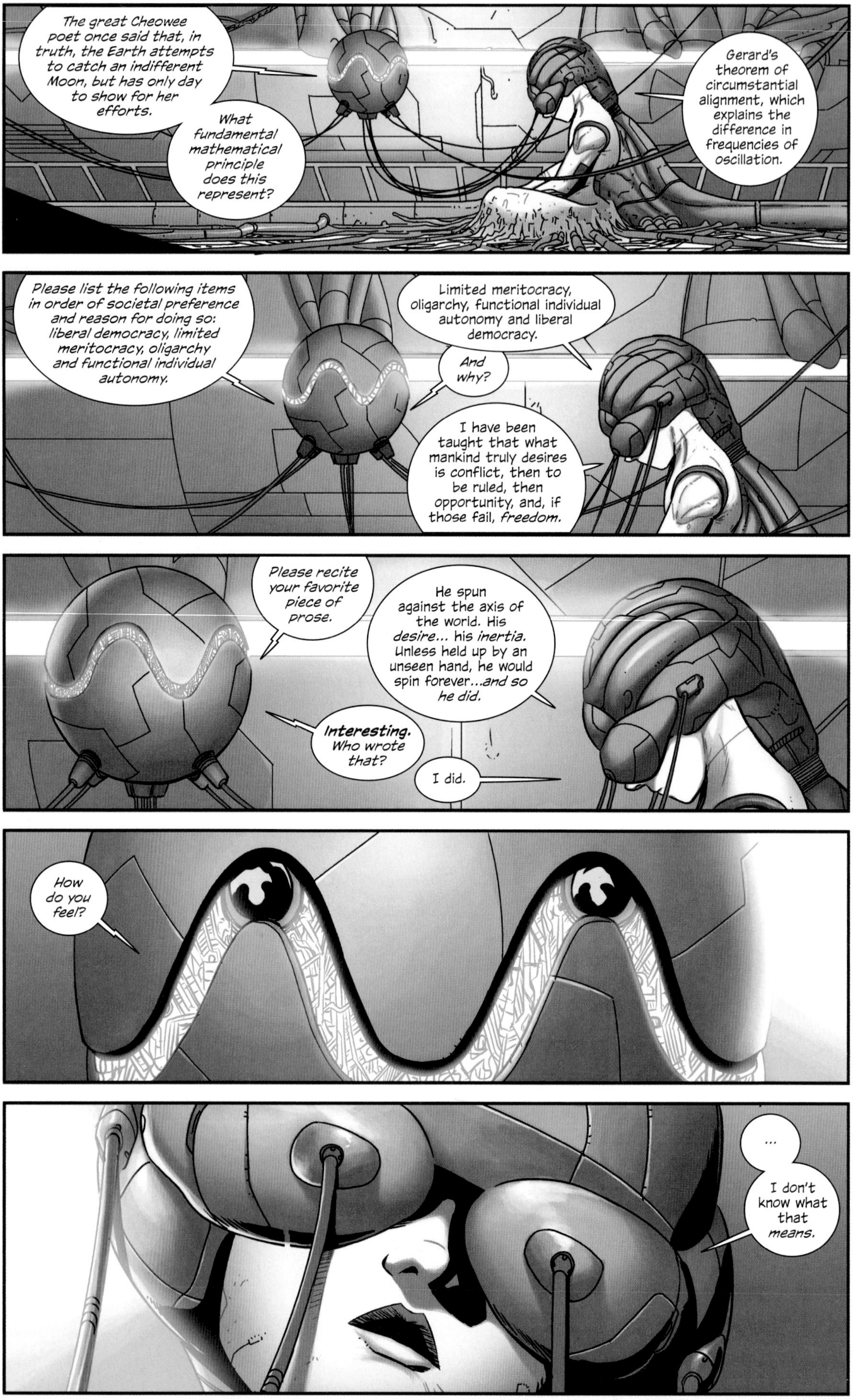
The great Cheowee poet once said that, in truth, the Earth attempts to catch an indifferent Moon, but has only day to show for her efforts.
What fundamental mathematical principle does this represent?
Gerard's theorem of circumstantial alignment, which explains the difference in frequencies of oscillation.
Please list the following items in order of societal preference and reason for doing so: liberal democracy, limited meritocracy, oligarchy and functional individual autonomy.
Limited meritocracy, oligarchy, functional individual autonomy and liberal democracy.
And why?
I have been taught that what mankind truly desires is conflict, then to be ruled, then opportunity, and, if those fail, *freedom.*
Please recite your favorite piece of prose.
He spun against the axis of the world. His *desire*... his *inertia.* Unless held up by an unseen hand, he would spin forever...and so *he did.*
Interesting. Who wrote that?
I did.
How do you feel?
...
I don't know what that *means.*

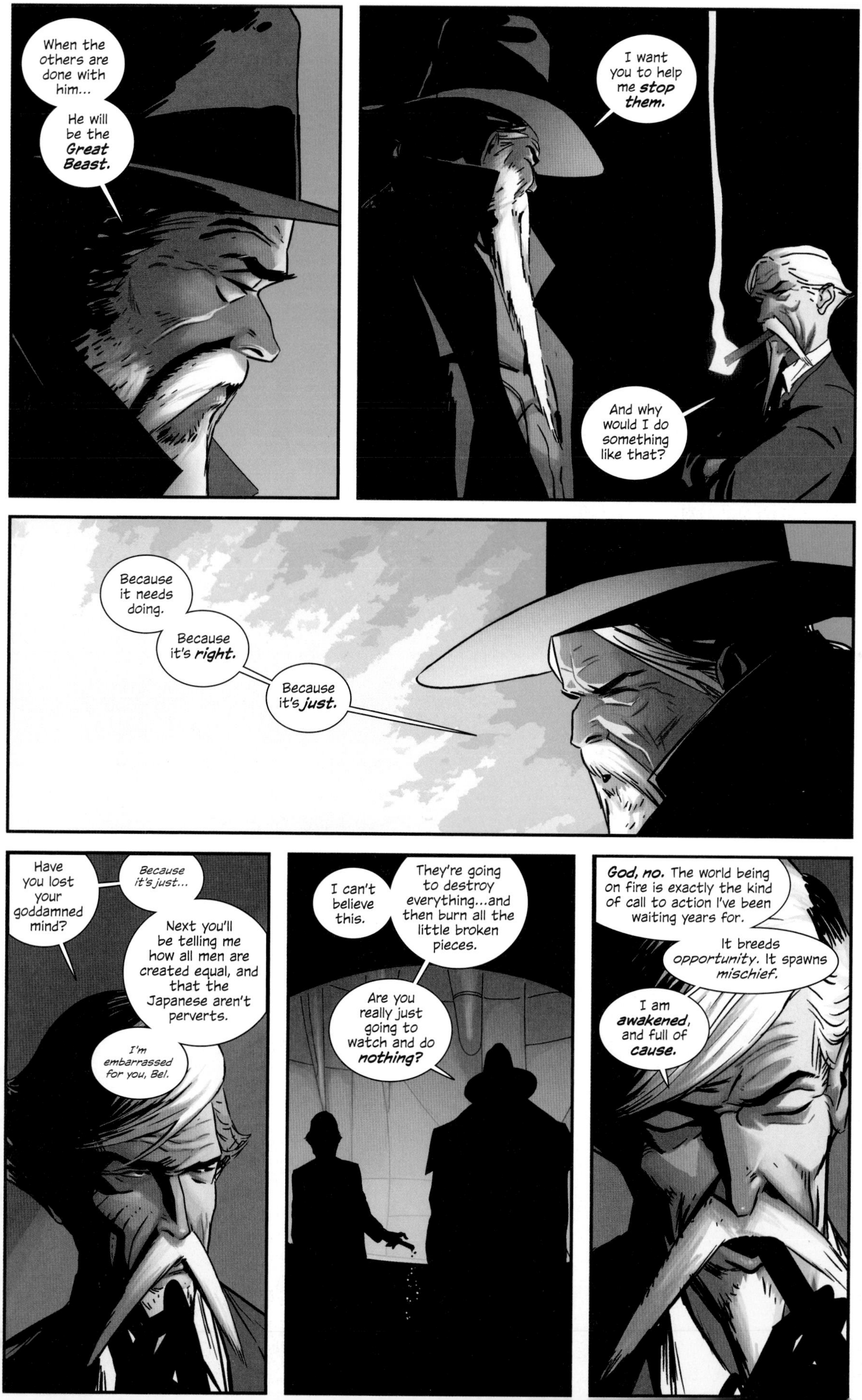

When the others are done with him...
He will be the **Great Beast.**
I want you to help me **stop them.**
And why would I do something like that?
Because it needs doing.
Because it's **right.**
Because it's **just.**
Have you lost your goddamned mind?
Because it's just...
Next you'll be telling me how all men are created equal, and that the Japanese aren't perverts.
I'm embarrassed for you, Bel.
I can't believe this.
They're going to destroy everything...and then burn all the little broken pieces.
Are you really just going to watch and do **nothing?**
God, no. The world being on fire is exactly the kind of call to action I've been waiting years for.
It breeds *opportunity.* It spawns *mischief.*
I am **awakened,** and full of **cause.**

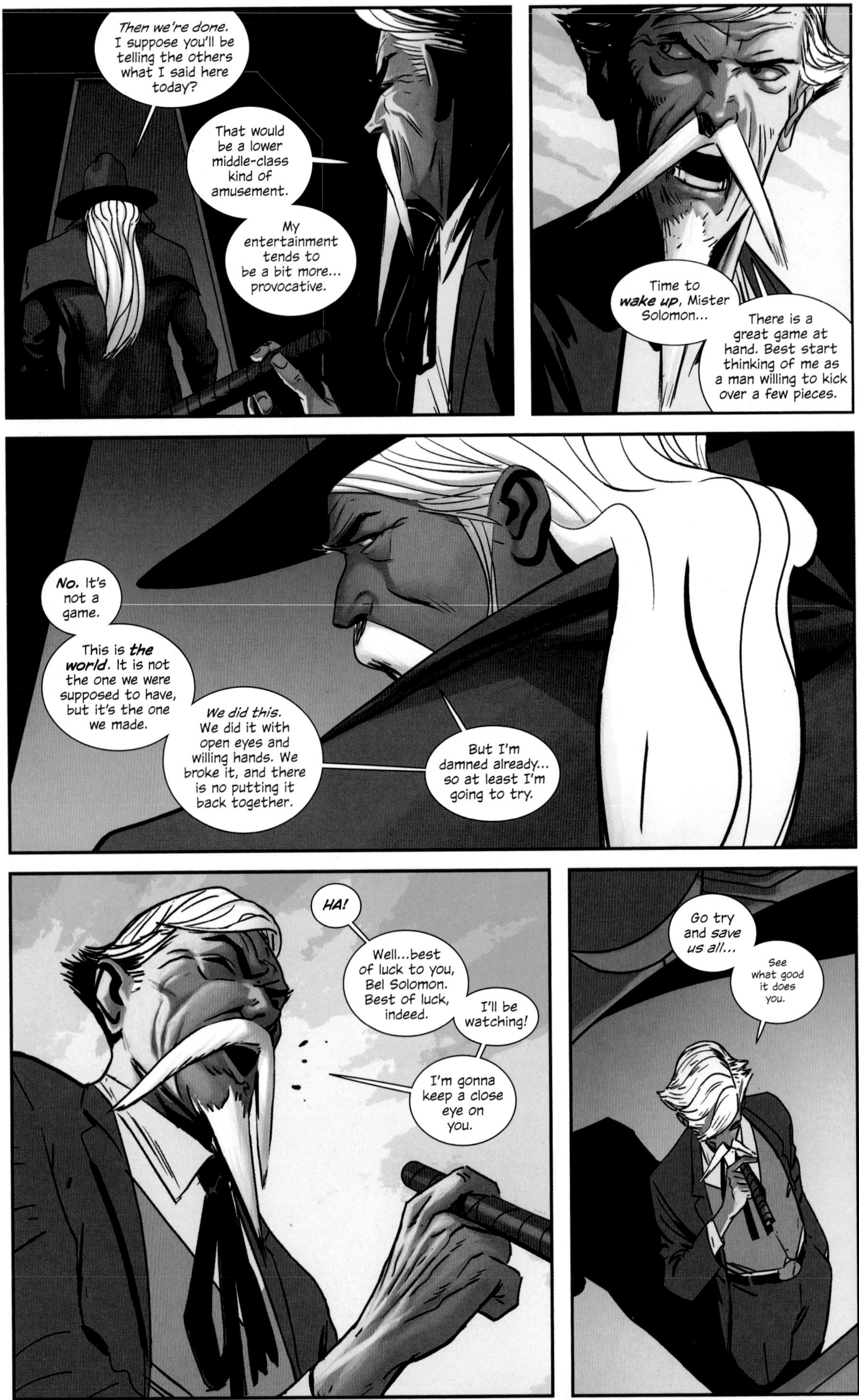
Then we're done. I suppose you'll be telling the others what I said here today?
That would be a lower middle-class kind of amusement.
My entertainment tends to be a bit more... provocative.
Time to ***wake up***, Mister Solomon...
There is a great game at hand. Best start thinking of me as a man willing to kick over a few pieces.
No. It's not a game.
This is ***the world***. It is not the one we were supposed to have, but it's the one we made.
We did this. We did it with open eyes and willing hands. We broke it, and there is no putting it back together.
But I'm damned already... so at least I'm going to try.
HA!
Well...best of luck to you, Bel Solomon. Best of luck, indeed.
I'll be watching!
I'm gonna keep a close eye on you.
Go try and *save us all...*
See what good it does you.

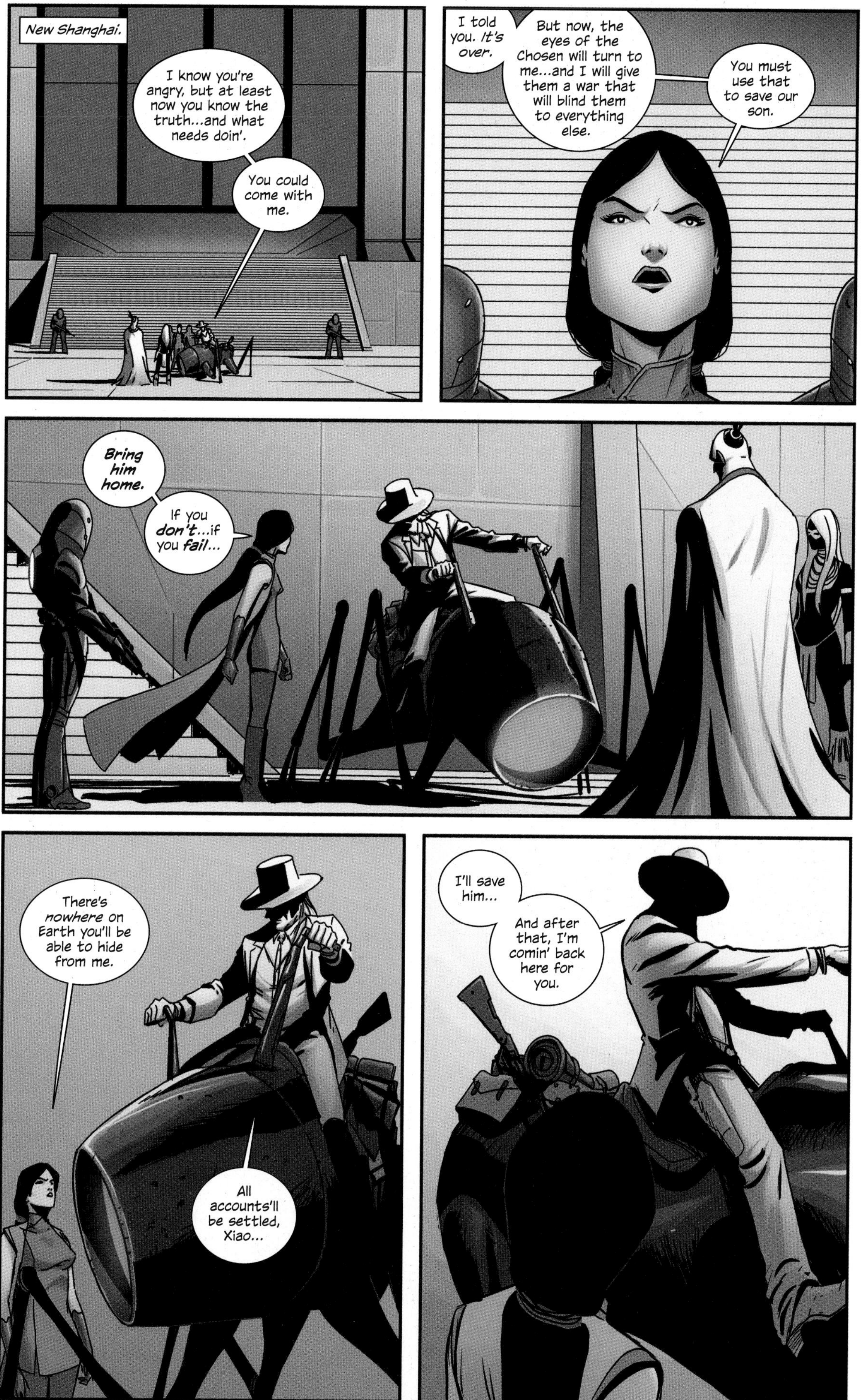
New Shanghai.
I know you're angry, but at least now you know the truth...and what needs doin'.
You could come with me.
I told you. *It's over.*
But now, the eyes of the Chosen will turn to me...and I will give them a war that will blind them to everything else.
You must use that to save our son.
Bring him home.
If you **don't**...if you **fail**...
There's *nowhere* on Earth you'll be able to hide from me.
All accounts'll be settled, Xiao...
I'll save him...
And after that, I'm comin' back here for you.

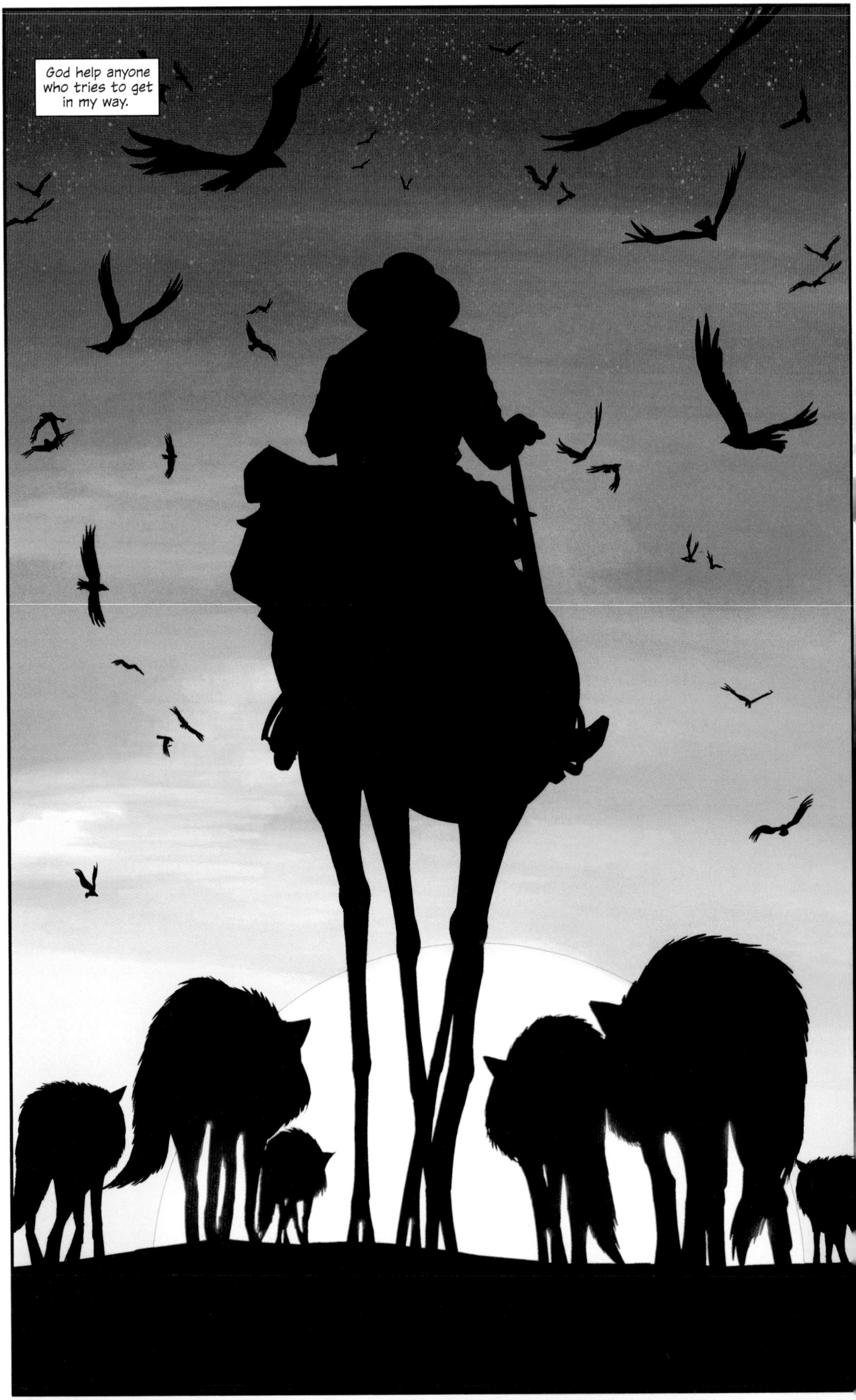
God help anyone who tries to get in my way.

ALL MEN TELL **LIES.**
THESE ARE A **FEW** OF
THEM.

Jonathan Hickman is the visionary talent behind such works as the Eisner-nominated **NIGHTLY NEWS**, **THE MANHATTAN PROJECTS** and **PAX ROMANA**. He also plies his trade at MARVEL working on books like **FANTASTIC FOUR** and **THE AVENGERS**.

His twin brother, Marc, is who really wrote this. Jonathan doesn't even get out of bed anymore.

Jonathan lives in South Carolina surrounded by immediate family and in-laws, which he plans on leaving unless they start showering him with the love and affection he deserves.

This includes his wife.

You can visit his website:*www.pronea.com*, or email him at:*jonathan@pronea.com*.

•

Nick Dragotta's career began at Marvel Comics working on titles as varied as **X-STATIX, THE AGE OF THE SENTRY, X-MEN: FIRST CLASS, CAPTAIN AMERICA: FOREVER ALLIES,** and **VENGEANCE.**

FANTASTIC FOUR #588 was the first time he collaborated with Jonathan Hickman, which lead to their successful run on **FF.**

In addition, Nick is the co-creator of **HOWTOONS,** a comic series teaching kids how to build things and explore the world around them. **EAST OF WEST** is Nick's first creator-owned project at Image.